SEARCHING
for
PEKPEK

D1737338

SEARCHING

for

PEKPEK

Cassowaries and Conservation in the New Guinea Rainforest

ANDREW L. MACK

CASSOWARY CONSERVATION & PUBLISHING, LLC.

Cassowary Conservation and Publishing, LLC
340 Love Hollow Road
New Florence, PA 15944 USA
http://www.CassowaryConservation.com

ISBN-13: 978-0-9893903-0-9
LCCN: 2013957998

Printed in the United States of America

Acknowledgments

In a narrative spanning so many years and from New Guinea to New Florence, there will be a huge number of people to thank. In this case there are even more because I truly depended on many people; not just for help and support, but really depended on them. My apologies to the many whom I've failed to include.

I can't begin to name all the Pawai'ia who helped. Indeed, given their affinity to changing their names from time to time ("my name is Cowboy now"), many who I would thank now go by a different name. Sadly many have died; life is hard and short for the Pawai'ia. Particularly outstanding among the several hundred who worked as research assistants and guided me in the forest, thanks to: Ben, Cowboy, Diwai, Joe, Jonah, Luke, Mayabe, Metea, Moai, Orei, Pero, Peter, Salape, Serao, and Simion. Among the Gimi, thanks to Amos, Avit Wako, Batanimi, Dorahau, Falau, and Smith.

Through the entire narrative my family, Ruth, Rus, Rich, and Freni, have been loving, encouraging, and supportive. Thanks to Sy Montgomery for motivation to resuscitate the manuscript and Jane Eklund and Jennifer Gehlar for editing. Mal Smith has been a great friend and supporter since day one in Papua New Guinea (PNG). The years Janine Watson and Silas Sutherland worked with us, they played a key role in getting our program rolling; the good times we shared could fill another book. Debra Wright made it all possible and shared the ups and downs; she provided many of the photos and helped edit the manuscript. Thanks to Samuel Price who made the maps.

In New Guinea over the years, thanks to research colleagues and friends: Gerry Allen, Allen Allison, Arison Arihafa, Michael Balke, Paul Barker, Larry Barnes, Bruce Beehler, Brett Benz, David Bickford, Robert Bino, Frank Bonaccorso, Peter Burke, Doug Cartan,

Andrea Chatfield, Matthew Chatfield, Wayne Crill, Richard Cuthbert, Chris Dahl, Jack and Isa Douglas, Gretchen Druliner, Jack Dumbacher, Eunice Dus, Phillipa Eckhardt, Pippa Ellis, John Ericho, Chris Filardi, Banak Gamui, Vidiro Gei, David Gillison, Hector Gomez de Silva Garza, Steve Hamilton, Lance Hill, Helen Fortune Hopkins, Mike Hopkins, Kalan Ickes, Paul Igag, Bulisa Iova, Nancy Irwin, Matthew Jebb, Heinrich Jessen, Josh Jones, Libby Jones, Enock Kale, Dan Kamien, Brian Kennedy, Michael Kigl, Susan Klimas, Anna Koki, Kepslok Kumilgo, Sarah Legge, Leo Legra, Silvia Lomascola, Caroline Macleod, Jane Mogina, Kurt Merg, Olivia Missa, Junior Novera, Vojtech Novotny, Onika Okena, Muse Opiang, Sandie Opiang, Steffen Oppel, Caroline Pannell, Bob Park, Eben Paxton, Dan Polhemus, Liz Pryde, Stephen Richards, John Richardson-Meyer, Katayo Sagata, Leo Salas, Mellie Samson, Doug Schaefer, Ed Scholes, Ross Sinclair, Robert Sine, Kevin Smith, Suzette Stephens, Miriam Supuma, Craig Symes, Wayne Takeuchi, Kore Tau, Ramona Visnak, Diatpain Warakai, Mark Watson, George Weiblen, Paige West, Ann Williams, Ken Yhuanje, Kamena Yoriene, Tanya Zeriga-Alone.

In the US, thanks to Kim Awbrey, Don Bruning, David Bickford, Rene Borges, Chuck Burg, Burke Burnett, Ricardo Calvo, Mo Donnelly, Margaret Fischer, Ted Fleming, Frank Gill, Joshua Ginsberg, Roger Gunther, Megan Hill, Carol Horvitz, Dave Janos, Cynthia Mackie, Doyle McKey, Patrick Osborne, Mary Pearl, and Jorgen Thomsen. All helped or played important roles in the story.

Financial support came from many sources and I refer anyone to the acknowledgments in my published papers for details about who funded what. Special thanks are due to The Christensen Fund and New England Biolabs for their ongoing support.

And a late entry to the overall story, but who I must thank the most for encouraging me to complete the manuscript and supporting me in innumerable ways—my loving and patient wife, Lydia.

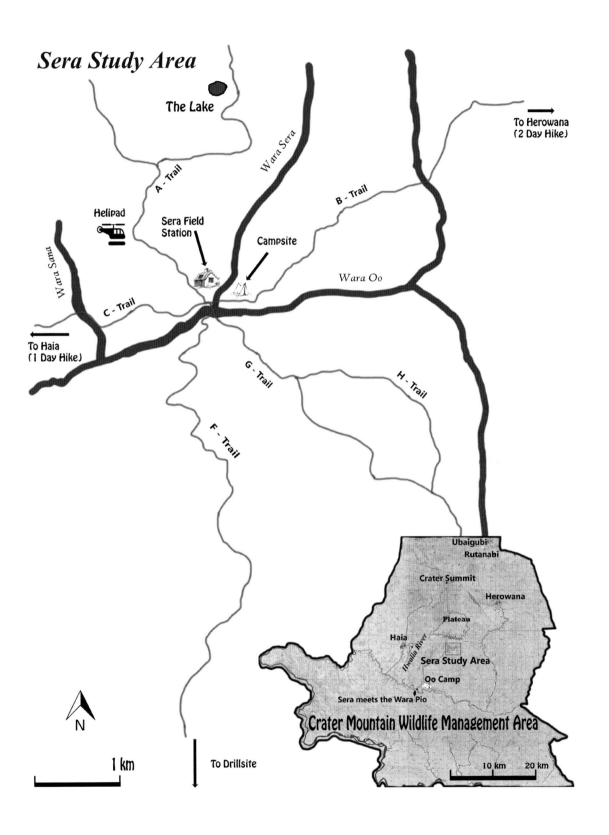

Sera Study Area

The Lake

To Herowana
(2 Day Hike)

A - Trail

Wara Sera

B - Trail

Helipad

Sera Field
Station

Campsite

Wara Oo

Wara Sana

C - Trail

To Haia
(1 Day Hike)

G - Trail

H - Trail

F - Trail

N

1 km

To Drillsite

Ubaigubi
Rutanabi

Crater Summit

Herowana

Plateau

Haia

Iwaia River

Sera Study Area

Oo Camp

Sera meets the Wara Pio

Crater Mountain Wildlife Management Area

10 km   20 km

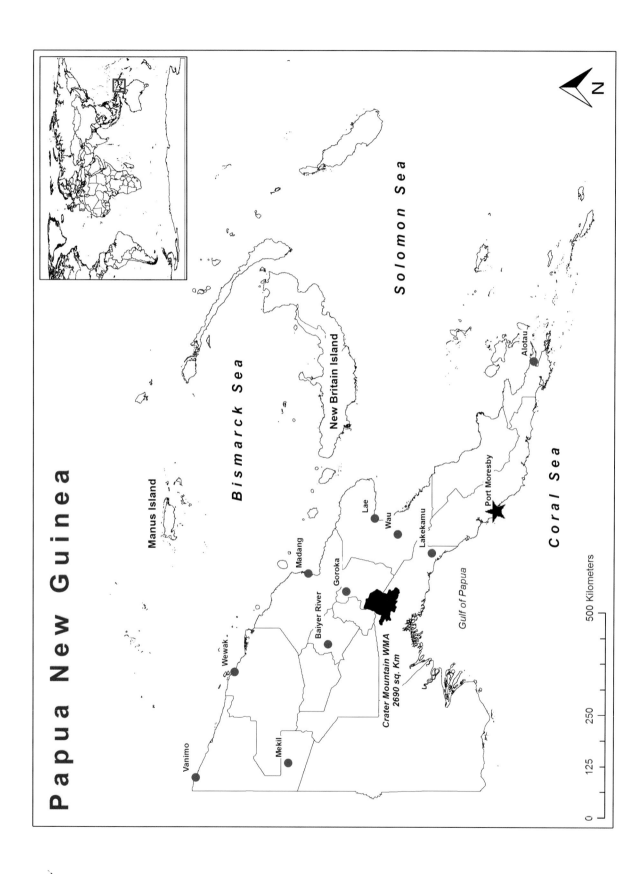

x

Contents

Introduction: Where? Why? My story xiii

Chapter 1. First time in Haia 1

Chapter 2. Gimi gunfire and bandits.. 14

Chapter 3. Droppings galore, a good camp and a flood 19

Chapter 4. Why fruits and droppings?... 32

Chapter 5. How did I get here?... 35

Chapter 6. Searching for a place to search for droppings...................................... 38

Chapter 7. Deb arrives 57

Chapter 8. Burglars and the Ubaigubi court system 63

Chapter 9. Choosing the study area when malaria strikes...................................... 72

Chapter 10 Building the station 84

Chapter 11. Blazing trails and exploring 98

Chapter 12. Cassowaries, chiggers and conservation.. 102

Chapter 13. Two cassowaries: Huey and Louie.. 107

Chapter 14. Big Reds and radio-tracking dung.. 120

Chapter 15. Some extraordinary help 127

Chapter 16. Big Reds and the last contribution of Huey and Louie...................... 133

Chapter 17. Back to Miami and life in the USA.. 143

Chapter 18. Data analysis in Miami and Big Red becomes "my" tree 146

Chapter 19. Finishing the dissertation and searching for a job 152

Chapter 20. Meanwhile, back at Sera 155

Chapter 21. Epiphany: transformation from research to conservation 162

Chapter 22. Hardships and danger 165

Chapter 23. Back to PNG at last and shedding baggage 172

Chapter 24. Finally, real conservation—capacity building 183

Chapter 25. InterOil arrives 193

Chapter 26. Spivs and liars 199

Chapter 27. Moving ahead despite InterOil 203

Chapter 28. The dealbreaker 211

Chapter 29. Things unravel quickly 215

Chapter 30. Regrouping, yet again 220

Chapter 31. Closing shop 225

Epilogue 230

About the author 235

Introduction

Where? Why? My story

Wanem ples? Bilong wanem? Stori bilong mi

From inside the cockpit, I could sense the vastness of the rainforest sucking the alien drone of the plane's engine out of the sky. This sound, this plane, and I did not belong here. Massive tectonic forces beneath New Guinea have folded and twisted the earth so violently that even the dense rainforest draped over them cannot conceal the sharp cliffs and ravines that make traversing the land on foot torturous. Like an insignificant gnat above some huge wrinkled beast, our slow flight over the treetops was of no consequence; were we to crash it would not register. Somewhere in there was the place I wanted to live. It was 1987 and I was looking for a spot where I could build a camp, and I intended to spend a few years focused on my research.

We'd been flying for half an hour and had seen no evidence of human beings other than a few tiny clearings, each containing a crude brown thatched hut. Not a single road, no bridges, nothing metallic or concrete marred the terrain; there were no power lines and certainly nothing so perverse as a billboard. In that expansive, unbroken forest canopy, anything more than a bit of thatch or an axe-cleared garden would have been obscene. Even in the sky through which we flew not a single vapor trail marked the passage of fellow humans above. From that vantage point, we seemed to be the only people in the world. We were flying transects over the third largest remaining tropical rainforest on the planet, one of the least-populated places on earth capable of sustaining agriculture.

Inside the forest lie dividing lines that are known and visible only to the indigenous. These lines mark boundaries between tribes, clans, and families. I was about to start my research in the country of the Pawai'ia, a semi-nomadic tribe of just a few thousand individuals with an enormous area to call home. It was a perfect place for my work and the Pawai'ia seemed an ideal group to work with and live among.

Much later, after living with them awhile, I learned that the Pawai'ia had a nickname for me—Andy Wee Seae. That in itself was not unusual. They liked to refer to my research assistants, particularly the pretty ones, by names that translated to such elegant phrases as "clouds in front of the full moon." My Pawai'ia nickname, by contrast, means "Andy cassowary shit." Cassowaries are large flightless birds that live in rainforests of New Guinea (one species can also be found in Australia). "Large" might seem an understatement to those familiar with the little brown birds that skulk in US gardens. Large in the case of cassowaries means fifty pounds for the smallest species and about a hundred and twenty for the largest—and when I say "largest," I'm talking about birds that can look me straight in the eye, and I'm about six feet tall. These are among the few birds that can easily kill people. Although all birds are the living relatives of dinosaurs, when you look at a cassowary this ancestry is viscerally evident.

"Cassowary shit" might seem an odd and even slightly derogatory nickname. But it's certainly accurate, given I spent about four years roaming the forests of the Pawai'ia searching for cassowary droppings. Each new dropping was either carefully examined and measured *en situ* or gleefully deposited in a plastic bag for more detailed sifting back at the research station—a couple of houses we built in the forest just so we could live there and study cassowaries over an extended period of time. To my Pawai'ia guides, my behavior was not only bizarre but also a waste of a perfectly good plastic bag—a Western commodity they could not easily obtain, as there was no store within days of walking and no money to spend even if they did walk for days. But I paid them well for what was probably one of the best jobs in the country—to leisurely roam the forests, making sure I did not get lost, and helping me carry my rucksack when it became weighed down with numbered plastic bags filled with the stuff that earned me my nickname.

A fresh "dual" cassowary *pekpek* from where the bird slept. They defecate once, go back to sleep, then shift a little and defecate again. Lens cap is about three inches and displayed for scale.

Why dung? Why cassowaries? Why Pawai'ia country? Why even Papua New Guinea, for that matter? Good questions, all. To answer them, I'll begin with the last, most general question, and then move on to specifics.

PNG, as everyone calls Papua New Guinea, is the eastern half of the island of New Guinea, split by a long past and a totally irrelevant colonial map. The western half of the island is now owned by Indonesia, which actually has no more legitimate claim to it than did the Dutch, who annexed that half of the island four hundred years ago. But the eastern half of the island, PNG, became an independent nation about thirty years ago, making it relatively young in the pantheon of former European colonies to gain independence.

The colonial mapmakers shaped the western boundary we see today, but inside PNG live over 800 tribal groups, each with its own culture and language. Not dialects, not varying accents (like Texas vs. Massachusetts), but full-blown languages. Many are as different as Spanish is from Chinese and Chinese is from Hindi. This small nation, roughly the size of California and home to roughly 30 percent of the world's languages, has an incredibly complex culture. Even veteran travelers on their first arrival in PNG can get the sense of having travelled in both space and time. When I first arrived, I felt I had stepped through a portal to a different time. For some, this sensation becomes a compulsion and they either stay or keep coming back. Others seem to hate it and can't wait to get out. Foreign visitors are rarely ambivalent about PNG.

Few countries are further from the beaten trail. There is not a single movie theater or fast food franchise in PNG. You won't find McDonald's or Pizza Hut. In my first year there, the country fired up its first television station to the tune of Sting's "I Want My MTV," because the network is called EMTV (it later had to stop using this theme song because apparently the station had never considered issues of copyright or royalties). EMTV broadcast for about four hours a day then; now it airs for about eighteen hours a day. Most parts of the country have no access to electricity, health care, roads, telephones, or police. A handful of hotels cater mostly to expatriate businessmen in the mining industry. Tourists are rare, numbering a few thousand per year. The tiny tropical island nation of Fiji might welcome more tourists in a good week than PNG sees in a year. This isn't to say that PNG is free of Western influence. When I first arrived there in 1987, many people asked me, "What church are you with?" assuming that, like most whites who live there, I was a missionary. The country still remains a stronghold of American missionaries with anachronistic Victorian-era mentalities, whose goal is to "save" heathen souls from damnation. So whether you are interested in saving souls or saving rainforests, PNG is one of the best places to be.

For me, on that first day in the co-pilot's seat of the Cessna, heading to the airstrip at Haia, was the culmination of a compulsion to dive ever deeper into rainforests. Starting from a bivouac on the summit of El Triunfo in Mexico when I was sixteen, through months in Costa Rica, Ecuador, Peru, and Borneo, my twenties were little more than a relentless drive to plunge ever deeper into pristine rainforest and ever further from the "normal" life of the USA. Flying in to Haia the first time in 1987, I was a 28-year-old biology grad student who thought he knew a bit about rainforests. I soon realized that I still had much to learn: about rainforests, about the coolest rainforest birds—cassowaries—and about PNG and its people. In the very long run I would learn some painful lessons about the nature of "big business" conservation. What I knew, as we banked and circled over green folds of the canopy, was that I was about as happy as I had ever been. A huge adventure lay ahead, but I had no way to predict how it would play out. It would be like a gourmand facing a feast of delicacies from around the world, none before tasted. Unlimited opportunity and new sensations spread before me, ready to be tasted, savored, and explored. It was wedding night with one's fantasized perfect match. Ahead lay the prospect of years with virtually no interactions with anyone other than a few of the semi-nomads who carved out those little gardens. Every day I could pursue the research that interested me; whatever questions tantalized me I could explore. Any beast, from ant-mimicking spider to Harpy Eagle, I could pause to observe as long as I liked. Unnamed plants and animals no biologist had seen before would surround me. I was stepping into the world of past explorers, like my hero Alfred Russel Wallace, who was the first biologist to see so many species and spectacles (like birds of paradise displaying) any person now can see on their televisions. I knew how fortunate I was; I was living in the last few decades of a centuries-long era of biological exploration. The end of this era will come in my lifetime. Few others will experience what I felt as we looked for the little airstrip in the jungle. The future never looked better; my dreams were about to come true and my time in New Guinea would extend to a couple decades. I never imagined the politics, conflicts, and violence that would find me, even in such a remote place.

Chapter One

First time in Haia

Nambawan taim long Haia

I'd been in PNG for several months already, looking for a suitable field study area. The search had proved difficult and my small grant for a pilot study was rapidly shrinking. I'd learned that proximity to a road offers undesirable risks and complications, and so Haia—an airstrip cut in the rainforest far from any road—seemed a potentially good option. Built in the 1970s by a missionary couple, the airstrip now formed the center of a village established by the widely scattered Pawai'ia to take advantage of the new possibilities it created. This little strip of grass was their first link to the outside world and the offerings the missionaries provided: the word of the Lord and some much-needed health care. The missionaries' goal was to translate a few books of the New Testament into Pawai'ia. (Fortunately, they also offered some nursing and other practical training.) They would be there a long time, as the Pawai'ia had no written language, no alphabet, and no tribesmen who could read in any language. To fulfill their mission, they had to learn Pawai'ia, come up with an alphabet for its bizarre vowel sounds, figure out spellings for every word, make up words for things the Pawai'ia had no word for (how, for instance, do you talk about a lion's den when the only large mammal the Pawai'ia knew was a pig?), create special characters for printing the new alphabet, translate Matthew, Mark, Luke, John, etc., and then find some willing locals and teach them to read this newly written New Testament. This same, to me absurd, mission is under way in hundreds of communities across New Guinea.

The entire village of Haia was thus an artificial construct created, ultimately, for the purpose of printing a handful of New Testaments in an unwritten language so a handful of Pawai'ia men could claim to be reading the word of the Lord. I guess I should be thankful to the missionaries, because without a decent airstrip the vast Pawai'ia lands would be accessible only via a very long hike or a helicopter, which I could not afford. At the time, two aviation carriers could take me there. One was the air service maintained by the New Tribes Mission (specializing in Bible translation), and the other was the more generic and public Mission Aviation Fellowship (MAF). Seventh Day Adventist planes were not allowed to land at Haia, I was told, because the sect "preached a false gospel." I found it incredible that missions could have such strong infrastructure and the money to maintain their own fleets of planes, pilots, engineers, hangars, spare parts inventory, and so on in such a remote country. I still marvel that so much money is available for translating the Bible when there is so little for medicine. While expensive new Bibles are churned out in obscure languages like Pawai'ia, children die for lack of a few cheap pills. In PNG, there are dozens of planes devoted to serving missionaries, but not one dedicated to delivering medical service. One missionary explained this to me: Their concern, he said, was people's souls and their afterlife, not this life.

After preliminary scrutiny of available maps, I was hopeful that the Haia area would be an ideal place to find cassowaries and conduct long-term research. Like a single divot in a football field, Haia was a little manmade gap in the dense rainforest canopy that stretched unbroken in every direction to the horizon. The vast surrounding area, the traditional land of the Pawai'ia people, looked promising. The forests were extensive, but the Pawai'ia were few in number. Their land spanned from sea level to near the summit of Crater Mountain on the south side of the central ranges. The dense human populations, such as those in Ubaigubi, where I'd begun my search a couple of months earlier, were over the ridge to the north in the big Central Valley. Europeans had not arrived in Goroka, the capital of PNG's Eastern Highlands Province, in any numbers until World War II. Travel to the fringes, like Pawai'ia country, came much later. For many Pawai'ia, the missionaries living in Haia were the only foreigners they'd had contact with. But before I settled on the area, I needed to do some reconnaissance overflights and scout things out on the ground. The abundance of forest looked promising, but would it offer an ample population of cassowaries?

At the MAF hangar in Goroka I booked a flight to Haia, the first of innumerable bush flights in my future. I would meet many bush pilots who would come and go on two- or five-year contracts. More than a few would die serving rural people like the Pawai'ia, providing their only tenuous link to the outside world. It was dangerous work with lousy pay. But the scenery was spectacular, and every day those pilots made a real difference in the lives of many people. For much of PNG, those pilots and bush planes are the nexus for health care, education, and economic development. Many pilots told me that after flying in New Guinea, every other place seemed mundane. A few went back to Australia or the US, only to return on new contracts because they found the flying in those places dull and pointless. Most of the pilots I met flew for the experience; the mission work or the money was secondary. They were there because it was PNG; I understand that compulsion.

The flight over the mountains was magnificent. After leaving Goroka, we skipped over a series of valleys where ridgetops stretched up to meet the plane then dropped into deep valleys. We skimmed the tops of the ridges so close we could see the smiles on the faces of waving kids, then a half mile farther the valley dropped away and we could not even make out people. From the air in PNG you can see the huge plates of the earth's crust that have been thrust up by subduction, a process wherein geologic massive plates collide, with one forced under and the other riding up to form mountains. Little shifts in this process, earthquakes, are frequent in PNG. We flew past Mt. Elimbari, a giant slab of the earth's crust shoved up in the air that offers on one side a gradual 30-degree slope any Cub Scout could ascend and on the other a vertical cliff that only a fearless technical climber would attempt. Further to the west, the more symmetric volcanic cone of Mt. Karimui poked up through the clouds. A short flight in PNG is the best geology course imaginable. You can envision the forces that lift these mountains. Some of New Guinea's ranges are the fastest rising in the world, inching upwards at roughly the rate fingernails grow. Some New Guinea geologic formations, like the terraces of the Huon Peninsula, are standard examples in geology textbooks. On the ground you often feel the earth shake and tremble. From the air you clearly see the cumulative effects of numerous earthquakes and volcanic eruptions. You can see and feel the massive forces that have shaped the surface of Earth.

Leaving the valleys behind, we approached Crater Mountain, a dark wall rising vertically and disappearing, as it usually does, in cloud. You never fly into clouds in PNG, as they often conceal "hard centers." The usual route to Haia skirts the west side of Crater via a notch between Crater and a lesser summit with ridges also vanishing into the low cloud. We squeezed through a little gap between these two mountains, pushed down to near treetop by the clouds above. Slipping through, the left wing was so close to the vertical wall of Crater I could see individual orchids clinging to the rock. Not far below the tops of trees whipped by. It was too tight to turn around—once committed to flying though a notch like this there is nowhere to go but forward. You hope to emerge on the other side, in clear skies, and not smack inside a low cloud. The bush pilots talk with each other to help get an idea of what conditions lay ahead. There is no Weather Channel with Doppler radar giving them up-to-the minute images. A tip from a pilot who passed a couple of hours prior on a run to Mt. Hagen provided our only information on what lay ahead. He'd seen blue skies to the south, so we felt safe to press on.

Just when I began to think, *Oh shit, I don't like this,* the bottom dropped out below us and the mountain angled off to the far left. Often the terrain changes so swiftly, it seems to be moving toward or away from what feels like a fixed position in the plane. Waterfalls too numerous to count plunged off the sheer sides of Crater. All signs of people and gardens vanished;

we had left the Central Valley and its numerous villages behind. Ahead of us stretched endless miles of rugged folds of land, all draped with unbroken closed forest. No smoke from a cook fire rose above the trees.

What blood is to red, rainforest is to green. Somewhere in this green, I hoped to find a study area and make my home. I searched in vain for anything resembling level or gentle terrain. It was clear that my knees, already the least cooperative part of my body, would take a beating wherever I ended up. Beyond the inhabited plateau aside the big volcano of Karimui twenty miles to the west, there was no level place large enough for a camp, much less a comfortable field area. One unexpected revelation during my time in PNG was that biologists might lend bias to their research because they tend to choose study locations that are easy to traverse on foot. Here, I'd be in a place where every plot or transect would be set on steep, slippery terrain—really hard on knees and ankles, and the sort of place few field biologists deliberately choose to work.

We flew over several valleys, each one looking more like the previous. The pilot must come here often, I told myself, bewildered. Nothing stood out as a landmark, and this was long before the days of GPS. This pilot was flying by memory. At this point in the flight to Haia, as I'd learn on later trips, pilots new to the region would unfold a map on their knee and then alternate between consulting the map and craning over the window, trying to tell which valley was which. After I'd flown in numerous times and had become familiar with the route, I could sometimes help a new pilot. But usually I kept my mouth shut. Usually I was not 100 percent certain where I was, even after dozens of flights over the same endless repetitions of valleys and ridges. There's something a bit disconcerting about sitting next to a pilot who is circling over the terrain, trying to figure out how it corresponds to his map. These guys never stop to ask directions. At such times I sometimes developed an unhealthy fixation on the fuel gauges. One had a typewritten note taped to the instrument panel that read "no more than 85 lbs at 1/4 tank," which meant the gauge didn't actually indicate the amount of fuel in the tank. I wondered which pilot was the first to discover the tank would go empty well before the gauge hit "E." Now and then the pilot would tap the gauge with his finger and, often, it would drop markedly when he did this. In a matter of a couple of seconds we'd go from half a tank to a quarter tank. Better not to think about these matters: You either put your trust in the pilots and their ground crews, or you go back to America.

After a few aerial switchbacks in search of potential study areas, the pilot, Graham, followed a direct trajectory to the small slit in the forest that was the Haia airstrip. We circled, dropping lower and dipping between the flanking hills for the final approach. I spied one metal roof on the missionaries' house and another shed with a metal roof that belonged to an incongruous agriculture extension project. Some two to three dozen houses, all with traditional palm thatch roofs, dotted the area around the airstrip. Twenty years later, on my final flight out of Haia, I would note more than twice as many houses, and several more buildings with metal roofs. But even now, most of the houses are unoccupied at any given time. The semi-nomadic Pawai'ia cannot settle and stay in one village. Aside from cultural reasons, the soil where they live will not sustain many consecutive years of harvest. They have to move on, or starve.

When the plane dropped from cruising elevation, we hit a zone where the air becomes hot and humid. The aroma of rainforest rises hundreds of feet up, and although much of it comes from decomposing vegetation, it is the rich smell of life. If colors have an odor, this is what green smells like. Details came into focus as we descended: each unique individual tree, then individual branches, then leaves. Birds—brilliant white cockatoos and ponderous hornbills—scattered from the canopy as the ground neared.

The MAF Cessna coming in to land at the Haia airstrip.
The approach entailed a circle around the surrounding hills and between peaks.

Flying into a grass landing strip for the first time can be a bit intimidating. You do not realize how fast you are going until you see the ground whizzing by in a blur just before the pilot makes that initial tentative bounce to test how muddy the strip is. What looks from the air like an extended length of runway seems insanely short when the plane touches down on it. The end of the strip, featuring some sturdy trees, rushes toward you at sixty miles per hour. Three little wheels with tiny brakes. I have larger tires on my lawnmower. Depending on the recent weather, water and mud spray up and the pilot coaxes and cajoles the plane into a controlled slide and then a stop. Fortunately, I knew what to expect as I'd flown in and out of a much shorter grass strip in Costa Rica—one that ended in weeds sporting the wrecked fuselage of a botched landing, tail-up, to remind approaching pilots to judge well. You reach a point of no return on these strips: You either land or wreck, but you can't change your mind and circle around for another approach. Attempting to do so would merely drive you at speed into the trees. In Costa Rica, the pilot would sometimes have to buzz the strip to scare off grazing horses. I think that scared the passengers more than the horses, who'd amble toward the edge in response. The Haia strip, I would learn, was well maintained, with good drainage, no ruts, and no livestock. Occasionally a dog would wander through while a plane was descending, causing the pilot to circle while the villagers chased it away.

As we landed, I could see a big crowd of people gathering. Planes did not touch down here often, especially unplanned landings by someone other than the resident missionaries. A major event for the entire village was about to happen, and I was it.

When this guy with long blond hair and a thick beard emerged from the cockpit— with intentions to stay awhile, judging from the number of rice bales in the cargo—speculations murmured through the crowd. As the plane took off, a mob of staring Pawai'ia surrounded me. I was left on my own, surrounded by my supplies and the Pawai'ia. I loved the sensation. After a couple of months in PNG and a few false starts, I had a better idea of what to do and my command of Tok Pisin, the *lingua franca* of PNG, had improved considerably since my first abrupt drop in Ubaigubi shortly after I arrived in PNG (more to come on this). The Pawai'ia seemed much more laid-back compared to the Gimi I encountered in Ubaigubi. In Haia, no one shouted; everyone gaped at me quietly. It made for a somewhat unsettling welcome—a hundred stares, murmurings in a language I did not understand, and a palpable hint of hostility toward a foreign intruder with unknown intentions. Plenty of older warriors, who undoubtedly had histories of brutally killing enemies in tribal war, glared. The crowd, as usual, was mostly men with the women too busy in the gardens or with children to tarry around the airstrip. A few naked boys ran around the feet of their elders or stood still clutching dad's knee and staring, usually with two streams of snot running down from their noses. The men generally wore filthy shorts and an even filthier ripped-up T-shirt, often with some incongruous message like "Visit Bermuda" or "The Ramones" barely visible under the grime. Everyone was lean and fit from a life of hard work and simple diet.

"Apinun olgeta! Gutpela dei!"

Having wished everyone a good afternoon and declared it a beautiful day, I smiled my biggest, stupidest smile. If you look and act like a moron, you can't be much of a threat. Lots of people smiled back politely, saying *"apinun."* They seemed relieved that I did not appear to be a government official or here to push an unwanted agenda. Instead, an idiot had landed in their village—an idiot with a lot of rice and tinned fish. A well-provisioned moron posed no threat, so reservations eased and curiosity swelled. Time to talk.

A guy from Kundiawa, the provincial capital, working on the agriculture extension project pushed out of the crowd and introduced himself. He was the closest thing to official government here, and the only educated person in the group, with some high school. So even though he was not Pawai'ia, the people deferred to him as initial spokesman. He offered me the use of a small storage shed, and I accepted gratefully. I could use it as a sort of base camp for my scouting forays into the forest, and staying with someone neutral, who was not a member of the community, made sense. I didn't want to start out showing any kind of favoritism, as I'd been required to do on my first foray into the bush up at Ubaigubi. (More on that later; I'd learned a lot about what NOT to do in my first sudden total immersion with the Gimi tribe, the Pawai'ia's neighbors to the north.)

That evening I roamed around a bit, but not far. I did not want to intrude and disrupt the quiet village life. I could not help but cause a stir anywhere I went. This village was more accustomed than many to odd white people thanks to the long-resident missionaries. People were curious and stared, but at least children did not scream and run crying for the safety of mother, as was usually the response when I wandered around Gimi villages in the previous couple of months. Houses were raised on stilts and had crude clapboard walls of hand-split logs punctuated with just one or two small windows and a door-less entryway. Inside, cook-fires glowed and smoke wafted out of the thatch. People paused and stared as I passed, then returned to their business. Hordes of kids did not follow me everywhere, and my presence did not seem to cause much of a commotion. I felt a bit less like an alien intruder in Haia than I had earlier in the highlands.

There is mind-numbingly little to do in a village for a biologist like me (my anthropologist friends have a very different sentiment). In Tok Pisin, conversation is fairly limited to niceties like "do you think it is going to rain?" In Haia this is about like speculating whether the sun will come up again. It generally is either raining or soon going to rain. The absence of conversation sometimes aggravated an already lonely feeling. My partner back home was not able, or inclined, to sally into the rainforest for long periods of time. We'd had a good relationship for years with off-and-on stress over my desire to spend longer and longer periods of time in the field. The pull and tug between a good relationship in the U.S. versus time in the field was a constant challenge for me. At times I was numbingly lonely and other times totally enthralled with the forest. After a few months in PNG, the pull to move deeper into the forest was winning. But if I became too idle, the yearning to be back home resumed. It was best to keep moving.

The next day I got started with arrangements to leave. The agriculture extension agent helped set me up with a few carriers and guides, with the goal of heading toward the area where my new friend Mal, whom I'd met in Goroka, told me some survey geologists had noticed (and casually mentioned to him) an abundance of cassowary droppings. I engaged four young men in their late teens to twenties. I chose single men ready for a bit of adventure, not concerned with leaving their families, and clearly able to carry heavy loads. Young PNG men have the muscular sculpted bodies you'd expect to see in muscle magazines in the US. I looked for good smiles, eye contact, and other hints from their body language that they would be willing and reliable companions in the field for a few weeks. Judging character relies on a lot of the same cues wherever you are in the world. John had an easy smile and calm demeanor. More than most, he took extra effort to explain things in Tok Pisin and ensure we understood each other. The usual tendency among Pawai'ia is to nod and agree, even when they have no idea what I am talking about. Orei was quiet but you could tell he was alert and others in the crowd were deferential to him. My favorite was Dupa. He was only about six years old, but I could tell he was smart. He asked questions and listened to the answers. He wanted to go for the experience and didn't care if he was paid. Dupa and Orei would prove to be supportive friends and allies through many ups and downs over the next twenty years.

We discussed the pay, how much food we'd need per day, and other specifics before concluding any obligations. I did this in front of plenty of eyewitnesses. I was being sure to avoid any opportunity for someone to claim I had underpaid him or otherwise reneged on an agreement. I knew the most important key to long-term success with the Pawai'ia would be their trust, and I knew they would not offer that easily and that I could lose it in an instant.

Early the next day while the air was still cool, after the morning fog lifted and some of the dew dried, we set off over a mountain, across a big river, and up over an even larger mountain. As is typical, the day started clear, but I knew it would likely turn to rain in the mid-afternoon. It pays to get moving early so one can get under shelter by the time the rain really sets in. It is funny for me to think back on this trip, to remember how deep into the wild I felt I was going. Later, when we established the field station, this section of trail would be the first four hours on the hike in. I would make it so often it would become a routine trudge and I would just wish for it to be over. But on that first trip it was invigorating to be walking out into a vast forest with no real clue where I was going or what I could expect to find. I can remember sights along that trail from that first trip better than the dozens of times I hiked it later. There was a very recent and large landslide that smothered the trail. We had to pluck our way along it, sometimes sinking into the soft overturned clay. At places we went through sago swamps, where you can sink in to your knees or above in soft gluey muck. The Pawai'ia toss in the large stems of the palm leaves and chunks of fallen trees to make an invisible walkway below the opaque water. In their bare feet they scamper along, feeling where to step. In my boots I could only guess where to step and when I missed the hidden bit of palm I'd quickly sink past my knees and struggle to keep from completely toppling and submerging my binoculars. When I got my footing back, the guides were long out of sight and I just followed the trail of freshly churned mud in the water they had left behind.

The first night, we stayed in a Pawai'ia house. As mentioned earlier, Pawai'ia houses are on stilts, often a good twenty feet in the air, whereas highlands houses are on the ground.

Typically, a tree trunk or two cut off at floor height gives a bit of stability to what otherwise looks like (and is) a rickety stick house tied together with vines. The thatch roof curves completely down the two side walls; the "front" and "back" walls are constructed of thick vertical logs and sticks lashed tightly together. Usually at the front, the floor and thatch roof protrude beyond the vertical wall to form a small "verandah" where you can sit and take in the view, because inside the house there is not much of a view except through the small door opening. The walls are made thus so the house's inhabitants can shoot arrows out through the cracks in the event of attack. The "floors" are a lattice of sticks, usually two inches or less in diameter, lashed to a few thicker bearers. I learned to be careful where I stepped, because often they are too thin in places to bear this white man's burden. The floors, too, had gaps through which arrows could be slung at enemies. Of course, these gaps also meant that if you dropped your flashlight or pencil or anything smaller than a breadbox, it would fall through down to the ground below, usually touching down in the freshest splat of pig manure. It did not take me long, that first night, to tie my pencil to my notebook, as note-writing could become a tedious cardio-exercise I did not need—down the "ladder," wipe off the pig shit, up the "ladder," write a paragraph, down the "ladder." Not a problem for the residents, who have no possessions to drop, but my bag was full of essential gadgets and devices, from rolls of film (which do, indeed, "roll") to expensive pesola scales, candles, batteries, and cutlery, all slightly thinner than the tightest gaps in the floor.

My first of many nights in such houses was typical and I eventually learned there is not a great deal of variation in Pawai'ia lodging. There's no power, TV, or playstation. There are no shelves to hold stuff, no closets, no artwork. Just the floor and the thatch. Sometimes you'll find jaw bones of pigs and other animals wedged in the thatch and well smoked by the fires—testimonies to the owners' hunting prowess. There are usually at least two fire pits— wooden trays filled with earth upon which the cook fires are built, one for men and another for women. The genders are separated by an invisible boundary, and when asked to bring something to the men, a girl will be quite timid about entering the male space, often just setting the item down at the edge of the invisible frontier.

The way up to the verandah/deck (the word "ladder" gives completely the wrong impression) is a single tree trunk leaning nearly vertical, with notches chopped in it for steps. A notch is typically slightly smaller than half my booted foot. I tiptoed up the tree. No handrail. Definitely not OSHA approved. Going up that first time was fairly easy once I stopped thinking about slipping and breaking my neck. The houses are fairly spacious inside, maybe twenty-five by forty feet; and without lights, windows, or interior walls, people seemed to disappear into the deep shadows. Even my team of seven carriers and the house's occupants seemed to melt away in the expanse. A few huddled near the fires and the rest were manifest only as disembodied voices from the deep shadows.

Once we were all inside the gloomy smoke-filled interior, one of my guides began to position massive slabs of tree trunk in a clever holding mechanism in the opening (calling it a door is misleading). I asked why he was doing this. Why on earth barricade the doors in the middle of nowhere? He replied that spirits traveled the river at night; they would kill you if you went out after dark, and they would come in while we slept if we did not bar the door. I refrained from pointing out that spirits probably would have no trouble slipping through the gaping holes in the floor where my dinner, a packet of crackers, had just escaped. Sunset comes around 6:30 p.m. at this latitude. It was going to be a long night.

The first thing you do when you get to a bush house is light the fire, after which the house quickly fills with smoke. The fire dries the thatch and discourages some of the biting insects, who, from what I could tell, instead find a perch outside to wait either for someone to come out or for the fire to die down while the people inside sleep. The smoke also makes breathing hard. When it got too bad, I would lie on the floor with my face pointed through a gap in the decking to suck up fresh air. I should have brought a snorkel. The Pawai'ia capacity to breathe smoke is amazing, but the depressing statistics for respiratory illness in PNG reveal the long-term effects. The men talk through the night in the deep shadows and haze, sitting forward into the light of the fire occasionally to stir it or relight newspaper-rolled sticks of tobacco then leaning back and vanishing in the darkness. That night, their quiet murmuring became gentle white noise and my half-inch foam pad a wonderful mattress. If you are tired enough, any place is comfortable.

I felt like I'd entered a portal to a different era in human evolution. With no "stuff" and no furnishings other than a few slabs of bark to sleep on, which also meant nothing to organize, clean, or tidy up, a Pawai'ia house really is a shelter—from rain, enemies, spirits. The forest is "home." Windowless, the inside is perpetually dark, even in mid-day. At night the smoke and thatch absorb the firelight. There is not a single reflective surface on the interior; everything has the patina of hundreds of hours of smoldering fires.

On one particular night I dug a couple candles out of my bag, lit them, and prepared to make my dinner of Wopa biscuits with peanut butter. Wopa biscuits resemble a three by three, quarter-inch thick piece of lumpy drywall, presumably made from flour. As I gathered my dinner accoutrements, Swiss army knife, Wopa biscuits, and peanut butter, I noticed a sound like raindrops inside the house. Plop, plop, plip, plipipip. . . . Numerous somethings were dropping out of the thatch. One dropped and put out my candle. (What are the odds?) Stuck in the hot wax was an inch-long cockroach. Hundreds of them were dropping out of the thatch. And they were hungry.

I pulled out my torch (what we call a flashlight in the U.S.) and shined it over my backpack and supplies. Hundreds of roaches scurried around. I was on the set of a cheap horror movie. They were everywhere and they were on the prowl for food. A few explored my hair and beard. I kept tight-mouthed for more than one reason. The roaches were so numerous that when I spread peanut butter on a biscuit resting on my thigh, by the time I put the knife aside and closed the jar, there were already two roaches gorging on my peanut butter cracker. All you can do is blow them off like so much dust and continue eating. Somehow, anything I dropped slipped right through the gaps in the floor, but it seemed every roach dropping from the thatch landed on something solid, with its head pointed toward the rich smell of my peanut butter.

That first night was a bit uncomfortable, coping with the roaches and then having to un-barricade the door and negotiate the notched tree in the dark in order to relieve myself. It would have been considered rude to simply make use of one of the gaps in the deck; I might have ended up peeing on one of the valuable sleeping pigs below. Most Pawai'ia have a few pigs that they buy and trade, using them as brideprice, to settle debts, and, on rare special occasions, to slaughter and eat. The pigs, perhaps also fearful of spirits, or more likely acquainted with scraps of food that sometimes fall from above, often sleep below the houses. Lacking a twelve-hour capacity bladder, I had to leave the house at night. My hosts looked at me like I was nuts to go out and face the spirits. I'd take spirits any day over roaches and smoke, and so I took my chances with them, the hungry mosquitoes, and the notched log ladder just to relieve myself.

The house was on the Wara Oo, a river that feeds into the Pio, which feeds into the Purari. The mighty Purari is only the third largest river in PNG, yet its freshwater output to the ocean exceeds all the fresh water coming off the continent of Australia. Someday Australians will want pipelines just to import New Guinean fresh water to their arid continent. It still seems odd that such a parched, dry continent can have such a wet and humid neighbor just a short hop away. I was happy, the next morning, to get away from the trail and garden clearing and explore the lush and dripping forest, where many trees were in fruit.

Almost right away I started seeing signs of cassowaries: fresh droppings full of large seeds, like the ones I envisioned as the topic of my research. Trees peppered the ground below with large fruits the cassowaries like to eat. For the first time, I found an abundance of what I had come to PNG to study. I was elated. With each new pile of *pekpek*, I grew more excited. Each dropping presented a sample of what a cassowary had eaten in the past several hours. Each pile had seeds of new species not seen in the previous pile. I sorted through them glee-fully, scribbling notes, while my Pawai'ia guides watched, puzzled by my exceptionally odd behavior. I was even stranger than the other whites who had been through here collecting ordinary rocks and sending them off in a helicopter. Was there anything whites did not find valuable and fascinating?

I spent a couple weeks in the area, sometimes in a camp, sometimes in a bush house. This was enough to use all the food we had brought and more than sufficient to determine that I could certainly do my research in the area. Everywhere I went I found both more cassowary droppings and more trees dropping beautiful fruits of red, orange, and blue. I could spend weeks cataloging what I found along just one mile of trail. But with an already diminishing supply of food, I had to go back to Goroka and buy provisions for a proper pilot study.

Rather than make the daylong hike back to Haia and then fly to Goroka, I decided to hike all the way to Ubaigubi (a village I'd been to earlier by road) and try to catch a ride to Goroka. My guides, John and Dupa, knew the way. It would mean an overnight on the trail, another overnight near the village of Herowana, which I'd visited earlier before coming to Haia, then another full day to reach the house at Rutanabi/Ubaigubi that had been my initial destination on first arriving in PNG. I had been told this house, built by a photographer and an anthropologist years ago, would be a suitable place to study cassowaries. I found in my first week that it was not, setting off the series of exploratory scouting trips I was now concluding. At Rutanabi I would sleep and await a ride on the next coffee truck to Goroka. It would be a lot of walking, but I would see some nice forest and save the cost and uncertain timing of catching a plane at Haia.

An hour into the hike I was doing what no white guy should do, which is try to walk in the rainforest while carrying a bushknife. I was balancing along a fallen tree over a small ravine when I fell. The fall resulted in a deep gash between my thumb and forefinger as the blade stopped in the ground and the hand holding it slid down along its edge. The old park guards in Costa Rica had a saying: "The most dangerous thing in the forest is a gringo with a machete." The painfully throbbing gash took some of the pleasure out of the long hike. My bush-style bandage of leaves and vines frequently needed readjusting. At least I learned not to hike nonchalantly holding a bushknife, something every male over the age of two could do without mishap in PNG.

The first night we stopped to camp near a stream. Massive trees at the site contributed to an odd, magical feel. Upstream, the water meandered through a level area, with every surface densely cloaked in mosses. Then, abruptly, the stream ended its quiet wandering and hurled itself over a precipice. The dark mossy forest interior provided a backdrop; the other direction offered a view of the tops of trees and water pounding down against polished boulders. I saw very little indication that anyone had been there before us or, for that matter, that anyone had been anywhere in the vicinity in recent decades. The "trail" we'd been following was almost invisible, merely an occasional ancient moss-covered knick from a bushknife made years before. I had the unusual and profound sensation of what earth would be like without humans.

As I'd been merely following the heels of John, I had no clue where I was. I find it very liberating to be camped in a rainforest with no sense of location. When I don't know where the nearest civilization is—because there is none near—I get a sense of calm. The part of the brain that tracks position can shut down, or maybe devote itself to awareness of where I actually am since that is all that matters. It is easier to forget about the outside world when you don't know where it is.

By now I was quite accustomed to the nightly rain. In Pawai'ia country there generally is a light rain every night punctuated with heavier downpours. That night was additionally exceptional because it did not rain and we could listen to the chorus of frogs and night insects all night long instead of the drum of rain pounding on a tarpaulin. We built a small fire and did what hunters do after dark: stare in the flames and listen to the forest. I had no idea that we were camped in what would two years later be part of my study area. And in two years, when we would chose the study site and lay out the trails, I would have no idea we were anywhere near where I had spent this idyllic night. Was it an odd coincidence that in 1989 I would unknowingly choose to live in the same place I'd had that one exceptionally pleasant camp in 1987? Or was that special night what destiny feels like?

Chapter Two

Gimi gunfire and bandits

Mi harim ol guns na bungim raskols bilong Gimi

The second day of the hike was a long haul to Herowana, with my bloody hand throbbing under my makeshift bandage of leaves and vines. Leaves just don't have the absorbent, clot-promoting properties of gauze. A hundred times on that hike I swore I'd always carry a good first-aid kit in the future, even when traveling light on a short patrol. I asked my guide if we were close to Herowana, and he replied "*klostu*," which can mean anything from one mile to ten miles. *Longway liklik* (*liklik* translates to "small") means anything from two miles to fifteen miles, and *longway tru* means anything from ten to fifty miles. And then there is the dreaded *longway nogut tru*, meaning too far to even think about. Right now Goroka was *longway nogut tru*. But Herowana was *klostu*. I needed to stop and rest.

As we approached, I began to hear what sounded like the popping of small arms fire, as if two mobs of gangsters were shooting it out in South Herowana. Dupa told me it was "*mambu*," which means bamboo, or pipe, or tube, or cylinder, and meant nothing to me in terms of explaining the noise. As we approached I could see what he meant. A few men, women, and children were clearing a new garden—cut right into the forest. They had their backs to us as they burned a thicket of bamboo, which popped like gunfire when the air inside the hollow internodes heated up and exploded. New Guinea fireworks. We were fairly close to the group when our guide sang out a greeting. You don't surprise people in places like this. We were Pawai'ia walking into Gimi territory. A few generations earlier an encounter could have been extremely dangerous for the Pawai'ia.

The group turned and a couple of the kids screamed in horror, clinging to their mother. Not only was I the first white person they'd ever seen but I was covered in facial hair, had a bloody hand (probably fresh from my last meal of child), and had emerged from the forest where all sorts of spirits dwell. The men, muscular and sweaty from their labor, all held axes. I hoped they were less superstitious than the wailing children.

Some of my Pawai'ia guides knew enough Gimi to explain why we were passing through. The Gimi had heard of me through the grapevine because of my earlier stays with Batanimi, one of the region's elder "bigmen," on the mountain to the north. But they never expected to see me emerge from the south. We went to their hut and they treated us generously, as most rural Papuans will do with a stranger, with offers of fruit and roast *kaukau*, the soft potato staple of the highlands. It was a treat after a couple of weeks of Wopa biscuits, peanut butter, and the occasional cockroach.

The ensuing hike from Herowana back to Rutanabi was uneventful. A couple of my Pawai'ia carriers came along, wanting to go to Goroka; the others turned back to socialize a little in Herowana (there were a few intermarriages between Herowana and Haia and I think a couple of the young men wanted to scope out the prospects for a bride). I had been paying them—for some this was the first cash they had ever earned—and they wanted to go to town to buy something. This seemed like a lot of effort just to get a new bushknife or a rice pot. They feared being robbed along the way, in town, or on the way back. But they wanted to go anyway. I admired their spirit. These were young men and their eyes were bright, as have been the eyes of millions of young men around the world for centuries when going to the "Big City" for the first time seeking adventure and fun. At Rutanabi, Falau and Dorahau, who'd been my first guides in PNG a couple of months earlier, greeted me like a long lost son. I still had supplies stashed in the house, so we ate well and rested while waiting for word about the next ride to Goroka. The Gimi and my Pawai'ia guides talked a lot. Power in both their societies often stemmed from allegiances with people of different clans and tribes. A tactical marriage here and there or the gift of a pig at the right time, and you might have an ally when you most need one.

There was one old vehicle in Ubaigubi—Jeffery's Land Cruiser, with which he made a small business by hauling passengers and 100–pound bags of green coffee beans to Goroka. Coffee was going for about fifteen cents a pound. (Think about that next time you get a three dollar espresso.) I could not fathom how Jeffery's cut could pay for even the fuel, much less maintenance. But on seeing the vehicle it was obvious not much went toward upkeep. It looked like it had been airdropped in World War II without the benefit of a parachute. It was covered with massive dents—not the kind of dents you get in the shopping center parking lot, the kind you get when you roll down a hill and are stopped by a tree. The windscreen was spider-webbed. In fact, the only smooth surfaces on the truck were the tires, which were like polished obsidian. Oh well, I thought, Jeffery makes the drive several times a month, so how bad could it be?

He loaded on so many bales of coffee that, if the truck still had a suspension, it would have snapped. Jeffery eyed it carefully and, judging it overloaded, dictated that two bags of beans be removed, despite the loud protests of the bags' owner. Satisfied that the truck was now at maximum load, he told us to get in—as if human cargo did not add to the weight. Twelve men piled on top of the coffee bags. Something metallic, like the frame, groaned. At least the weight will provide some traction, I thought, and we have enough strong men to push the Land Cruiser out of the mud holes when we get bogged.

As the *"masta,"* I was offered the prestigious passenger's seat. But I demurred and allowed the usual Number Two to have his spot beside Jeffery. I'd been on this road before and had good reason to want to sit on the back. About an hour into the ride, my caution paid off. We were moving along the side of the mountain where the road sloped downhill, "downhill" being a euphemism for a huge cliff with the distant sound of rapids roaring invisibly far below. The truck started to slide toward the edge and Jeffery did what my Driver Ed. teacher in high school taught us never to do. He gunned the engine and swung the wheels away from the edge. This sent the rear of the truck, where we were sitting, swinging wildly toward the cliff. We all jumped for safety, fully expecting to see Jeffery and the dented Land Cruiser slide out of sight over the precipice. A few twisted wrecks at the base of this mountain testify that such events are not unheard of. Miraculously, the truck stopped, like in a carefully staged movie cliffhanger. Jeffery was an unusually large and muscular Gimi warrior, but he looked pretty pale. I was glad I'd opted not to ride up front with him. I probably would have needed to change my pants right about then.

The riders and Jeffery started shouting in Gimi, even louder than usual. The problem, as it appeared to me, was they needed men to stand on the very brink of the precipice and push uphill so the truck could pull away without sliding further sideways and over the edge. But if it did slide sideways, the guys pushing could be pushed over themselves, with a truck following on top of them. I could see why they were shouting, though Gimi shout about anything. ("THAT'S A CRICKET!" "NO, IT'S A GRASSHOPPER!") No one asked my opinion, and I was not about to volunteer to get between the truck and the cliff edge.

Some men found rocks and gravel to shove under the wheels, and we wedged them in so the truck would be less likely to slide backwards, after which we pulled as best we could from the uphill side, using a natty length of rope, as Jeffery gently inched the vehicle away from the edge. This was no time to gun the engine. He kept the door open in case he needed to leap free. The truck crept back from the brink and onto the road. Laughing, everyone jumped back on board, and smokes were passed around. I inhaled deeply on mine. I kept a wary eye on the edge of the road as we continued on the narrow track, poised to bail out again if necessary.

Bailing out is a common safety feature on many open-bed Public Motor Vehicles (PMVs), as taxis and buses are called. Safety belts could be a big mistake. Once I read in the paper of a handful of people who died when they bailed out of a PMV rolling down the highway at high speed. Thinking the vehicle had caught on fire, they just leapt off. It isn't easy in PNG to make the transition to the late twentieth century in a couple of generations. Kids who grew up in a society that resembles what Europe might have looked like fifty thousand years ago can find themselves as adults on the back of a truck rolling down a highway. Not understanding that you can't jump off a speeding truck is symbolic of the whole difficult transition PNG has gone through. Our world in the US has changed dramatically in my lifetime. Imagine the change if the starting point were not the United States of the 1960s, but North America of 1,000 BC.

A little farther down the road we connected to the stretch that the UN-funded machines had upgraded. Earlier, when I came up this road, workers were busily trying to make it passable, all the while acknowledging it was an expensive exercise in futility. Here Jeffery could sometimes shift to second gear and we all relaxed a bit, thanks to the recent work of the heavy machines. When a truck approached from the other direction, the two drivers stopped to discuss the hazards each had yet to face. There was especially animated discussion in what sounded like three languages as the passengers on our truck shouted to the passengers on the other truck.

None of it was intelligible to me, but by their body language I could tell something was up. One of the guys told me the oncoming truck had just been robbed by a group of bandits (*raskols* in Tok Pisin), who were waiting just ahead. He suggested I hide my money and pocket knife, as they would really want my pocket knife. I was with about fifteen of the most muscly guys you can imagine. I asked, "Would they rob Jeffery's truck with so many strong men aboard?" The response: the bandits had bushknives, two shotguns, and a pistol. The rules changed when guns were involved. Every sane person in PNG dreaded the increasing numbers of firearms. The bandits, we were told, were at a landslide that had blocked most of the road; you had to stop. Great, I thought. Who would they want to rob out of this crowd? I shoved most of my cash into my crotch, leaving a few bills in my pockets for the thieves. I wondered why we didn't at least wait a few hours in case the bandits tired of waiting for another load of victims.

I'd already heard all sorts of horror stories about *raskols* in PNG—about how they'd just as soon chop your wallet out of your hand as take it, about the homemade shotguns that accidentally went off, about victims brutalized for no apparent reason. I did not have much choice; I could not walk to Goroka alone and expect to be safer. As we came up to the landslide, I saw no sign of the armed robbers. They were probably lurking in the nearby undergrowth. An old man cleared the loose earth from the road with a flattened stick. Probably their lookout. As we pulled up to him and stopped, the old man asked for some small change, and Jeffery gave him some *toea* for his work making the road passable. Some small kids played nearby. Everything was calm.

This was the same "robbery" the people in the passing truck had endured and survived to tell us about. I learned a lesson here that I would constantly need to re-learn:

many Papua New Guineans, especially the Gimi, have the capacity to so exaggerate and twist a story to the point that it bears no resemblance to what I might consider the truth. But even the most outrageous distortion will be considered true if the telling of it serves some purpose. Not every culture defines "truth" the same way, which can create huge misunderstandings. So the gang of robbers with bushknives, two shotguns, and a pistol turned out to be a few kids and an old man with a stick. The only truth I could see to the story was that there had, indeed, been a landslide.

Having survived a near fall off a cliff and a "band of armed thugs," and after the Land Cruiser's incessant jarring and violent rocking in the ruts of the road, we all grinned ear to ear when we pulled onto the paved Highlands Highway. We went farther in the last thirty minutes of our trip than in the first four hours. Jeffery kindly dropped me off at the Lutheran Guest House. I quickly made tracks for the Aero Club and a few cold beers with my friend Mal and the other pilots that would undoubtedly be there. Mal was a long-term expat in PNG, an Aussie chopper pilot who had landed here after a stint in Vietnam and stayed to build a thriving helicopter charter business. This club had been my initial point of entry into PNG and every night it housed the community of expatriates and pilots who were becoming my friends, or at least occasional drinking buddies. In the past few weeks I'd barely spoken at all, just the basics of camp life and discussions about *pekpek* in Tok Pisin. I looked forward to a few rounds of drinks, called *helikoptas* because you ordered another one by twirling your finger like a chopper rotor. The banter with the hard-drinking Aussies and chilled *helikoptas* would be a welcome diversion while I planned the next step in my research.

Chapter Three

Droppings galore, a good camp and a flood

Plenti pekpek, gutpela ples, na wara tait

My story of looking for a study site, getting government and landowner permissions, and struggling for funding is atypical among biologists. In much of the world there are well-established field research stations, parks, or other entities that support research. Some eco-tourism facilities sponsor biologists who do their research between guiding visiting tours. I thought I was coming to such an arrangement when I first got the invitation to PNG, something I'll describe later. But that tourist lodge proved to be a chimera when I got here. I had to work through difficult preliminaries many young biologists avoid simply by going to any of the many well-established research sites around the world, none of which happen to be in the world's third-largest rainforest, New Guinea.

These established sites typically offer electricity, running water, housing, a kitchen, and real lab space. Often there are support staff who cook, buy supplies, maintain the buildings, and even do your laundry. Well-groomed trails are laid out and mapped. There are permanent vegetation plots and someone has done the hard work of identifying at least the dominant plants in the forest. Often populations of birds and other animals have already been tagged, banded, or somehow marked, ready for study. There are detailed topographic maps, censuses, and inventories of all sorts of organisms. And, most importantly, there are alumni of the site who have encountered and can help you solve almost any problem that might come up, from a failing water pump to government paperwork and permits. I had none of these benefits.

An idealized trajectory for a graduate student in biology is to: 1) identify some interesting questions (like my questions about seed dispersal); 2) identify a good system to study those questions (as I had determined cassowaries would be ideal); 3) choose the research site that best suits the study of the system and questions; and 4) find the funding, go to the selected location, and do the study. I call this the "idealized" trajectory because more often than graduate advisors like, students approach it differently. For example, they might already have a passion for pythons, so they seek a question they can study with pythons, or they might have a passion for a particular place and so they seek the questions and organisms they can study at that place. Some purists say this is the wrong way to pursue a PhD, but I disagree. People should follow their passions, not just the sterile intellectual exercise of a good question. Of course for some, their passion is answering questions and the organisms or places are irrelevant.

Usually this trajectory can land a student anywhere from a viable study site to a super-cushy field station, like Barro Colorado Island, where there are cold drinks in vending machines and enough lab equipment for a small college. All my questions and passions led me to PNG, where unfortunately there was no cushy field station, not even a Spartan camp used by some ecologist before me. Indeed, when I came to PNG there had been hardly any long-term ecological studies of any sort. Only one person had banded birds for any period of time on the world's second largest island. There were no permanent vegetation plots (other than some widely scattered plots across the country of the PNG Forestry Division). No checklist of plants I could consult, no habituated animals, no grid of mapped trails, and certainly no one to shop and cook for me.

I faced a many-layered series of barriers and hindrances that essentially discouraged anyone from doing long-term ecological research in the region. Graduate students normally have just a couple years to get their data and start writing. Who can afford to spend two years just setting up a study site? More senior researchers need to publish or perish to keep the funding coming. Who can stop publishing for a couple years to set up a study site? The situation in PNG was a negative feedback loop; each passing year channeled the world's researchers to other countries with better research facilities. This hurt PNG in many ways, most significantly in that it eliminated the places and opportunities that provide the training grounds for indigenous biologists. At the established research stations in Costa Rica, Panama, etc., you meet many national students and biologists along with foreign biologists. Through the years these students become top biologists themselves; many get scholarships to top universities around the world and go home to build and mentor scientific capacity in their home countries.

Look at the thriving academic biology communities in places like Costa Rica, and the scientifically managed and effective conservation in such countries, then look back in time and you will find subtle links back to research stations and the researchers who used them. In 1987 the modus operandi of biological research in PNG was still like that of the first half of the century—a short expedition from abroad in which a series of specimens or other data are collected, after which they are analyzed and written up back in the U.S., Australia, or Europe. Hardly anyone stayed for any length of time to study ecology. Hardly anyone had the chance to mentor and train a PNG student in the field.

Every hardship and challenge I encountered getting started in PNG heightened my resolve to do something more than just collect my data and get out. I knew the way to do something more significant than simply generate a nice dissertation was to build a research station that would endure long beyond my study and become a center where PNG students and foreign researchers mixed while they did long-term studies. The kernel of this strategy took shape in the months ahead; particularly after I was joined by Deb (chapter 7), who encouraged and developed a grander vision (most of which I kept concealed from my graduate committee back home).

Establishing a new research station required more than just putting up some buildings or completing a passable dissertation. I would have to demonstrate to the skeptics, like the ones who had warned me off PNG the previous year, that one really can do long-term field studies in Papua New Guinea. For those who had come up through the relatively easy path provided by established stations in easy-to-work countries like Costa Rica and Panama, what I would attempt seemed foolhardy. Many friends and colleagues warned me against coming here. I'd end up with nothing, they'd say: it was too risky, I'd waste all my time on logistics, it was too expensive, I'd be killed or die of malaria. . . . The vast majority of US tropical biologists worked in the New World tropics. In 1987 you could find more US tropical biologists in one Costa Rican research station in one month than in all of Papua New Guinea over a year. The equivalent for marine biologists would be to study the Atlantic Ocean but ignore the Pacific Ocean. Marine biologists don't do this. But then, their research stations can sail around the world.

But the cassowary work was the engine that drove the larger agenda. Few donors would fund a new research station, especially in a place without a proven track record of successful research. It was a classic case of what comes first, the *pekpek* or the tree? But I could find donors to support a study of seed dispersal and what happens in a cassowary dropping. I needed to get my research rolling and the rest would hopefully follow.

Back in Goroka, after a night at the Aero Club trying to prove a Yank can keep with the Aussies, and maybe sleeping in a little later than usual at the Lutheran Guest House, I set about stocking up on a Cessna-load of supplies to go back to Haia for a pilot study. The two food staples are rice and tinned mackerel; with these and a few flavorings you can live for weeks and meet the expectations of guides and carriers. PNG is the largest per capita consumer of canned mackerel. The key to a successful camp assistant is his full belly. Variety and flavor count much less among people who just want a really big meal with some protein. I bought new tarps and a larger cookpot for the rice. I packed my key research gear in two Pelican cases. Unlike nearly everything that seemed to break or fail in the harsh PNG conditions,

I had few problems with Pelican cases. I even lit one on fire by accident as I listened to Dorahau, my assistant in Ubaigubi, drone on about village politics while a candle burned down to the case and ignited it behind me. My first clue that my tent was about to go up in flames around me was that Dorahau actually stopped talking! I hope by now the manufacturers have changed to a polymer that is not so inflammable.

For this trip and many more over the next ten years I had no car in Goroka. Visiting researchers like me had to either carry everything by hand to the MAF hangar or cajole shop owners to give us a lift for heavy purchases. Most were willing to help. Goroka was wrapped around the nearly mile-long airstrip. So to get from one side of town to the other, you had to walk around the airstrip. Most of the shops are on the east side. The MAF hangar, of course, was on the west. I could kill several days walking, shopping, and lugging.

A chartered Cessna holds about 450 kilograms (about half a ton), including passengers—more than enough for the supplies on this early pilot study, but later work would require several planeloads. You can go more cheaply as a passenger, but then you are limited to about twenty pounds of belongings. Even though MAF subsidized their flights so poor rural people could get to town for medical care or to their missions, charters were still expensive. Chartered planes cut into my small remnant of grant dollars. As we flew into Haia I tried to reconnoiter as the pilot flew a couple extra circuits over the general area. But with the rugged terrain cloaked in forest and no outstanding landmarks, it was impossible to identify potential field sites from the air. It all looked too hilly and steep. I'd been in the country over three months already, mostly just looking for a place to do research. I was tiring of looking for a study area and eager to actually get started studying cassowaries.

The gear was off-loaded and the Cessna roared away, skimming just above the trees at the end of the airstrip and up into the closing clouds. I was again met with that silent moment, standing alone with cartons of food and gear. Once again I stepped out of the Western world and solidly into Papuan village life. I was finding that once that plane faded into the sky, I could feel the weight of appointments, schedules, and the hundreds of things that dictate our days slipping away. My internal clock shifted to a more sane and relaxed measure of the passage of time. In town there seemed to be a million externalities assaulting one's senses, demanding alertness (*Watch out for the traffic*) or constantly niggling in my mind (*Remember to buy cheese to take to dinner tonight at Mal's house at 7 . . . and what should I wear? Do I have time to do laundry? If I go to the bank before it closes at 4, how long will the line be? . . .*). These sorts of thoughts constantly run through our minds in our society. Every moment is defined by expectations placed upon us.

Upon arrival at the airstrip, the transition from Goroka to fieldwork was finally complete. A bunch of men and kids grabbed the various cartons and bales of rice and carried them up to the agriculture agent's little office. As happens in the tropics, dusk sank quickly; and as happens in Haia, a light rain pattered on the tin roof. I had arranged with a couple of the men to go back to the area I had visited earlier for a more extended stay. They could see by the amount of food, I meant to stay a longer time. They could not be happier. I paid a good daily wage for the easiest work imaginable—walking in the forest looking for cassowary *pekpek*. When I first visited Mexico as a teenager, the important first words of Spanish I had learned were *cerveza fria*, cold beer. In PNG, my first words in Tok Pisin were *pekpek bilong muruk*, shit of the cassowary.

Getting the proper landowner permissions is essential to working in harmony in PNG. Without first learning the local language and then spending a year mapping genealogies and the myriad invisible boundaries that crisscross the landscape, it is virtually impossible to know what ground belongs to whom. The best I could do was to try to pick out the people who would be honest and helpful and then assign them as deputies to choose my workers and get the proper permissions. If you hire a guy from one clan to work on land that belongs to another clan, you can encounter a major snafu. Unfortunately, Pawai'ia culture inhibits anyone from readily telling you you've made a bad hire. So more than once I've made a camp with a crew of workers and after a few days someone comes and tells me the *papa graun* (elder landowner) is mad that I've hired so-and-so and either wants me to fire the worker or get off his ground.

"Why didn't you tell me this when I hired them?"

"You didn't ask."

I picked out John, who had demonstrated his intelligence and eagerness to communicate on my first patrol. Someone who makes the effort to explain complexities through the language barrier is surprisingly rare, but essential. John helped me pick out seven guys to stay in camp with me. This was more than I really needed, but the politics of employment often mean you hire more manpower than you need. A few more carriers would return to their homes after shuttling supplies to the campsite. All this had to be worked out in advance and explicitly, because it is difficult, to put it mildly, to be in camp with eighteen men and have to disappoint eleven of them by sending them home. Among the group with me was Dupa, the young boy who had wanted to come on my first patrol. He would turn out to be about the hardest worker in the bunch, and later prove to be one of the best workers in the community throughout the next twenty years. I would watch him grow to become a young man with a family of his own and grieve for him each time one of his children died, a shamefully common occurrence in rural PNG.

The next morning as I finished my breakfast of Wopa biscuits, the designated men, along with John and Dupa, arrived to take up their loads. No one had high-tech backpacks like you see on the Appalachian Trail on the backs of intrepid hikers. These guys literally shouldered the loads, be it a twenty-kilogram bale of rice or an even heavier carton of tinned fish. Although all were shorter than me by a foot, they all had more muscle and not a gram of fat. Their sinewy muscles rippled and bulged when they hoisted their loads and glided toward the forest edge. With a lot of laughter and joking we set off. Soon I would be huffing through the sago swamp quagmire and then gasping for oxygen up the first ridge, but the carriers contin-ued laughing and talking as though they were still taking their first steps out of the village.

John had a place in mind for our camp. He knew I wanted an area with lots of *pekpek bilong muruk* and level enough so one could move freely, not be constrained to ridgetops as I'd been on my earlier forays around Herowana. He had the ideal site in mind, which also just happened to be on his clan's property. When we got there it seemed well chosen. It was fairly level and right along the lower Wara Oo (*wara is* Tok Pisin for "river"), not far from its junc-tion with the Wara Pio. Here the riverbed was quite wide, easily eighty meters in places, and filled with large stones and small boulders. The actual river with water in it was only about twenty meters across and varied from slow idyllic swimming holes to rapids over the shallows that were difficult to ford. It was getting late so we set up a temporary camp before a light rain set in. The men quickly got a fire going. I've had all sorts of miserably wet camps in PNG, often setting up just as night falls. We've never been without a fire, even though no one carries anything more than a few matches and sometimes not even that. In the early days of my work someone carried a few carefully wrapped hot embers that were used to start the next cook fire. Now, lighters and matches are widespread.

I set up my two-man tent, mainly to keep out sandflies and provide a bit of privacy. Before turning in, I to my tent and the others to the ground by the fire under the largest tarp, we chatted around the fire. Well, they chatted in Pawai'ia. I listened and let the sound of the chatter act as a background to my internal thoughts about how to pursue my research the next day. I turned in tired but excited to finally have things in place to start serious research. I was at the edge of a forest full of cassowaries, with a month or more of food, and no other distrac-tions. At last I could *really* get started without further interruptions. Or so I foolishly thought.

The next morning I paid the carriers and sent them off to Haia, happy to have some cash and something new to talk about. After they left, the remaining men started building a better campsite. I thought for a moment we might be too close to the river in case it flooded. But I figured these guys grew up here and knew their bush better than I ever would. While they improved the camp, Dupa, another man, and I set off to look for *pekpek*. We wandered in a fairly random way, seeking out places where we expected to find *pekpek*. The terrain was rolling along the river and then abutted the flank of a ridge. But here the side of the ridge was a fairly gentle incline and one could work on it all the way to the top. I did not make it to the top that day, as we found so many droppings and fallen fruit, I was busy with a new discovery every fifty yards.

Wherever we found a dropping I would stop and collect data about it, all recorded in a rainproof notebook with waterproof ink or pencil. It rained at least some every day, and some days it rained a lot. Sometimes the driest spot on your body was the roof of your mouth. Everything had to be waterproof and sealed in Ziploc bags, and these stored inside a plastic garbage bag inside my backpack. So depending on the weather, each bit of work could be preceded by several minutes of extracting notebook, camera, tape measure, etc., from their plastic bags and then concluded with the same process in reverse. Not knowing when I would find the next dropping, leaving something unwrapped could mean it was wet and ruined by the next time I stopped. The plastic bag is the single greatest invention for rainforest biologists. Most *pekpek* I put into a Ziplock bag to take back to the camp for more detailed analysis. I am sure this facet of my odd behavior gave the Pawai'ia the most to talk and speculate about.

I sorted through each bagged dropping, counting how many seeds of each species I found. For each type of seed I would make descriptive notes, save some as vouchers, and assign it an identifying number beginning with my initials. Before too long I would be able to enumerate the contents of a dropping: 17 AM #4s; 2 AM #27s; 6 AM #12s. The goal then was to find the trees of all the species of seeds I found in droppings, collect vouchers of them (preserved leaves, flowers, and fruits) that I could then take to botanists and have identified. Eventually I would change the AM numbers to scientific names and know that in a particular dropping I had 17 *Cryptocarya papuensis*, 2 *Cerbera floribunda*, 12 *Chlaenandra ovata*, etc.

I also began learning the name in Pawai'ia for each species, so I would know a dropping had seeds of *Sa-ah*, *Orai*, and *Bobbohsah*. The Pawai'ia could identify the species in the field using their language, but those names were meaningless to the scientific community. So I had to initially put a number to everything and eventually tie that to its local (*tok ples*) name and its scientific (Latin) name. Science requires an unambiguous name for something, and a great deal of my time was devoted just to figuring out what to call different organisms.

Dupa, an exceptional tree climber, proved a great aid. I could find a fallen fruit and need a specimen of its leaves. Dupa would find a way up into the canopy and drop a sample to me. Sometimes this meant climbing up the vine-encrusted bole of one tree then moving through the canopy horizontally across several trees to get to the desired place. Often he would be completely out of sight from the ground. He and I shouted back and forth, like I was talking to the trees themselves, until the sample I wanted came spiraling down from high in the canopy. It was nerve-wracking to watch, but his skill and ease were so evident I became comfortable with his climbing. I never specifically told him, or any climber, to climb anything. I asked if he could get a sample and he was free to choose what was viable and what was not. Every now and then a tree or vine proved too difficult for him. But he would remember and sometimes days later point out a tree and say, "this is the same kind as the one I could not climb before, but this one I can climb." It was this kind of initiative that made Dupa particularly stand out among the hundreds of Pawai'ia I would employ over the years.

Collecting the samples in the field was only the first step. I would take them back to camp then sort through the *pekpek*, tabulating their contents. I described and illustrated new seeds and fresh fruits. Fruiting plant leaf samples I pressed and dried in newspaper. I also separated fruit pulp samples from the seeds of freshly fallen fruit and strived to dry them in the sun. All of these tasks were difficult in a bush camp. I had the guys fabricate a table from bush materials, with a bench to sit at so I had at least a bit of comfort. But it was rough and tiring. The tables were made of saplings lashed together with vines, so when I set something down there was a 50 percent chance it would slip through a gap and I'd have to waste twenty minutes sorting through the leaf litter and detritus looking for it. Even after raking the ground clear, I'd find that things have a way of vanishing. If there was even a slight crack in the soil, that is where my forceps would land out of sight. I swore that when I built a research station the three priorities had to be a good roof, a good floor, and a good work surface. After that, the rest would follow.

Because of the biting insects and the tedium of being watched incessantly by my camp mates, I sometimes hunched in my little tent to work. The Pelican case would be my tabletop and I would write my notes into the night by candlelight. It was a tranquil time to myself.

One evening, in a light rain just at dusk, Dupa came to my tent, and with a mischievous big grin he said, "*Wara i kamap nau*," which meant the river was rising. I did not really understand the implications of this, but he repeated it several times for emphasis. Then I heard it. At first it sounded like the rumble of ocean surf in the distance. The difference was, unlike the ocean, this rumble was moving toward us. There is something primal about rumbling low-frequency noises that increase in power as they move toward you. It almost invariably means you are in some kind of trouble, and the autonomic reflexes start kicking in. My gut turned sick and my pulse quickened. I climbed out of my tent into the light rain. How could such a light rain cause this? I looked to the north and saw the mountains buried in roiling, angry black clouds. A heavy rain was dumping in the headwaters and we were about to see how quickly water rolled off those steep slopes.

I could see water filling in the low places between the rocks, but the main river was still half a football field away across the dry rocky riverbed. Then a low wall of water actually moved down the river, and in a minute the 80 yards of dry rock bed was covered in fast-moving water rushing to the Pio. Dupa watched with an excited grin. He found this entertaining, but I was getting a little nervous. My tent was on the top of the embankment. It had been about fifty yards away from the water and about fifteen feet higher than the riverbed, but now that fifty-yard buffer was gone and I was only about ten feet higher than the water level. I could stand at the edge of my tent and look down at fast-moving water where a few minutes ago there had been dry rocks.

I asked the guys, now wishing I had asked this when we set the camp, were they *sure* this was a safe spot? They all smiled and laughed and assured me it was okay. Their part of the camp was about fifteen yards farther from the edge but no higher than my tent site. I liked to set myself a little apart so I did not have to breathe campfire smoke and listen to chatter all night long. If the river topped its bank, my tent, and everything in it, would be the first thing to go.

I went back by my tent. The river was now much higher and had transformed from fast to raging. Entire trees were washing down, spinning like toy boats in a bathtub. It soon became dark, and heavier rain further reduced visibility. I could see the raging river with my flashlight; it was only about four feet below me now. I looked back and saw the men smoking and laughing under their tarp. This was reassuring. As long as they were calm, I figured I was okay. Then that heavy rain that had been upstream arrived; it pounded down in buckets. I retreated inside my tent.

The roaring river was literally a few feet away and rain thundered on my tent. A couple times I poked my head out with the flashlight and saw the water only about a foot below me. It was racing by. I lay back in my tent. Great. I got out my trusty pocketknife and kept it open in hand. My worry now was that the swift current could undercut the bank and I would collapse into the river zipped in my tent, like a ready-made bodybag. I had the knife clutched in hand in case this happened. I thought I might have time to cut through the tent and escape if I felt the bank beginning to slip. One likes to pretend he is prepared. The pounding rain on the tent and the roaring of the river fused into a single roar. I felt like I was inside a waterfall.

After a while I stuck my head out again and shone my torch over to the men's camp to see how they were faring. My stomach tightened another notch when I saw they were gone. The tarp was gone, their stuff was gone, and the fire long since doused by the rain.

Things are just getting better and better, I thought. They had fled into the night without me. So much for the bonding around the campfire. If I slipped into that river now, and the guys did not report it, it would be months before anyone else in PNG would even think to ask, "Hey, what ever happened to that Yank who looks at cassowary shit?" I had to get out, but I could not carry much. I envisioned all my supplies, my tent, clothes, everything, washed away. Maybe those skeptics back home had been right. PNG *is* too difficult. I made sure I had my most valuable items in the two Pelican cases—my notebooks, my camera, my passport and money, and my plane ticket home. I'd probably need it soon. The specimens would have to meet their fate along with all the food, camp gear, and my tent.

Just as I began moving away from the tent, looking for the best route into the forest, Dupa materialized from the dark, his big smile still firmly planted. In the light of the flashlight I could see he was as soaked as me. Dupa wore only a ragged T-shirt and shorts; there was no point in even wearing a raincoat in this kind of rain. It is weird when your salvation comes from a six-year-old. He said it was time to go, "*yumi go nau.*"

I gave him my flashlight and followed, carrying my two precious cases. We moved up the hillside, deeper into the forest, and came to a little bluff, where we set up a quick make-shift camp: a ridgepole with the men's tarp draped over it. The men huddled beneath it, with no fire for once, watching the water lash down on all sides. At least the roar of the river was muted and replaced by the sound of raindrops on a million leaves. Even in such uncomfortable conditions, the men were in good humor and joking. They explained that they decided the river might overflow its banks and wash us away, so they moved uphill. They had wanted to get a tarp up before coming back to get me so I could move straight under shelter. I appreciated their consideration, but wished they'd at least told me they wanted to move camp.

We leaned together for warmth, none of us sleeping. I shared the soggy blanket of a raincoat with Dupa; a couple of the men had their rain-soaked blankets sogged around them too. Sometime around 4 a.m., the rain eased up enough that we could hear the river. I tried to discern if it had moved twenty feet closer and washed away our camp but it was impossible to tell. There was nothing we could do now, so we waited until dawn. We made our way back to camp through the soaked and dripping undergrowth. I was dreading what I would find. But to my relief, everything was still there. It looked like the river had barely reached the top of the embankment. All our gear was soaked and sitting in pools of water, but nothing had been washed away.

One of my early camps on the Wara Oo. The river rose in a matter of hours and nearly washed us away.

Almost as fast as the river had come up, it receded. By afternoon we had everything out on rocks in the re-exposed riverbed, drying in the tropical sun. The specimens had been wrapped in plastic and survived. Very little was actually damaged; being meticulous about always keeping things wrapped in plastic paid off. That afternoon I moved my tent farther uphill. The next day I was back to searching the forest for *pekpek* and fruit. Every new experience seemed a lesson pointing to the same conclusion: I would need a real structure for long-term work. I knew if I ever built one, it would not be in a scenic and sunny spot beside a river! Given the way water collected on the forest floor, anyplace could flood. Now I understood another reason why Pawai'ia houses were on stilts. They were not just defense against marauding neighbors or spirits in the night. Being up off the ground not only kept you away from the sodden earth, it allowed a breeze through that helped keep the interior dry. As my research design improved with every *pekpek* and fruit, so did my nascent thoughts for a research station with every new discomfort and calamity.

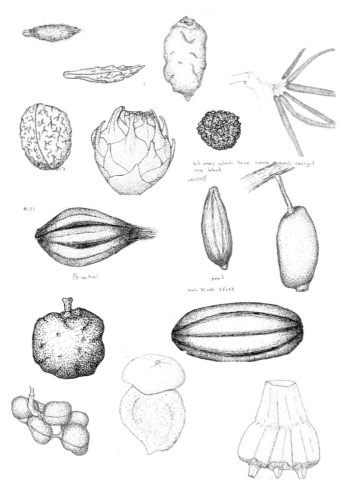

I made field sketches like these for many of the fruits and seeds I found in the forest and in *pekpek*.
The sketches helped me catalog the amazing diversity of plant species that cassowaries eat.

The time at the Wara Oo Camp helped me solidify my research plans. Many of the things I had anticipated doing were finally looking feasible. Even though cassowaries were very difficult to see, I often found fresh droppings, sometimes still warm. Occasionally they were so fresh, the gut parasites shed with the seeds still writhed in the hot, moist equivalent of seedy fruit salad. Work with the droppings would yield good data, but I could not count on direct observation of the birds. Even my assistants, like the ever-active Dupa, did not see the birds often. But the list of seeds and species they consumed grew every day. I spent many hours sketching seeds. Film was expensive and I had time to sketch, though this would change as things like building maintenance were added to my plate. I could carry my field book with me and compare sketches in the field. But even after documenting seeds of several dozen plant species in *pekpek*, every day I had more first-encounters. It seemed the forest was so diverse the birds could eat different food every day. The birds themselves formed a way of sampling the rainforest flora. They efficiently sought out and discovered a much greater diversity of fruiting plants than I could find on my own, walking and searching the forest floor.

After finishing up my supplies of food at Wara Oo, I returned to Haia to catch a plane back to Goroka. I moved into the agriculture extension agent's tiny two-room office off the west end of the airstrip. When I arrived there I found three women from Simbu Province who had come to the village as part of a women's training program. They were waiting to get a plane to Kundiawa, the provincial capital, about as far away as my destination, Goroka, in Eastern Highlands Province. The four of us shared the cramped space in good humor; they had a little stove and generously shared their hot food with me.

At Haia, the clear skies required for landing planes are unpredictable. If the missionaries were at home, they would radio to the MAF hangar in Goroka with a weather update. Without good visibility and a high ceiling with some holes showing blue sky, it was not safe to land. Pilots preferred not to leave Goroka without some indication that the weather was okay on our side of the mountains. At this time, it was raining, the ceiling was about 8 feet, and blue skies were only a memory. We were, as the Aussie pilots termed it, "clagged in" for days. I asked the Pawai'ia men hanging around if maybe I could hike back to Rutanabi and leave that way; a three-day walk would beat sitting there indefinitely waiting for clouds to lift. They said the rivers were too high; we would not even be able to cross the first river, the Hwalia, which was only a couple of miles away. No one was going anywhere.

The Simbu ladies were educated and spoke good English, but eventually we ran out of things to talk about. We would sit listening to the crescendo and decrescendo of rain on the tin roof as it pounded and eased, pounded and eased. I read and wrote letters while waiting.

Once, the leader of their threesome asked me, "What is Priscilla doing?"

I said, "Huh?"

She repeated, "What is Priscilla doing now?"

I apologized, saying I had no idea what she was talking about.

"You are from America, aren't you?"

I acknowledged my ancestry, but said I still didn't understand.

"Priscilla, you know, Priscilla. The wife of The King. What is she doing since he died?"

There huddled in a damp shack in the pounding rain at the edge of the New Guinea rainforest, Elvis was still "The King," and people worried about his widow, Priscilla.

The flow of cultural exchange between the US and PNG pretty much moves in only one direction. She knew more about "The King" and his wife than I did. I hadn't known he had a widow.

When waiting for a plane, clagged-in at a little airstrip, you can't wander off. You never know when the clouds might part enough and a plane will drop in. Without any radio connection to MAF, I could not do anything more than read, write, and think. It began to sink in what a daunting task lie ahead of me. For although droppings were abundant and easy to find, I would need to find perhaps hundreds before I could have a sample that included enough of any one plant species to calculate even the simplest of the statistics required by my PhD committee back in Miami. This is precisely why pilot studies like this are so important. As well as learning what I would need to succeed in PNG in terms of logistics, cultural considerations, and health (mental and physical), I was also learning what kind of sampling I would need to do, what would produce results, and what would not. Anything that relied on a large sample of cassowary droppings would be fairly doable. Anything that required a large sample of a particular plant species dispersed by cassowaries would require more time in the field, but could be doable. Back in Miami, when initially pitching my project to my committee, my best guesses for some aspects of the work had been weeks to months. It was quickly becoming evident that the timeline would extend to several years. A whole new set of challenges emerged.

Chapter Four

Why fruits and droppings?

Bilong wanim ol prut na pekpek?

Fruit might be good for us, but why is it good for the plant? Why does fruit exist? What use is the nutritious pulp surrounding a seed? That pulp does nothing to nurture the embryo within the seed. Just like mammals, plants have mothers and progeny. Evolution favors mothers that invest in their progeny. Mammalian mothers provide nurture first via the umbilical cord, and then with milk. Mother plants nurture embryos with the nutrients stored in the seeds, but when the seed leaves the mother, a process called abscission, there is no coming back to the teat. The reserves the mother puts in the endosperm—the meat of the nut or grain—are all the seedling gets. So why further surround that seed with a fleshy pulp like that of a plum, cherry, or apple if it does not nourish the embryo? Wouldn't it make more sense for the mother to invest those nutrients in the endosperm so the embryo has a little more cushion before it is completely on its own? Why produce nutritious fruit pulp?

These are the sorts of questions evolutionary biologists ask. Broadly speaking, the fruit pulp is crucial to the spatial positioning of the plants in a population, it determines the embryo's chances of taking root, it affects gene movement within a population, and it feeds a large component of the animal community (e.g., primates like us). The interactions between plants and frugivores (animals that consume fruit) play a major role in determining the overall structure and composition of rainforests. These questions are not sterile exercises. They help answer key questions: Why is the forest the way it is? How do forests maintain themselves over millennia? Practically speaking, how can we keep from damaging or destroying them when we harvest forest products like timber?

One key difference between a plant and a mammal is that the young mammal deliberately moves away from the mother. We call this dispersal; parents of college-bound teenagers are familiar with the concept. We want them to go and they need to go; they won't thrive and mature properly when constantly shaded by their parents. But we also want them to go to the right place. We want them to disperse to a safe place where they will be able to flourish on their own. Survival of one's progeny depends in large part on where they land after dispersal; this is true for any organism, plant or animal. Better a dormitory at Harvard than a crack house in a less affluent section of Boston. And that is where the fruit pulp comes in. Plants don't walk, fly, swim, or drive away from mom. The pulp is the plant's means for moving its baby off to a new place. The pulp's job is to entice some animal, usually a bird or mammal, to eat the fruit and then, sometime later, to defecate or regurgitate the seed in a good place—hopefully the plant equivalent of the dorm as opposed to the crack house.

Dispersal is a crucial determinant in the life history and success of plants. Once dispersed, unlike animals, plants generally have no way to relocate if they land in the wrong spot. But dispersal is also one of the hardest phases in a plant's history to study. It is easy to monitor growth and survivorship of a tree—it stays put. But when a seed disperses, it typically travels in the gut of some animal we cannot easily follow, and lands somewhere we cannot easily find. Biologists have studied frugivores as they eat fruit. But we lumbering, clumsy bipeds are hard put to follow the frugivores when they subsequently fly or run away. We see the seeds go into the feeding birds, but we don't see where they defecate or regurgitate the seeds. I had come to PNG to study this particularly difficult phase of a plant's life history. Some might think it was particularly stupid to come to such a logistically challenging place to take on such a formidable subject. At times I would be in total agreement with that assessment. Did it make sense to tackle these tough questions in a situation where I had to start completely from scratch, including first building a place in which to live and clearing the trails on which to walk?

But it did make sense, thanks to the special attributes of cassowaries, their diet, and the unique features of the Papuan rainforest. This forest system has the ideal set of plants and the ideal disperser to study aspects of seed dispersal virtually impossible to tackle in most other systems. Cassowaries are the largest animal that dine almost entirely on fruit. There are other larger animals that eat fruit, elephants among them, but they also consume large amounts of leaves, grasses, and the like. So their behavior, movements, diet, and evolutionary history are also strongly determined by things other than fruit. Studying an animal that eats only fruit eliminates many potential complications.

Other advantages to studying cassowaries are related to their size. Even the smallest of the three species of cassowary, the Dwarf Cassowary that I studied, weighs about fifty pounds. They cannot fly and they do not live in the canopy. They're found right down on the ground, where I am. Since, like the cassowary, I am a large biped, I could go anywhere they could—a feat in itself biologists would find difficult to duplicate with a monkey or hornbill. While many frugivorous birds forage over vast distances in a single day, cassowaries do not. Being large also means they have to eat a lot of fruit. There are other specialist frugivores, many of which weigh less than a single fruit a cassowary could eat; none begin to approach the heft of a full-grown cassowary. Many of the fruits eaten by cassowaries are large and avocado-like with big seeds that are easy to study. Many birds, from tiny berrypeckers to huge cassowaries, eat small-seeded fruits like figs. But in New Guinea, only cassowaries can move the largest seeds, so my research didn't have to account for the possibility that multiple frugivore species might have dispersed these seeds. For these large, avocado-like species, when I find a seedling, sapling, or tree in the forest, I can be reasonably confident that at some crucial moment in the past, a cassowary defecated in that spot. Through this lens, I have come to see the forest as the end result of many scats and regurgitations by many species of frugivore over hundreds of years. Every tree has a story to tell, of storms, landslides, attack by wood-borers, and competition with neighbors over decades and decades; and all those stories begin with a splat.

The real advantage to studying cassowaries: their scats are big, easy to find, and full of seeds. Thus originated my Pawai'ia nickname "cassowary shit," and the chopper pilot–comedians in Goroka make a conspicuous show of checking the soles of their shoes whenever I walked into the Aero Club. Finding *pekpek* in the forest offered the opportunity to see exactly where those dispersed seeds landed and how they fared. Which sites were good or bad for the survival of the seed and its long ordeal to become a tree? Did cassowaries deposit a mother plant's seeds preferentially in good sites, poor sites, or randomly? What advantage did the parent plant gain by producing a huge fruit that only a cassowary could disperse? If I could answer some of these questions, I would have a handle on an important set of issues in rainforest ecology. In the rainforests of the world, usually more than 90 percent of trees produce fleshy fruits that frugivores eat. It is not so in temperate forests, where wind-dispersed seeds are much more common—think of the winged seeds maples produce or the drifting plumed seeds of milkweed. This is why frugivores like toucans predominantly inhabit the tropics and more seed eaters like cardinals live in the temperate zone.

Overall, I was convinced my proposed seed dispersal research was a good project, viable, and of interest to the broader scientific community. I was a graduate student, and had worked on a number of projects as an assistant to other ecologists and ornithologists. But this was the first big project that was wholly mine. Even if I felt in my heart I could undertake it and come back with interesting results, would I be able to convince my advisor, my committee, and—most difficult of all—donors to share my convictions and take the risk of supporting me? My best hope for getting the backing I needed came from this pilot study. If I could assemble enough preliminary data and could present hard numeric and photographic evidence that the project was feasible, I might be able to get the backing to return for the long term.

Chapter Five

How did I get here?

Wanem samting kamap long mi stap hia?

For twenty years people have asked me, "Why Papua New Guinea?" It's a good question, and I wish I could answer that I tactically chose the most interesting project in the world and then went to the best place to do it. But that's not how science works. My landing in PNG, like so many outcomes in science and in life, was the culmination of a series of random events, misunderstandings, and personality conflicts, guided by a general sense of direction and a big pinch of serendipity.

When I began graduate school at the University of Miami in 1985, I had considerable field experience in rainforests, particularly those of Costa Rica, Mexico, Ecuador, and Borneo. Among a small group of ornithologists I had the reputation of being a good rainforest worker; namely, I could endure a good deal of discomfort and didn't need to be paid to do so. If you work in deep rainforest, you are going to itch. You will put on wet clothes most mornings and all manner of fungi and bacteria will thank you for it by dining on your epidermis. Insects will be your constant companions. Relationships falter. You deal with it.

One day Don Bruning, the curator of birds at the Bronx Zoo, called to ask if I would like to go to Papua New Guinea. I did not then know Don, but he'd learned of my rainforest compulsions through a mutual friend. A small ecotourism project in the Eastern Highlands needed a manager, he said; it came with funding from the zoo's conservation arm, Wildlife Conservation International (WCI), and I'd have most of my time free for research.

"I need to think about it," I said.

To a young aspiring rainforest biologist, this call was manna from heaven. New Guinea holds the third largest rainforest remaining on earth. These tropical forests are the least studied of any. Few, if any, ecological studies lasting longer than a few months had ever been done there. What better place for an ambitious graduate student looking to make his mark?

"Of course," Don said. "When should we talk again?"

"I've thought about it," I replied. "I'll do it."

And in that moment the direction of my life was set.

With Don promising support for travel to PNG, I developed plans to study cassowaries, then spent the next year entangled in bureaucratic red tape and the science community's lack of communication. Don assured me I did not need to submit any sort of research proposal. I was his man. Getting a visa and then getting my passport stamped by the PNG embassy in Washington, D.C., took many agonizing months. When finally my visa was in hand, I called Don to get things rolling. Don assured me my research would still be funded.

"Just send your budget to WCI," he said.

Turns out there were a few minor details of which I'd been happily ignorant. Don didn't actually have the authority to promise me WCI funds. He'd also never mentioned me, or my research plans, to the WCI folks controlling funds. Some WCI bosses were, shall we say, a tad miffed to receive a budget for ten thousand dollars in research funding from an unknown and impertinent graduate student, without so much as a proposal to go with it. I had a miserable time in Miami as it dawned on me I'd wasted a year with only an unfunded project concept, a research visa, and a huge knot in my stomach to show for it. Bailing on PNG now would put me in my second year of grad school without so much as a viable research plan.

Finally, in an effort to resolve the misunderstandings, I went to New York and met with the WCI powers that be in a paneled conference room lined with trophy heads hunted by the likes of Teddy Roosevelt. While I sat trying to explain how I came to be in this situation, I pictured my impudent head mounted there next to the wildebeest, who'd certainly done less to warrant decapitation than I. The tone of the meeting slowly warmed and they decided to fund a pilot study—if only because they wanted me to go away. And PNG was about as far away from that conference room as you could get.

We all knew I was lucky to have this offer. There was no work with the ecotourism project; apparently it had been defunct even when Don first pitched the opportunity to me. Even so, it would be several more years before WCI stopped mentioning that project as a success in the glossy literature meant to entice donors. I was beginning to see how the façade shown to the conservation-minded public and donors differed from the conservation reality in far-off Papua New Guinea.

But at the moment all that mattered was that I had enough grant money to bet my future on. With $10K I could get something started in PNG that I could then use to leverage more grant support elsewhere, even if WCI just wanted me to disappear. I had a great advisor, Ted Fleming, who had a long career of hard-core fieldwork under his belt. He understood the risks and the dividends and was always supportive of my decisions. If I was willing to gamble, he was not going to stop me.

Cassowaries are huge but elusive birds. No one knew anything about them. Often the standard advice to beginning students is not to take on a project unless you know it is workable. We learn as students not to risk failure, usually with the coda that "later in your career when you are established, *then* you can take risks." But often by the time academicians are nicely established, they are there by virtue of not taking risks and are not about to start. Such entrainment for safety is not limited to academicians either. But I find a sure thing boring.

I'm a bit embarrassed to admit my career in Papua New Guinea began as a breakdown in communication at WCI. Were it not for Don Bruning trying to push the organization to get involved in PNG, and without the compassion of Dr. Mary Pearl, who was then overseeing WCI's Asia programs, as a beginning graduate student, I might never have landed in Papua New Guinea. Although for a while Don put me in an uncomfortable situation, he was the one with the vision to get something going in PNG and pushed the slow organization to act. Eventually, WCI would become a very strong backer of my work there . . . at least for a while.

Chapter Six

Searching for a place to search for droppings

Painim ples long painim pekpek

When I finally arrived in PNG in July 1987, at the old Jackson's Airport outside Port Moresby, I landed in a scene straight out of *Casablanca*. The airport's creaky old wooden building, warped by humidity and heat, was a large hall with grimy windows that never opened along one wall and a hundred and fourteen fans on the ceiling. One of the pastimes while waiting in the long Immigration queues was counting the ceiling fans, then counting how many were actually working. Anything to take your mind off the heat and the heavy smell of perspiration, the two things that immediately greeted visitors to PNG. In the days before computers, every passport was inspected by hand and checked against typewritten carbon copies of approved visitor documentation. People did not visit PNG on a whim. Every step of getting into the country was a test of stamina, right up to the long, hot wait for the final stamp in the passport—after thirty-plus hours on airplanes.

Frequent travelers in the developing world will know what I mean when I say one of the best sounds in the world is that double thump of a rubber stamp, first on the inkpad and then on your passport. Thunk thump, you're in. That's the sound you love to hear both on your way in to a place like PNG and on your way out. Thunk thump, you're out. You never quite feel confident in PNG that the Immigration officials aren't going to inspect your passport and then pause, glare at you, and say, "please follow me." It has happened to me on border crossings. I hold my breath for that thunk, thump of acceptance. Nothing good ever happens after an Immigration or Customs official says "please follow me."

I had no plans to live in Pawai'ia country or to build a research station. Don Bruning had recommended a village along the southern edge of the central valley of the PNG Highlands, and I made my way there. I soon learned the place was wonderful, but not well suited for studying cassowaries. It was, however, the ideal setting to get a sudden shock, full-immersion lesson in the unfathomable complexities of village politics.

The village Ubaigubi (mentioned earlier) sounded to me like a place out of a Tarzan movie. To get there, I met up with Mal, the helicopter pilot, in a bar in Goroka. He took me to a house where Kevin, a United Nations–funded engineer, was living. As Mal hollered, every dog in Goroka howled along; believe me, one has no idea how many dogs are in Goroka until they all start howling at 1 a.m.

When Kevin appeared on the verandah in his skivvies and obviously none too amused, Mal introduced me and asked if Kevin would give me a ride down the road he was working on, which ended in Ubaigubi. I was glad to be outside a security fence topped with razor wire. Had we actually been on his verandah knocking at the door, I think Kevin would have thrown us off. In an obvious effort to get rid of us so he could go back to bed, he agreed to drive me up to Ubaigubi.

"See, I told you I could get you a ride," Mal said as we left. The guy had connections and a knack for getting things done, even if it meant waking up half the town. Thirteen years later he would be the governor of the province and still helping me get things done.

Kevin picked me up before dawn in his four-wheel-drive Toyota HiLux. I had a couple of months' worth of rice and canned mackerel with me, along with my field gear. We started out along the paved Highlands Highway. Traveling from Goroka to Ubaigubi is like experiencing, in reverse, the evolution of the road. From the highway we turned to graded dirt, then ungraded, and for the last few miles we followed a foot path that only a few intrepid folks had driven along. The UN had sent Kevin to turn this devolving road into a real road with drainage ditches and bridges. By chewing into the side of the mountain the crew strove for a wee margin of error on the edges of cliffs and gorges. The rusted belly-up remnants of a few vehicles far below testified to why widening the road might be a good idea.

But Kevin explained to me why it was not such a good idea and was, in fact, a pointless waste of money. Some expert in an office somewhere had identified the road improvement as a good development project, and about ten million dollars was allocated (big money in PNG in 1987). Kevin, the contractor, was doing his best. But as the workers pushed farther along the track, more machinery had to be diverted back to clear recent landslides blocking the improved stretch. Kevin noted that in such young mountains, erosion and unstable land meant nearly constant maintenance, and the province had no money or equipment for such upkeep. Just completing the road was proving difficult. Kevin predicted the road would again be virtually impassable within a few years after the completion of this work.

Although PNG is called "the land of the unexpected," Kevin's expectations came true. Not long after the UN money was spent and the equipment taken elsewhere, landslips and erosion turned sections of the road back into little more than walking tracks. Although much is unpredictable in PNG, the experts' decisions on how to improve things there seem to predictably waste millions of aid dollars.

The little truck bucked and jolted as the wheels spun in and out of axle-deep ruts. Kevin kept the engine screaming in low gear and never stopped. Kids, dogs, and chickens along the way seemed to understand this and jumped for safety as we approached. A gutsy small truck can get to places that Detroit-style pickups and SUVS could never reach. Still, the trip was slow and uncomfortable. I then realized Kevin's initial reluctance to serve as my chauffeur had less to do with the hour and the canine symphony and more to do with the realities of the drive. "Four-wheeling" is fine as an occasional weekend diversion, but when it's a necessary spine-jarring component of your daily work, it gets old fast.

The road to Ubaigubi was often a quagmire. "Four-wheeling" is not an adventure when it is a necessity.

About fifteen miles and three hours after we'd left Goroka, we eased into Ubaigubi. The engine let up its whining and my fingers relaxed their grip on the dashboard. The truck entered a large communal area flattened and smoothed by hundreds of bare feet packing the clay every day. I eagerly hopped out the door, then momentarily staggered as I regained my land legs. As I started to gather my wits, Kevin tossed out all my food and gear and I heard the racing engine whine as he sunk back down the mountain. He had work to do.

Suddenly I felt very alone. A crowd of several hundred people closed around me and my little pile of food. These were highland warriors, their faces deeply etched and furrowed in a manner characteristic of New Guinea's highlanders. Most held axes or bush knives (the PNG machete), and a few clutched bows and arrows. Children caught between fear and curiosity clung to their fathers' legs or milled around behind the crowd. There were very few women; most were already at work in the gardens. A few gray-haired old women stared quietly with opaque, cataract-clouded eyes. I could tell they had experienced a lot in their lives, and the arrival of a white kid with a hundred kilograms of rice was unremarkable. No one spoke a word of English and I spoke not a word of Gimi or Tok Pisin.

Men hanging around in Ubaigubi. Back then men usually had their bow and arrows or at least a bushknife on hand. Note the cool hat made of an onion bag on the guy in front and the guy in "arse grass" at the back.

Some just stared. Many had entered an animated discussion. I imagined they could be saying, "Let's just take all that food and tell this bozo to walk back down the mountain." Others were probably arguing that they might get in some sort of trouble if they did. What they didn't know was that in the whole world, Kevin and Mal were the only people who knew where I was, and they had no expectations of ever seeing me again. At that moment, and hundreds more like it in the years ahead, someone could have made me disappear with no repercussions. But why would anyone want to harm a nice guy like me? In PNG the best assurance of security comes from not being a jerk and from treating people fairly—a stratagem that has eluded many foreign visitors and expats, to their eventual dismay.

There were already arguments developing. I hoped they were arguing about who would get to help me rather than who would get helpings of my precious rice and canned fish. Far up on the ridgetops, men bellowed something in Gimi through the cool mountain air. I could faintly hear someone on the next ridgetop passing the message on to listeners miles away. A little voice in my head said, "you're completely on your own, kiddo." And I found this the most exhilarating sensation. I was hooked.

Don, the ornithologist at the Bronx Zoo, had suggested Ubaigubi because artist/photographer David Gillison had lived there a decade earlier with his family. His then-wife was an anthropologist. I'd arranged in a phone conversation with David to use the little house he had built above Ubaigubi in a hamlet called Rutanabi. The house had a caretaker named Falau. So my only utterance to the congregation pressing around me was "Falau?"

This generated more discussion. I could hear the word "Falau" now and then in the banter. I hoped I had remembered the name right, and had not, instead, said something inane in their language like "Puddle?" So I waited and grinned like a moron. Morons are unintimidating. The crowd tightened around me and stared.

Papuans do not have the cultural taboo we have about staring. You'll never hear Papuan parents tell their child "It's not polite to stare;" in fact, they are usually too busy staring themselves to even notice their kid is staring. As one of the few white people (or *masta* in Tok Pisin—a linguistic hangover from colonial days) they'd seen in Ubaigubi, I realized I'd just have to try to get used to being stared at (I never really did). Sometimes I'd see people staring into space just for practice. After what felt like hours but was only about fifteen minutes, the crowd parted a bit and a wizened man wearing dingy shorts and a (once) cream-colored dinner jacket strode up. Someone pointed at him with his nose (this is how many Papuans point; not with their fingers) and said, "Falau."

Falau walked up across the clay courtyard. Like everyone in the village, he'd never worn shoes and his feet were about as wide as his head. He stopped and we shook hands. I tried a few words in Tok Pisin. I said something like "Puddle. My Andy is name. Talking house said David stay can in I."

He pulled a smoke—a leaf of local tobacco called *brus* rolled in a long narrow strip of newspaper—from behind his ear and an ancient metal lighter from a pocket of the dinner jacket. This was obviously Falau's moment in the village and he was milking it for all it was worth. Indeed, I'd learn as I went just how much my entry into the delicate village politics anywhere in PNG could alter or upset the tenuous social hierarchy and pecking orders. Clearly, Falau's status and social position was soaring up. The money machine had rolled into town and asked for him.

Falau's furrowed face was exceptional, even by PNG standards. He could squint like no one I've met and he was now directing that squint at me, revealing nothing about what was going on behind those slits while he calculated and sized up the situation. Falau never simply reacted—in Ubaigubi every action has repercussions that require careful consideration. What he said and did at this point mattered. Probably everything from a bear hug welcome to telling me to piss off ran through his head. I'd spend the next couple of months with him and we would become good friends, but when the shutters were down, there was no seeing into that squint. He stared at me, my pile of stuff, and the crowd staring back. But having taken in the situation for several long minutes, General Falau took charge.

Gimi is a language spoken at only two volumes: the conspiratorial whisper or the top-of-the-lungs shout. This was a time for the latter. Falau shouted out orders. Designated young men stepped into my small circle of neutral ground and picked up the bales of rice, cartons of tinned fish, and bags of gear, hoisted them on their shoulders and started off with them. I hoped they were taking them to David's old house. I followed the ragged line of carriers, Falau periodically barking orders. The telegraph signalers up on the ridgetop kept up the live relay. This was their version of "breaking news" with instantaneous updates. If I so much as scratched my nose, the entire mountain would know within seconds. A few of the carriers wore just "ass grass"—a handful of leaves tucked in a vine belt at the front and back to conceal the important bits. In a few years this dying tradition would be entirely gone, replaced by the much less sanitary rugby shorts and filthy Rambo T-shirts.

The hike up to the house in Rutanabi took me along a roaring stream with gardens and traditional houses with grass roofs leaking smoke from cook fires. Although it seemed the entire village had encircled me down where the truck dropped me off, I came across many more people along the way. Children peered from the dark doors of the houses, many running out to join the train of carriers. The women were mostly at work in the gardens and had no time for the stranger in their midst. Their toil fed the family and they could not afford the leisure of the men to make a fuss and act self-important. They would pause, watch me pass, and return to weeding or digging. They'd seen white guys come and go before, but the need to grow food never ended. A few women carrying huge loads of firewood stacked high on their backs passed me coming down the trail. It was becoming obvious who did most of the work in Gimi society.

The house I was to live in had a small yard fenced to keep pigs out. It was the only building with a metal roof, other than a couple of community houses, like the aid post, in the main village. Unlike the traditional round houses, it was rectangular and sat low to the ground on short posts. The walls were made of woven, flattened bamboo. Falau produced a key from a dirty string around his neck and with dramatic flair opened the door. He was the official caretaker for the house and he'd been waiting for someone to return for years.

I stepped into the dark interior as Falau opened the small, shuttered windows, which let in just enough light to see. There was a main room and kitchen and two small bedrooms. It was more comfortable than I could have hoped for. I sat down on a wooden bench, tired from the long ride and stress. I'd been preparing for this for two years—planning a project, finding the funding, and wangling with PNG Immigration for a research visa. My arrival signified the end of a long struggle and I realized that perhaps I had landed at the beginning of a much larger struggle. But at least I had made step one. I was legally in PNG with the appropriate visa, in a house I had been told sat right on the edge of primary forest, and I had a small grant to get me started. I was pretty well out of touch so could lay aside personal and relationship issues back home. There was not much to do other than my research. At last I could really get started, or so I thought.

The tourist lodge at Ubaigubi, of which Don and the WCI staff had spoken, was closed. All that remained was the shell of the building on the hill above the village and the myth being spread in the US that ecotourism thrived in PNG. Because the project was defunct I was free to explore the entire country for a suitable study area—which was a good thing, because the house at Rutanabi was not, as I had been led to believe, "right on the edge of primary forest." I could not just step out into the trees and begin to look for cassowaries. The house was in a small cluster of traditional Gimi houses surrounded by gardens, which in turn were surrounded by forests heavily disturbed by daily wood cutting. Any cassowary that came within a mile would likely end up as dinner. After a few days of hiking around Rutanabi, it became clear I needed to find a better place.

At least seventy-five boys hung around outside the house at all times. They peered in through the open windows, they crowded at the door looking in, and they found gaps in the woven bamboo walls through which to watch me. When I was in the house I was nothing more than an exotic animal in a cage, perhaps an appropriate situation for a researcher sponsored by a zoo. If I stayed immobile reading for a half hour, a few onlookers would get bored and wander off to other pursuits. But as soon as I sneezed, stood up, or even turned a page too quickly, the onlookers would send out the news flash at the top of their lungs. The kids, or in Tok Pisin *pikininis,* who had strayed from their vigil would dash back to the door, windows, and cracks in the wall to see what the *masta* did next (Tok Pisin is not a politically correct language, showing the footprint of PNG's colonial era). The boys were constantly murmuring in Gimi and jostling for position all around the house.

They crowded so tightly in the door (which had to be left open to let light in) that sometimes those in the back would push and a small kid in the front would fall inside. This would elicit a look of utter terror, as if he had fallen into a tiger cage. The panicking kid would fight his way out through the laughing mob; what good fun. If I *raused* them (Tok Pisin) or told them to "piss off" (Australian), they would all run screaming around the yard, tripping over each other and laughing. This was a great game, and soon double the number would be back, leaning through the door and windows, waiting for the chase. There seemed to be an infinite supply of little boys. I imagined them walking for days from distant villages just to peer at this odd wonder. I hoped with time they would tire of me and grow bored. But the crowd never diminished. My only respite came at dusk when small children returned to the safety of their homes, away from the spirits that roamed at night.

A few of the young warriors displaying their weaponry at Ubaigubi.

The children not only challenged my sanity, but they interfered with my research. Gimi boys are rarely disciplined. Once, when Jeffery's dilapidated truck could not leave because all the tires were flat, the owner said it was because the children let the air out. Again. He said it in the same resigned way you would say, "because it rained last night." Like the weather, the hordes of children were a natural phenomenon that could not be altered.

Near the house at Rutanabi I found a nest of a Blue Bird of Paradise, arguably one of the most beautiful birds of paradise. Like nearly every species in New Guinea, it had never been properly studied. So with the help of Falau and his sidekick Dorahau, we built a very well-concealed hide. I could monitor the nest through a little hole they cleverly constructed in the grasses and leaves. The hole was so small I could see only the nest and the incubating bird. Moreover, the children could not see me sitting there with my notebook and binoculars. The hide blended into the undergrowth so well I could barely tell it was there. It was as good as invisible.

Every day I slipped into the hide before dawn and stayed into the afternoon. I wanted to learn how long the female incubated the egg, whether the male ever contributed to the effort, and what the young would be fed. I eagerly waited for the egg to hatch, and for the monotony to be broken (watching a motionless, incubating bird is not particularly thrilling after a few days). One day as I watched the female, I noticed a slight tremor in the nest tree. The female began to look around and then flew off—something she did every hour to feed. Then I saw a little hand reaching up to the nest to take the egg. A kid had seen the nest from the ground, but not the hide, and had climbed up to get the egg. Rural PNG kids will catch and eat just about any small animal they can get their hands on. This one was about to eat my research subject.

I burst out of the hide, which sat ten feet away up the steep slope, and yelled at the kid to "come down, now, *RAUS!*" If the boy left right away, maybe the female would not abandon the nest. But instead of climbing down the tree, the poor kid burst into tears and began wailing at the top of his lungs. He trembled so violently his knees knocked together. I was afraid he'd lose his grasp and fall. I tried for ten minutes to convince him that I was not a hungry demon, but his wailing did not cease. The more I tried to calm him and coax him down, the louder he wailed.

So much for not disturbing the incubating female. Eventually a father or uncle appeared, thinking this was the funniest thing ever. No apology or explanation—kids were a force of nature. He talked the kid down and they scampered back to the village, one sniffling and the other guffawing. I went back to my hide, but the female never returned to the nest. A couple of days later I climbed up to find the egg stone cold. Despite the abrupt and premature conclusion of my little side project, I had still obtained enough new information for a small publication. This is one of the advantages of working where so few biologists had traversed. Because it was so hard to get any research done, and because so few really tried, anything I did was potentially new.

Falau had been joined by a cousin named Dorahau, who boasted that he too had worked for David Gillison. These two became my lieutenants. They helped me learn Tok Pisin and they supervised when I needed to hire carriers and guides or get permission to traverse someone's land. Beside the kids making Rutanabi unsuitable, all the habitat within a couple of hours' walk was heavily modified. Dogs ran free. People hunted, cut trees for fuel, and regularly carved new gardens out of the forest. All those kids would soon need to feed their own families. As in most villages across PNG, population growth drove new expansion into forest. Any long-term research site would need to be far from a village because villages are dynamic, moving entities.

Me with Falau, the caretaker of the house at Rutanabi, and Dorahau (on left),
who directed carriers and field assistants (whether direction was needed or not).

Falau and Dorahau helped me organize a scouting trip over the mountain, where a much smaller and younger village, Herowana, was surrounded by much more extensive primary forest. I thought I'd be more likely to find cassowaries there. Gillison had given me the name of a friendly "bigman" from Herowana. Falau sent word that I wanted to explore. "Bush telegraph" worked amazingly well, as there were always people moving among the villages and hamlets in the highlands. The next day a message came back from Herowana: I could meet Batanimi.

Finally, I was getting deep into cassowary country! We organized men to carry the food and camp supplies and set off one morning. The logistics of exploration in New Guinea are not simple: How much food you carry depends on how many carriers you have to feed, and how many carriers you need depends on how much food you carry. If you decide to bring an extra piece of equipment, you need to hire an extra carrier to bring the food the equipment carrier will need—and then someone has to carry the food for that extra carrier. One additional day of trekking means an additional day's ration for every carrier, which means more carriers. Falau was really good at making all these calculations without benefit of pencil and paper. He would just think and squint and then say how many bales of rice and how many men.

When the calculations and preparations were finalized, we set off. Up we climbed for a couple of hours; then we crested the ridge behind Rutanabi at a low pass. Later when I would fly over these mountains, the Cessna or chopper would often squeeze under the clouds at this very pass. But at that time there was no airstrip at Herowana and the only way in was to walk, or to fly in one of Mal's choppers if you had the money, which I certainly did not. We pushed up the muddy trail, me slipping and struggling for traction in my fancy hiking boots while the bare-footed Gimi porters never missed a step.

We stopped at the top. In a ritual I would replay hundreds of times in the years to come, I collapsed, out of breath and exhausted, while the carriers blithely dropped their fifty-pound loads like bags of pillows. They'd then roll the potent tobacco called *brus* in a rectangle of newspaper, light it, and have a chat while I gasped for oxygen. I later spent years hiking these mountains and got into pretty good shape, but even at my fittest I never approached their stamina and lung power. Ancient barefoot men smoking and coughing from chronic TB would politely pass me with their heavy loads on our treks. Few things keep one as humble as a trek through the mountains of PNG.

We descended the other side, which meant constant braking on a sharp descent. The pain shifted from my lungs to my knees. In New Guinea, the concept of a switchback has never caught on. No one can see any reason to zigzag between two points on a mountain when everyone knows the shortest distance is a straight line. You ascend straight up and descend straight down.

Eventually the trail leveled out a bit, to the relief of my knees. Somewhere along the way we were to meet up with Batanimi. After a couple of hours we came to a smoldering fire. From this Falau knew to turn left, so we set out through the forest for another hour. After crossing a fairy-tale stream with moss-covered stones, we found Batanimi, who was preparing a campsite for us. He had the physique of an older man who had once been extremely strong and buff. Though a bit wrinkled, he still brandished a heavy axe one-handed, as I might a butter knife. He had a broad, semi-toothed smile and eyes that twinkled with intelligence and possibly mischief.

Batanimi was my first guide in PNG and taught me a great deal.
Here he holds a mammal he caught and is readying for the cookpot.

We finished building the camp and had dinner of rice and canned mackerel before curling up under a lean-to. The next morning I sent everyone home except Batanimi and a couple of the kids. It was a simple, quiet camp surrounded by a vast forest with a thousand mysteries to unfold. By now my Tok Pisin was passable, but it did not matter with Batanimi. He was old school, a real woodsman, and did not speak Tok Pisin. In fact, he rarely spoke at all, even with the other Gimi in camp. We stayed there for two weeks, communicating with gestures and grunts and the occasional assistance of a younger translator. He taught me a great deal about cassowaries and his forest.

Each day Batanimi and I walked through the forest. He'd detect some small sign of cassowary—a track, a broken twig—and would intuitively know where it had gone. We'd follow the imperceptible signs that eventually I too would learn to recognize, and come to places where the bird ate fallen fruit, or where it rested, or, most importantly for me, where it defecated. My research centered on learning what fruits the birds ate and where they voided the seeds. At this stage I was not so much learning about cassowaries, but learning how they could be studied.

Every new pile of scat brought exclamations of delight from me and an amused look from Batanimi. He was the first of hundreds of Papua New Guineans who over the years would see me sit in the mud beside a bird dropping and delightedly pick through its contents, scribbling in a notebook and often scooping it up into a plastic bag I then stashed in my back-pack. What could possibly have been stranger than a guy traveling from so far, from a land so rich, just to sift through bird droppings?

Batanimi also schooled me in the Gimi names for fruiting trees and the places for catching wild game, which he would demonstrate whenever he could for the sake of augmenting the rice and canned mackerel. I'd never before seen people hunt by catching animals by hand. He would climb up a tree and reach into any hole or cavity to extract its inhabitants, no matter whether they bit him, then bash them with his axe. I had a window into an ancient way of life and a body of knowledge learned through generations of subsistence hunting. Batanimi seemed able to spot from fifty yards away a tiny hole that indicated some hapless marsupial's den.

When I could, I collected fresh fruits before the cassowaries got to them, then dried them for later nutrient analysis. One day I was cleaning fruits and drying a pulp sample in the sun of a small clearing when Batanimi—a guy who didn't flinch when animals bit him and who could sit still by a campfire all night without speaking—got a little animated. He jabbered and poked a stick at the fruits I was handling. One of his sons translated. If I so much as tasted those fruits, first all my teeth would fall out and then I would die a slow, painful death. I went down to the river to wash thoroughly, holding my sticky hands out in front of me like a zombie.

We worked out of several camps around Herowana, exploring Batanimi's extensive lands. I considered myself very lucky to have such a knowledgeable and affable host. But the numbers of cassowaries were lower than I'd hoped for and the terrain was incredibly rough. The location was not ideal for a long-term study. Getting provisions to the site meant a dodgy day in a truck to get to Ubaigubi and then a day to hike supplies over the mountain. Later, a bigman in Herowana named Avit Wako would build an airstrip. He would become a great friend and supporter in later years, but I had no way of knowing that in 1989. So despite how much I liked Batanimi, I decided I better explore some other sites as potential study areas.

Doing my research in PNG was proving to be even harder than I thought. I could not just step out of the house at Rutanabi and begin sifting through *pekpek*. Hiking half a day over the mountain to Batanimi's forest was not quite viable either. Cassowaries were not plentiful there; neither were the large-seeded tree species I wanted to study. Falau described the way cassowaries migrated in and out of these higher elevation forests. When a particular species of tree came into fruit, the cassowaries appeared. I pieced together crucial information by interviewing experienced hunters like Falau and Batanimi. Were I working on a new project in Costa Rica or Panama, there would be dozens of field biologists who could provide technical information I needed. In PNG I was on my own and relied upon the traditional knowledge of local guides, which was not always easy to interpret. For example, should you cast your eyes upon a particular type of tree in the forest, you would immediately die; therefore, no one knew what the tree looked like. That community asked me if I could study that tree for them. I wonder if there was a subtle message for me there?

Three established sites at a distance from Crater Mountain offered research possibilities. I visited them all. At Varirata National Park I stayed in a first-aid hut for a week and searched for cassowaries. I did find some, but the park is very small, many people use it, and it's located just outside of Port Moresby, the crime capital of the Pacific. Even though the logistics of getting to Varirata were easy, I opted not to work there, partially due to the potential presence of *raskols*. I wanted a secure long-term study site and the indications in 1987 were that Varirata would not be safe over the long term. Events would prove me correct. In later years *raskols* robbed people at gunpoint in the park, two birdwatchers I knew were pushed off a cliff and narrowly escaped death, and another friend was carjacked. My need to avoid "civilization" in order to find cassowaries would prove advantageous in other ways.

I also made my way to the well-known Wau Ecology Institute, the closest thing to a research station in PNG and the most likely candidate among the existing facilities. But WEI is on the grounds of a coffee plantation right on the edge of the town of Wau. This place too had significant *raskol* problems that clearly were getting worse. Security was becoming as important an issue in the choice of a study area as the presence of cassowaries. It seemed any place accessible to a road was also dangerous. Earlier researchers at Wau had conducted fieldwork on the side of nearby Mt. Missim, a place then considered safe. I visited Thane Pratt's former camp with him and another ornithologist, Bruce Beehler, the authors of the field guide to New Guinea birds. I learned that even up on Mt. Missim, miles from town, a researcher had been assaulted. Since then no researchers had been back. How far did I have to go to get away from *raskols*? And *could* I get away from them?

The third place on my list of potential study areas was the Baiyer River Sanctuary, located north of Mount Hagen—a town with a reputation for lawlessness. I arranged to meet Dennis, who was then the manager of the sanctuary, through several scratchy phone calls. The sanctuary was PNG's zoo; it had developed an international reputation for breeding birds of paradise and was even home to the only known captive-breeding dwarf cassowaries. I was told forest was accessible from the zoo.

The road to the sanctuary traversed an area known for tribal fighting and highway bandits. Dennis offered to give me a ride to the sanctuary on his weekly trip to Hagen for supplies. He diplomatically suggested it would not be a good idea for me to try to make it to Baiyer River on my own right then due to unrest along highway. I was to wait in Hagen town for him to arrive. I wondered why Dennis did not have to worry about highway bandits on his weekly trip to town for supplies and his staff payroll.

When I rendezvoused with him, I began to understand why he might be safe from *raskols*. Dennis was a large, muscular highlander, clearly a man of warrior status and not one *raskols* would casually rob. But even the toughest warriors are not immune to *raskol* bands. Dennis drove a mid-sized dump truck, its bed loaded down with food and other supplies for the staff and many animals in the sanctuary. A load of food like this, not to mention the payroll, would be a prime target for highway robbers. But that would mean stopping the truck first. As we left town, Dennis kicked in the supercharger, or so it seemed, and like a scene straight out of the film *Mad Max*, we rocketed down the dirt road. From my elevated perch in the bed, atop a mound of cartons and bales of rice, I could see the surrounding terrain. In front of us the ubiquitous pedestrians scattered. Women stooped in their gardens straightened up to watch the juggernaut pass. Children ran from us, jumping in the ditch. Behind us a cloud of dust rose and blotted out the horizon. I could trace our wake by the lingering cloud of dust that wound above and obliterated the road. I hung on with my face in the wind. Thunder-dome, here we come. The truck's suspension and tires must have taken an incredible beating with a weekly trip like this. But at least the brakes would be in good shape, because I don't think Dennis touched them once until we turned onto the Baiyer River Sanctuary grounds.

Dennis later explained to me that there were tensions between the sanctuary land-owners and those whose land the road passed through—a pervasive theme that often para-lyzes PNG, where nearly all land is owned by its traditional landholders. At Baiyer River, the landowners of the sanctuary justifiably felt they should be the ones employed by the sanctuary. They also did not want landowners from neighboring tribes, traditional enemies in warfare, on their land. But since the road to the sanctuary passed through the lands of those former enemies, those other tribes felt they should also share the benefit of employment at the sanc-tuary. This tension was evident when I visited the sanctuary, which seemed to exist thanks to complex diplomacy, the threat of tribal retaliation, and one unstoppable dump truck.

Baiyer River was clearly not a secure place for a long-term research project. Any fail-ure in the constant diplomatic efforts among tribes could spell disaster. In fact, within a year the sanctuary buildings would all be burnt to the ground and the animals eaten, lost, or sold. Something failed.

Not only would I have to find a site that was safe from *raskols*, but it would also have to be entirely within undisputed territories. Traversing lands of one tribe to work on the lands of another could pose an intractable problem. Through the years, issues of ownership and control would frequently and inevitably arise. I would spend many hundreds of hours in discussion and negotiation with landowners. It's part of the cost of business in PNG, just like zoning boards and bureaucracy are part of doing business in the United States.

What I did not yet fully grasp, and learned through many difficult and sometimes tense encounters, is that tribal and clan boundaries are not discrete. What is one person's land and what is another's is usually ambiguous; rarely are any two people in full agreement on the finer details. Boundaries are fluid and differ due to many variables. Most land has a *papa graun*—the senior landowner. But often there are multiple claims for this authority, and trying to figure out who was the *real* landowner was a bit like the old TV show *To Tell the Truth*. You could not count on an honest or impartial assessment from a third party, because there are no impartial members of PNG communities. If people don't have their own agenda, they know not to weigh in on one side or another of a generations-long simmering land ownership dispute. Sometimes in protracted negotiations around the fire or in a village square where one, then another, then another, claimed to be the *papa graun*, I wanted to blurt out, "Will the real *papa graun* please stand up?" But since none of them had seen television, much less *To Tell the Truth* re-runs, I thought the humor would be lost on them.

Here's a typical scenario: I hire the *papa graun* Orei as my guide and to ensure I have permission to be where I am. I camp on Orei's land with his full and enthusiastic permission. Weeks later a hunter from miles away named Simka shows up and says, "You are on my ground. Pay up or get out." It turns out Simka is Orei's brother but lives far away and hasn't visited this ground for decades.

"Orei, why didn't you tell me Simka also owns this land?"

"You didn't ask."

It sounds like a cheap vaudeville joke. But many Pawai'ia and other tribal people with whom I worked did not seem to fully appreciate that something that was common knowledge for them would not be common knowledge for me as well. They grow up hearing information transmitted orally and seem to assume everyone has heard the same stories.

"You never asked" sometimes had the potential to be dangerous. You camp under a tree, a massive branch falls off and nearly kills you while you sleep, and your local guides *then* say, "Oh, you should never camp under that kind of tree, very dangerous."

"Why didn't you tell me when you saw me putting my tent there?"

"You didn't ask."

By now a good chunk of my ten thousand dollars was consumed. Not only were my funds running out, but I was lonely. I was spending a lot of time in camps with hunters with whom I had little in common, or alone on PMVs and in guest houses as I scouted the country. I was beginning to feel a little anxious. I still had not found a good place to study cassowaries, nor had I fully developed some of the field methods I needed to put to trial.

Back in Goroka, I met up with Mal. By then he had taken me under his wing and was acting like a big brother. PNG has a very fluid expatriate community. Twenty years later, when this story ends, Mal was one of two whites remaining in Goroka that I'd met in 1987. His support would be invaluable through the years in many ways, including several medical emergency evacuations for me and my students and friends.

Mal lives in a wonderful house on the side of a hill looking out into a magnificent garden and the opposing mountains that hem in the valley. In that house, usually after a few icy beers, I often got the benefit of advice based on his years of experience. But PNG is such a different place; new lessons were presented every day.

My friend Mal after he became governor giving a speech. He was making payments to community family groups that worked on maintenance of the road. He tried to spend money directly in the community rather than hire external contractors.

On one of my first days in Goroka, housed in the Lutheran Guest House, two rather exhausted guests arrived. One of the cooks, who seemed to know everything happening in Goroka, told me the two were passengers in a small plane that had crashed on the mountain just outside of town—practically within sight of the airport. As the wreckage was plastered to the side of a cliff, rescuers were unable to reach it easily. The Cessna's pilot died in the crash. I was stunned that victims of a crash at a known location so close to town, with readily available rescuers, would be stuck out in the cold for two nights. The boundary between "civilization" and "wilderness" in PNG is often sharp. And in contrast to most of the United States (other than Alaska), most of the terrain is wild with tiny islands of "civilization" sitting lonely and isolated. In PNG, the surrounding wilderness and isolation is accepted as a part of life.

In the States a story of crash survivors stranded on a cliff while rescuers tried to reach them would have been the stuff of front pages and late-breaking network updates. But in PNG I learned about the event from the cook. Later in the week the national newspaper barely devoted a few sentences to the story. "Rescuers had difficulty extracting two survivors of a plane crash near Goroka due to steep terrain. The pilot died in the accident." Nothing to fuss about.

Air travel was dangerous and crashes frequent enough that only the more spectacular ones merited more than a mention in the daily papers. A few of the chopper and fixed-wing pilots I met in the years that followed died in crashes. They were disturbingly frequent, but perhaps that's to be expected in a country where few places can be reached by road.

Mal, still flying after many others in PNG have come and gone, is the best pilot imaginable. It seems a bit incongruous, because on land he is a devil-may-care free spirit, full of laughter and practical jokes. I downed many rounds of drinks (*helikoptas*) and joked around with Mal through the years. But the moment he gets into a chopper it is serious business. I've seen Mal subtly adjust his path to a distant soaring bird long before I spotted the bird as a tiny speck. As in almost any dangerous profession, the macho, tough young cowboy bush pilots who think they are hot stuff often have shorter life expectancies. I like flying with old pilots.

One night at Mal's house, after a few *helikoptas*, he stopped kidding around and asked about the progress of my research. He thought the funniest thing in the world was that some Yankee would come all the way to PNG just to look for cassowary shit. I described my dilemma—that I was unable to find a place with lots of cassowaries and suitably situated in terms of security and land tenure issues. Mal had been almost everywhere in PNG, something that can be achieved only by helicopter. He leaned backed, thought a moment while he sipped, and came up with a suggestion that would set my direction for the next twenty years.

"There's a little airstrip called Haia, a pretty good airstrip too, on the other side of Crater Mountain in Pawai'ia country." He knew some geologists who had done transits through the area. He'd drop them off on a riverbed one day and several days later pick up their rucksacks filled with rock samples and drop off food supplies at a different rendezvous as they made their transect. A few repeats of this and he would pick them up miles away, at the end of their fieldwork, and typically bring them straight back to the Aero Club for a few cold ones.

The team crossing Pawai'ia country had commented on the unusually high numbers of cassowary droppings they saw. Although they were just chatting over beers, Mal had retained this particularly useless bit of information in case it might one day come in handy. Some years later, here I was, wondering where in PNG I could find a surfeit of cassowary droppings.

Thanks to Mal's years of flying in the bush and his contact with many tribes, he could recommend the Pawai'ia as low-key and reserved, and so far from civilization there would not be any crime problems. It sounded like a good prospect. If someone not even interested in cassowaries noticed lots of *pekpek*, I should be able to find what I needed. I had a potential destination. I had checked out all the established research sites—Baiyer River, Wau Ecology Institute, Mt. Missim, Varirata, Herowana, and Ubaigubi. None were suitable. I was going to have to find a place where no one had done biological research before and start from scratch.

Chapter Seven

Deb arrives

Deb i kam nau

The greatest personal challenge thus far was not the threat of various tropical diseases, legions of chiggers, constant rain, skin fungus, or other such physical maladies. The largest obstacles came from inside my head. Four months into my pilot session, I had spent most of my time in small camps with a few local guys, alone in the house at Rutanabi (not counting the seventy-five kids staring at me), or at cheap guest houses in town. My social life thus far consisted of occasional nights with Mal and his then-partner, Christine, at their house or the Aero Club. These social events centered heavily on consumption of large quantities of alcoholic beverages and usually took place after I'd had a few weeks of relative solitude and total sobriety. I joined right in. But conversation rarely touched seriously on the science and research I was there to undertake. Very few pilots and helicopter engineers cared to discuss the finer issues of seed dispersal by cassowaries. Yet they could go on for hours about rugby or cricket, topics as alien to me as seed dispersal to them.

My first taste of the tropics came in high school, when I traveled with a group of birdwatchers to the cloud forest of El Triunfo in Chiapas, Mexico. That trip left me with a life-long hankering for the rainforest. Being in PNG was the culmination of years of ever-longer trips to ever-more-remote forests. I leapt when opportunities arose, and I also worked hard to make trips happen. That first trip to Mexico required working weekends and nights after school in a restaurant for over a year. The next big trip required a year working construction full time while I put college on hold after my first year at the University of Arizona (chosen for its proximity to Mexico). I spent ten years completing my undergraduate education, mainly due to "distractions" in Costa Rica, Ecuador, Peru, and Borneo. Feeding this compulsion, like many compulsions, is hard on relationships.

PNG was more remote than any place I'd ever been. Yet despite a gnawing loneliness after just a few months, I planned returning for even longer stays. Studying cassowary seed dispersal in a place as remote and expensive to reach as Pawai'ia country could not be done in two-month excursions punctuated with adequate time in the US to maintain a life there. As my vision and dreams developed, they were turning my personal life into a train wreck. I did not see any way to pursue the vision and salvage my relationship back home. Something was going to give.

At the time, airmail was the most practical form of communicating with people back home. I marveled that a missive could often get from the US to me in under two weeks. In the evenings, by candlelight, I often wrote letters. I carried pre-stamped envelopes and aerograms in a Ziploc bag with a little desiccant so they would not self-seal in the humidity. The completed letters would accumulate in my Pelican case in a different plastic bag. On occasions when someone headed off to town, or a plane came through, I could pass off the stamped, addressed letters. Mail came to me care of Mal at his company, Pacific Helicopters.

When I got to town I would drop in at his office and his secretary would turn over a pile of letters. (Once, she handed me one that had been in her desk drawer for more than two years.) I would carry my pile of letters to a quiet place and feel a connection with the people I missed. Occasionally I would make a phone call, but these were expensive and profoundly ungratifying. When you hung up, it was over. Did it really happen? Phone calls are so transient, and what was communicated begins to morph immediately. But letters can be reread and savored. New nuances appear after several readings. Even the handwriting is revealing. I carried letters with me into the field and on lonely nights I would read them again and write my replies. Such communication reduced the sense of isolation, but could not stave off loneliness.

Among the letters I read in my camps were some from Deb Wright who I had first met in Costa Rica earlier in the year. Deb was a graduate student at the University of Florida. She was a hardcore fieldworker, smart, fun, and beautiful. Like me, the more remote and rustic a place, the more she liked it. We'd hit it off quickly in Costa Rica and became closer while exchanging letters. One day a letter came from her suggesting she could end her semester early and come to PNG. I had some big decisions looming.

I had a pretty good idea where it would lead if I said "Yes, do come." It would not bode well for my current relationship. But then, I felt that was doomed already due to my plans for long-term work in PNG. Deb's idea was very hard for me to resist. I tentatively drafted a letter back saying, "Yes, do come." I could always decide not to mail it when I got to town, I told myself. But at some level deep inside, I was pretty sure I would not avoid the outgoing mail slot when I got to Goroka. This decision was made with much vacillation and mental torment, unlike the nearly instantaneous, "Yes, I'll go!" I had given to Don Bruning when he asked if Papua New Guinea interested me. But this "yes," like the one I'd given Don, would completely alter the course of my life. It would lead to a long-term collaboration that continues to this day and a marriage that did not last quite as long.

I now had a new set of issues. I was about to make the transition from PNG newbie to expert and guide. Until now my travels had been fairly casual and relaxed because I did not feel responsible for the safety and comfort of anyone other than myself. PNG already had a nasty reputation for lawlessness, with bands of *raskols* robbing, murdering, and raping. Although not yet a major problem in rural areas, "getting *raskoled*" was a much more tangible risk in the towns and on the highway. I would need to consider the risk to Deb when deciding what to do and where to go. Although I was willing to face the possibility of robbery, like my brush with "armed *raskols*" on the road to Ubaigubi, I was not willing to subject someone else, particularly someone new to the country, to the level of risk I could accept for myself. Different people perceive risk differently, so what Deb or I might find OK, others might not. This would become an even greater concern over the years as we developed a research program that attracted new students and researchers from around the world. I have struggled to honestly answer the "Is PNG safe?" question from prospective visitors at least a hundred times.

From the mid-1980s, PNG seemed to slowly but relentlessly sink into greater lawlessness. The safety of colleagues, students, and staff was always the first consideration in every decision. From avoiding *raskols* to treating malaria to heli-evacuating a graduate student with appendicitis to sheltering battered women from their husbands, doing research and conservation in PNG demanded much more than would a comparable position in the US, and much more than a fine university education offered.

Port Moresby was, and still is, the epicenter of *raskol* activity. Restaurants in the city feature secure parking and armed guards to escort you to and from your car. They stand at the door of the establishment and attempt to prevent gang-style holdups in which armed *raskols* enter a restaurant, robbing it and all its clients. Banks station men with trained attack dogs at their doors; customers are buzzed in through double doors to see a teller. The US Embassy housing is like a fortress with steel doors and escape hatches in the bedrooms so staff can get away if *raskols* start battering down the front door. Every house and business is fenced with razor wire. Guard dogs are so prized there is a black market for stolen security dogs. What kind of beast do you use to guard your Rottweiler? One study found that over half the domestic economy of Port Moresby is based on crime. Nine of ten women in PNG have been raped. The chief of police in Port Moresby publicly stated that the best course of action in a carjacking was to run over the *raskols*. Though Moresby's roads are paved, people with means drive large, weighty four-wheel-drive vehicles with heavy steel grills. Moresby is the only entry point for overseas visitors, so these security precautions form many visitors' introduction to PNG. They do not always make for a good first impression. In order to be sure no misdeeds occurred, I would have to leave the relative serenity of Goroka and meet Deb in Moresby when she arrived.

I did not mind a trip to Port Moresby. I had been befriended by two faculty at the University of Papua New Guinea who hailed from the UK. Botanist Helen Fortune Hopkins was about as pleasant and good humored a person as you could ever hope to meet. Her husband, Mike, had a dry sense of humor and a keen interest in the birds of New Guinea. Visiting them meant I was among people with whom I could talk about my research and science. As the years went by, unfortunately, expatriate faculty at UPNG became scarcer as pay scales went down and *raskol* events increased. More than one faculty member was attacked in university-provided housing, and some brutal assaults even came from disgruntled students not quite happy about their grades. These risks reduce the pool of people willing to work in such a place. And when those with better options elsewhere leave, the city's downward spiral increases.

At that time, the PNG Bird Society held field trips and regular meetings. I made several expat friends through a mutual interest in birds. The expat community was very active in arts and science in Moresby. But that community diminished as, one by one, longtime expats who were the driving forces behind such groups as the PNG Bird Society wearied of being robbed and of living like prisoners inside razor wire fences. As skilled experts like Mike and Helen left PNG, their replacements came on short contracts. The exodus of trained expatriates magnified the need and urgency for what would become the priority for my programs in PNG in the years ahead—building national capacity for conservation. Although Mike and Helen told me of the importance of capacity building, it took me some time in the country to fully appreciate how important this was.

The foreign professionals working short-term contracts develop little or biased understanding of the nation before shuttling off to some other country for a different contract. Such shorter-term visitors do not invest in clubs, societies, or theater groups. My time in PNG straddled this transition. For decades, expatriates had committed to the place with a sense of permanence. They developed programs at the university and promoted arts and sciences by, for instance, forming ornithological societies. This era ended as increasingly the expatriates huddled together behind razor wire drinking copious amounts of booze. They became ever more insular and invested less in the country and people. Instead of building lasting programs, many of this new generation of short-termers counted their days, collected their hazard pay, and complained about anything and everything. More than once at social gatherings densely populated by foreigners grousing about how bad things were in PNG, I would suggest that perhaps they should just leave and let someone from PNG or at least someone who *liked* PNG take their job. Not surprisingly, I received fewer invitations to such gatherings. Some people would rather be unhappy and complain about it than actually make changes.

Crime (including the theft of government funds by a burgeoning caste of parasitic civil servants) fed the disintegration of the University of PNG. The UPNG had high-quality faculty like Helen and Mike, who were educated at Cambridge; it featured a modern library and an excellent bookstore that I visited every chance I got. Helen and Mike would cite crime and diminishing university budgets as major factors in their decisions to leave. The library lost its acquisitions budget in the late 1980s, and since then has accessioned books only through gifts. You can visit the stacks now and see nice long journal runs ending in 1987. Eventually the bookstore closed because it failed to pay publishers, who then stopped sending books to the university. Professors increasingly were drawn from even poorer countries where people were desperate to find a better life. Many soon moved on, realizing Moresby was not much of an improvement over tough cities like Lagos or Karachi. Witnessing the disintegration of the university over the years due to the exodus of trained faculty helped me appreciate how fundamentally important it was for PNG to develop its own intellectual capacity. No nation should be so dependent on foreign expertise.

Eventually, many faculty were barely qualified to teach at the university level—through no fault of their own. Many were bright and hard working. But the university could not offer competitive pay or promise decent security. Lecturers struggled to get by with no budget or books. Instructors carried their own chalk sticks as there was no money to buy more. Student strikes often shut down classes. Watching the university melt down and seeing good students cheated of an education helped lead to the training program Deb and I would develop together. But in 1987 I was still new to the country and full of energy and enthusiasm primarily directed toward research. Deb arrived with an even greater reservoir of eagerness. We were ready to build programs and undertake research at a time when many of the old timers were stepping away. I wondered if we would last. Or, would we try and then give up and return to safer field sites in Florida?

The arrival process at the old Jacksons Airport gave Deb a good introduction to PNG. When the plane landed she waited an interminable time until the ground crew wheeled up rickety steps. The minute the door opened, PNG sucked all the cool air out of the plane; even those in the back row felt the immediate blast of hot air. Once outside, the heat shimmering off the tarmac hit the passengers like a wall. By the time they walked to the terminal under the beating sun, they were dripping with perspiration. As they approached the terminal, they passed a long chain-link fence. On the other side of the fence, a crushing crowd scoped out every arriving passenger. People at the front of the crowd acquired the diamond imprint of chain-link on their faces as they were pressed against the bulging fence by the crowd behind. Everyone was trying to see the arrivals—you'd think there must be some celebrity coming.

The mob included the relatives—and PNG families are large—of arriving passengers. But the airport also attracted the curious with nothing better to do. In Port Moresby there are a lot of curious people with little to do. People hang out everywhere, talking, smoking, chewing betel nut, and just passing the day. Some people think nothing of going to the airport in the morning and just lingering until afternoon when a relative might be coming in. If the relative doesn't arrive, the routine is repeated the next day . . . and the next. Once a day the airport provided fertile material for entertainment: a planeload of strangers.

Deb, obviously happy to be there, bounced from the plane toward the Immigration and Customs Hall. She spotted me buried deep in the mass behind the fence and waved. I guess the fact that I was a foot taller than the locals, white skinned, bearded, and blonde made me a little easier to find. I waved back, genuinely happy to see her and wondering where her arrival would take me. Both of our lives were changing rapidly and unpredictably.

I've never met a visitor, long-term expatriate or first-time tourist, who is ambivalent about PNG. People generally either love the place or hate it, and most begin their fascination or their loathing shortly after disembarking from the plane. They're met by hills cloaked with savanna scrub, an unusual pocket of dryness in a very wet nation. Houses are haphazardly scattered around the hills and each has its gardens cut into the steep slopes, waiting hopefully for rain. Not far to the east looms the vertical front of the Sogeri Plateau and behind it, when there isn't too much haze or dust in the air, the virtually impassable Owen Stanley Range. Deb took it all in, excited despite many tedious hours of flying coupled with jetlag. She entered the terminal building to swelter in the long sluggish Immigration lines under immobile ceiling fans, an appropriate introduction to the country.

After all the passengers disappeared into the terminal, I shuffled along as the crowd relocated to the building's exit, where the mass of people formed a dense phalanx around the door. There you could watch the weary travelers emerge one by one from the Immigration and Customs ordeal. Newcomers often wore stunned and curious expressions while old timers were sanguine. Everyone looked exhausted and relieved. Deb finally appeared, smiling and excited. She'd brought a mountain of baggage for such a short visit, most of it traps. She wanted to see what she could catch in the forest. She studied the sole marsupial species found in North America, the opossum. New Guinea has some seventy species of marsupial, and no one had ever done a field study of any of them. It was the land of opportunity for her too.

We spent a little time in Moresby and Varirata with Mike and Helen, then headed straight back to Goroka, where Mal's then-partner, Christine, took a liking to Deb right away. Christine was French and in her sexy slinky style took me aside, saying, "Ahhh dahling, thees is soo good for you, I can tell she is purrrfect for you."

From here onwards, the story, the hard work, the dreams, gratifying successes, and crushing failures, are Deb's as well as mine (though I tell it from my perspective and I'll take credit for any errors in the narrative). We would share it all, as co-investigators, as husband and wife, and as co-directors of a program we established. Her commitment became as strong as mine, and even though the husband-and-wife component would eventually crash and burn, we still share the dedication to the people and country we would come to call home.

Chapter Eight

Burglars and the Ubaigubi court system

Man i savi stil na courtim em long Ubaigubi

I wanted to return to Herowana to revisit *pekpek* I'd left *en situ* (those I left in place to monitor). I wanted to see what was germinating and growing from these piles of seeds (from little things, big things grow). For my pilot study I needed to show that I could not only find *pekpek*, but that I could study what grew out of it—assess competition, growth rates, survivorship, seed predation, and so on. In Herowana I could check some of the droppings I'd tagged a few months earlier.

Deb wanted to trap mammals. She had wiggled out of her semester early and still had a couple of assignments due. I believe she baked a few pies and provided them to key faculty as part of the wiggling. Advice to new graduate students: never underestimate the power of a well-made dessert delivered to the right person at the right time. My particular weakness is cookies. At the Rutanabi house she wrote her essays longhand, the pies having bought her time but not exemption. Later, in Goroka, she borrowed a manual typewriter to make the final copies she posted to her professors in Gainesville.

We bummed a ride in a huge flatbed truck with Kevin's construction crew to within a few miles of Ubaigubi. We sat in the cab; the bed held a steamroller anchored in place by two chain binders. Slow going: we were in low first gear for hours, and I marveled that the truck could climb some of the steep hills. By now I was developing a pretty good sense of the sometimes casual attitude Papua New Guineans had toward safety. Most workmen in the country had not grown up with things mechanical. I was raised in a world of steel and plastic, but most in PNG grow up with wood and vines. Thus I had an acquired sense of the load steel could bear and the strength of tools. Later, I'd watch Pawai'ia workmen tighten a nut until the bolt snapped, only to look surprised, replace it, and snap the replacement. It never occurred to them that they had over tightened; they thought there was something wrong with the bolts.

The community in Haia would eat through water supply projects installed by well-meaning development organizations over the years. Every kind of tap and valve failed due to being turned too tightly or pulled too hard. Each new project crew installed more solid and durable fixtures, which only seemed to buy a little time until someone broke them. Solid concrete pads now support black iron pipes in Haia, but no water runs through the pipes because the hardware at each end—the steel and brass valves—have all long since snapped, jammed, or otherwise succumbed. The average American would never subject plumbing to such treatment. Things broke often and were rarely maintained in PNG due to the paucity of people with any experience of mechanical and electrical goods. Put an American in Haia and we'd be just as hopeless at making a thatch roof or splitting wood. This is changing as new generations grow up with Western technologies, but it is tough to catch up given the pace of change. Now folks who grew up with basic plumbing and maybe a generator for power are asked to make computers work. The wrench and hammer used to service the generator are not quite right for a laptop computer. Debacles similar to the Haia community water service still happen, and every business and government office now has a back room filled with mangled and broken computers.

As the flatbed climbed one hill, I happened to look out the mirror on my side and saw one of the roller's chain binders swinging freely. We were on a steep incline with only one chain securing the roller to the truck bed. There were not even wedges under the rollers. I said to the driver, "Um, I think you might want to check the load. Something looks like it could go wrong," which, in Tok Pisin, translated to something along the lines of *Mi tinktink em gutpela taim long sekim masin. Sampela samting klostu i bagarap.*

The driver leaned forward to look in the mirror and saw the dangling chain. Perhaps if the mirror had been positioned in a way that he could see behind without leaning way forward, he would have noticed it earlier. At least we did not have to look for a place to pull over. He stopped immediately and clamped down the roller. I double-checked to make sure none of our gear, stowed beside the steamroller, was in danger of being flattened if the machinery shifted.

From our drop-off point, we could get people to help carry everything up to Rutanabi. Willing hands abounded in Papua New Guinea. Up on the ridgetops, Gimi men shouted the news across the valley, from whence it was relayed to the next valley: PNG yodeling. By the time we set off on foot toward Rutanabi, everyone for miles knew I was back with a white *meri* (woman). There was a new fish in the bowl to watch.

What a joy to introduce Deb to PNG! Her wonder and enthusiasm reminded me what a unique experience it was to spend time there. As the years passed, sharing PNG with new arrivals helped keep it fun. When first-time visitors came, researchers new to PNG, I always relived a bit of the thrill I felt those early months. Years later, I would get to reverse the experience by bringing some of my PNG students to the US for their first trip out of PNG.

That first time I introduced Deb to the Gimi, I would not have thought it possible but the crowd of onlookers around the house grew even larger. The local women had not been comfortable stopping by when I stayed there on my own, but now that Deb had joined me, some of them began showing up, too. The addition of a woman to the show seemed to attract and hold every kid within miles. And if there is one thing in abundance in a PNG highlands village, it is children. Many of the men don't have a lot to do, with the women handling the gardening and tribal fighting banned by the government. More children seemed to be one of the results of their increased leisure time.

Mal would sometimes argue, tongue-in-cheek, that the way to tame PNG's runaway population growth would be to put televisions in the villages. With twenty-four hour satellite TV, he said, the men would have a significant distraction from their other main recreational activity. Joking aside, with controls to screen out violent and incendiary shows, many lives could be saved and improved with educational health and safety programs. Fast-forward twenty years, and you can now find a television powered by a generator in many communities. But there is no satellite link for educational programs. Instead, you will find abundant Rambo-esque killing spree movies on bootleg videocassettes, and the ever-popular Chuck Norris beat-up fests. In these communities you also sometimes find, perhaps not coincidentally, gangs of teenagers sporting dark shades, camo, a Rambo attitude, and, sometimes, high-powered rifles and semi-automatic weapons. Might things have been different if these same young men had instead grown up on a fare of Sesame Street, documentaries, and educational programming instead of Rambo and Chuck Norris?

After a short stay at Rutanabi, we schlepped over the mountain to meet up with Batanimi. I especially wanted Deb to meet him, as he had shown me so much about the mammal life in the area. He showed considerable interest in Deb's mammal live traps, and helped set them up along the nearly invisible game trails and den holes that he could spot so readily. We had reasonable success catching a few of the larger marsupials, but rarely with the traps: Batanimi demonstrated that he could search out and grab some of them by hand with more success.

At the time, no radio telemetry studies of mammals had been done on the island of New Guinea. With a mammal fauna that was 80 percent endemic to New Guinea, this represented a huge opportunity for Deb. Although trapping large marsupials did not prove a stunning success, her smaller live traps for rodents yielded a high capture rate. New Guinea's terrestrial mammal fauna is entirely composed of marsupials, rodents, and bats. There are no native deer, ungulates, tapirs, monkeys, cats, and so on that are fixtures of all other tropical forests around the world. An extraordinary study could be made of small mammals, and it would be the first for New Guinea. Although Deb's research would not move in this direction, she would eventually train and supervise a PNG student, Enock Kale (the first person from Herowana to go to college), who would trap small mammals for his thesis. Even in these first few weeks in PNG, we identified many gold mines of research we would never be able to take on, but we could someday support students to undertake. The common thread was that such studies required a permanent research station to serve as a base. All indicators—for my research, for Deb's research, and for our ideas for other researchers—pointed to the need for a permanent station. One had to have a good place to live and work in order to collect long-term data comfortably and safely. This vast and unique rainforest was unstudied in part because it was almost impossible to work efficiently and comfortably for more than a few weeks. Most researchers who tent-camp in such conditions find the discomforts of constant rain, bugs, and fungus excessive and eventually discourage longer residence.

In this field session I wanted to compare Herowana forests to those around Haia. Batanimi's forest had several potential advantages. It sat at a higher elevation and was thus pleasantly cool and well away from the malaria zone. The health risks would probably be lower. There were a lot of sickly people in Haia, but many fewer in Herowana. The Gimi were generally (perhaps not unrelated to the prevalence of parasites) a bit more energetic and hard-working than the Pawai'ia. But they were also quite intense and not as laid back; it was more stressful to work in Gimi country. This forest was within a day's walk from the end of a road and thus cheaper to reach than Haia, which required plane travel. I still had access to the comfortable house David Gillison built at Rutanabi, which could serve as a staging area. The higher forest had a number of interesting bird of paradise species and marsupials not found at lower elevations. But there were just not as many cassowary droppings and many of the cassowaries' food plants in the higher elevations were small-seeded. This higher forest was in extremely rugged terrain and more difficult to work than forests around my camp on the Wara Oo. So although perhaps better-suited for an eventual research station in general, it was not as good a fit for my research. I leaned toward the Haia area as the place to study cassowaries and build a long-term program. This pilot study was wrapping up as my ten thousand dollar grant was dwindling. When we dismantled our camp, I did not know if I would see Batanimi again. I would miss his broad smile and the protective way he looked out for me in the field.

On our last day he went out on his own gathering firewood. He came back bare-chested, carrying the dirty raggedy T-shirt he had worn every day in his hands. Now shredded into tatters, it looked as if a tiger had used it for a toy. He made a few particularly hard-to-understand hand gestures and grunts. Through his son, I asked in Tok Pisin what had happened. Batanimi said something back to him in Gimi, which I thought would be some story of a close encounter with a wild pig, but what he probably told his son was, "See what you can get out of him." He was a sly old man. His son said his shirt had caught on a vine and ripped. I looked at the shirt. It must have been attacked by one of those man-eating vines out of the old Tarzan movies; it looked more like confetti than a shirt. I realized what the game was. I would soon be leaving this cool and foggy forest for the US. I took off my Gore-Tex raincoat and offered it to him. He beamed and accepted. Proud and old school, Batanimi didn't just straight-out ask for things. Younger men I would work with in the future would have no compunctions about asking me to give them anything they fancied. I fully knew that in the poor communities I visited, I represented a potential source of vast wealth to be exploited one way or another. I also knew I could give away everything I had and still make no dent in the poverty around me. Unfortunately, giving something to one person implied favoritism. Simply making a small gift or reward for someone's help could alter the delicate village politics and clan power struggles in ways I could not imagine. I appreciated the graceful way Batanimi had made his request, even though he had gambled what appeared to be his only shirt. He had earned the exchange through his friendship and sharing his knowledge of cassowaries.

We hiked back to Rutanabi, where Falau and Dorahau greeted us. Dorahau especially doted on me. It had not taken me long to realize he was low in the local pecking order. Gimi society has "bigmen" who gather wealth, wives, prestige, pigs, and power. Men were constantly working the system to move toward becoming a bigman, or creating alliances with bigmen for their mutual benefit. By positioning himself as my assistant, Dorahau sent his stock soaring in the community. He had access to the wealth I carried.

All land in PNG is under traditional ownership, meaning the government does not own the land and cannot acquire land through eminent domain. Land that had belonged to a tribe for generations stayed in the hands of the tribe when PNG was colonized and then became a nation—a bit different from how things were handled in North America. Wherever researchers go, they have to work with the traditional landowners. So wherever they go, they alter the power base and hierarchies. This provides a level of complexity to fieldwork that most of my colleagues back in the US would not comprehend. You can easily spend weeks of a field session embroiled in political negotiations rather than actual research. I was about to get a crash course in village politics.

When we arrived at Rutanabi, Dorahau told me the house had been robbed while we were over the mountain with Batanimi. Deb and I had left a few supplies and items we did not need in the field, plus a small cache of food. I assessed what was stolen; it amounted to very little. The thief, probably a kid who could not carry off much, had climbed through a small window. Some pencils and other trivial items were taken. Fortunately, no specimens or field notes were missing. Dorahau and Falau were very upset and wanted to make a federal case out of it. I was more sanguine—petty theft can occur anywhere. But Dorahau was adamant that if we let this go, it would be worse next time. He said we had to make it known we were unhappy. In retrospect, I think this was more about him and Falau confronting the threat to their status posed by the theft than anything to do with "law and order" or my ability to study there.

Tired and hungry after the hike, I told him we could talk about it the next day. Somehow he took this as authorization to take whatever steps he deemed necessary, steps I would have much preferred to avoid. When he came to the house the following morning, he told me he had arranged for a village court to hear the case. The word was out. I was being played and matters were out of my control. I had no idea what to expect from the village court. Knowing the Gimi people, I pictured correctly that it would entail a *lot* of talking.

By 10 a.m. the crowd started to assemble in the yard outside the house—and not the usual horde of peering kids. These were the adult males, most of whom I had never seen before. When it seemed the yard could hold no more, Dorahau told me court was in session.

I went out into the crowd and, like everyone else assembled there, sat on the grass. I could imagine few less pleasant ways to spend a beautiful day with blue skies and billowing white clouds. The crowd shifted so I sat in a doughnut hole of green grass with a ring of men around me, loosely clumped in clusters I assumed represented clans or house lines. Around them sat an even larger crowd of children and women. Dogs wandered among the groups. I heard a constant undercurrent of Gimi murmuring. Now and then a baby cried, soon silenced by mother's breast.

Dorahau began a long speech in Gimi. Others replied in Gimi. The speech-like orations were directed at the crowd. It appeared the entire male population served as judge and jury. A few older men seemed to have some authority. Not understanding Gimi, I could only guess what was being said. It became clear I was merely a passive observer; this was all their show. I managed to occasionally get Falau to translate some fragments of the discussions into Tok Pisin. He was carefully taking in every word and who said it—this had much to do with his status. It seemed every house line had something to say. I wondered how so many men could be concerned about the theft of a few pencils.

After the first hour, with virtually nothing communicated to me, I realized court would not be over soon. Deb went back in the house to finish some assignments. Gimi can't discuss something for long without raising their voices. It often seems persuasion among the Gimi is accomplished not by reason or logic, but by the strength of one's voice. Along with the raising voices and tempo of the discussion, I heard some undertones of anger. One person might speak quietly for five minutes, only to be rebuked by a shouting man from a different clan. Something was happening in terms of local politics far more important than the loss of my pencils. Dorahau also brought up any other minor grievance I might have had in the past months, most importantly that when I had once set mist nets some kids had come and taken the captured birds, killing them for food. The discussions became more about me and less about the theft.

The debates ensued for hours. I was sunburned, thirsty, and tired. No one seemed to care that I could not understand a word being said. My presence was completely superfluous, other than to act as a focal point for the ebb and flow of power struggles around me. The tone raised and lowered; the talk went back and forth and on and on. If there is one thing a society with no written language can do, it's talk . . . and talk . . . and talk. Even I could perceive that a lot of the same things were being said over and over. I looked around. I seemed to be the only one finding this a waste of time; everyone else was dead serious. The charges were weighty, but were not discussed with me. Kafka comes to Ubaigubi.

Eventually the pace began to slow and I could sense some sort of consensus developing. I began to see more heads nodding in agreement and fewer angry bulging veins in temples. The various clans and house lines were finding common ground. Finally, the deliberations wound down and the verdicts were communicated to me in Tok Pisin. The consensus was that I had not done enough for them. The one thing everyone in the community could agree upon was that they had not become rich with my arrival.

They all agreed that the responsibility for the theft was mine. If I had hired more people to guard the house when I was away, no one would have been able to break in. Furthermore, they were happy to have me study birds by mist netting them. But I would have to hire a guard for each net to make sure no children stole birds from them. Additionally, I had not bought enough firewood from them. Even though I could burn only so much in a night, I needed to buy more from other clans. Each load of wood would be a hundred kina, a huge sum equal to a hundred dollars then and about what a worker would make for six weeks of fulltime labor.

White people come from a world of unfathomable affluence—trucks, helicopters, nice clothing, canned foods. All this represents a vast wealth that should be shared. There was no point explaining that I had only a small, fixed amount of money. The broader community saw me as a huge ATM cash machine. How on earth could I explain what a grant is? How could I make them see that, while I had ridden in trucks and planes, these were not *my* vehicles or part of *my* wealth? I was white. The people driving those vehicles were white. How could I tell them that my grant funds must be spent on certain things and not others? I could not pay for things unrelated to my research. Their village was poor and mine was phenomenally rich. I was a guest and stingy.

In retrospect, I suspect Dorahau had been boasting of my wealth in order to boost his own status as my assistant. But it was also clear that the community saw any white person as a potential fountain of money. I think they believed I could tap the wealth of all other white people the way they could tap the wealth of their clan. The planes, helicopters, and cars used by my white clan were assets I could access if I wanted to, just as a Gimi male could borrow the axe of his cousin.

When the pronouncement was made that I needed to buy more firewood and hire more guards, watchmen, and workers, I learned many important lessons. One was that if I were ever robbed again, my first action would be to fire whoever was supposed to be guarding the house. If the logic was that robbery meant my security was inadequate, then the first step should be to fire my security. This reaction would be perceived as fair in a similar situation in the future.

The trial convinced me to avoid research on Gimi land. This decision would prove a huge financial benefit to the Pawai'ia and an equal loss to the Gimi. Deb and I would have many good years among the Pawai'ia. But even on Pawai'ia land and working with Pawai'ia landowners, the bloated sense of entitlement of some Gimi would eventually reach deep into Pawai'ia territory to harm us.

The rest of my work would be done on Pawai'ia land. Not long after the conclusion of the court, we made a quick trip to Wau then returned to Moresby. We stored some things, confident of returning to PNG, but not knowing how or when. With very mixed emotions we flew back to the US. I knew I wanted to come back and stay a long time in the remote and very wet rainforests near Haia. I had difficult personal decisions to make about relationships. Daunting fundraising challenges lay ahead. I had to sell my vision to a potentially skeptical graduate committee. But I had passed a point of no return. I could not be happy now if I had to switch to a project in south Florida, or even in Costa Rica. If I could not pull off the dream of building a research station and living in the New Guinea rainforest for an extended period, I had no other appealing options.

In 1989 Deb enrolled at the University of Miami joining me as a graduate student. We soon married, and my PNG pursuits became joint ventures—and adventures. We shared the vision and the experience. Deb decided to work with cassowaries as well. I admit I was a bit reluctant about this. I had mapped out a number of projects, and I wanted to take them on. There were so many things to study in PNG, and she was encroaching on me! Realistically, though, I knew I could not do everything I wanted to do, at least for my dissertation, so doubling up offered a real advantage. We agreed to split the study, a decision that sometimes led to strife between us. Loosely, we decided that she would focus on factors leading up to a cassowary eating a fruit: diet, fruit selection, and fruit availability. I would study what fascinated me most, the process after the seeds came out of the cassowary: how far and to where seeds are moved, and what happens to the seeds and the seedlings.

Although we were a research team and a married couple, we each had our individual work and our individual perspectives. Often they complemented each other, but sometimes we conflicted.

After the 1987 scouting trip, I kicked butt raising money. A few small foundations chipped in and I got a dissertation improvement grant from the National Science Foundation, a Fulbright Scholarship, and more. Deb landed a three-year scholarship from the University of Miami to cover expenses in Papua New Guinea and an NSF grant as well. Together we had raised enough to build a modest research station and support a couple of years of research in PNG, if we could stretch the pennies. But we also knew we could continue applying for funds once we were established. After we had the station up and running and results were coming in, additional funding might be easier to secure. We also jointly had a research grant, from Wildlife Conservation International. It was by no means the majority of our funding, but we hoped WCI might consider renewals if we started producing good results. Thanks to David Gillison, Don Bruning, and the attempt at ecotourism at Ubaigubi, WCI had an interest in the Crater Mountain area.

I was on my way to a huge rainforest, dramatically different from all other rainforests in the world—one without a single research station. We had enough money on hand to build a good station and shared the dream of making it happen. We had both seen the movie *Field of Dreams* and liked to joke about the line "If you build it, they will come." If we were going to learn anything about cassowaries we would have to stay where the cassowaries were for a long time, and doing so required at minimum a good roof and a solid floor. I'd guess we had some of the most complicated and difficult logistics to master of any contemporary graduate students. But we would build it, and "they" did come.

Chapter 9

Choosing the study area when malaria strikes

Painim ples long wokim studi long ples bigpela sik malaria

In the second half of 1989, Deb and I returned to PNG. We opened a bank account, transferred money from the US, and started the work of building a research station. We agreed that establishing our base in Pawai'ia country made the best sense in terms of cassowary research and avoiding the unrealistic expectations and politics that could overwhelm us on Gimi land. We gathered a Cessna-load of food and supplies for a recon trip. Among the supplies were some rudimentary construction tools—axes, shovels, pick, and a digging iron. We would literally work from the ground up.

Before leaving Goroka, we consulted with the pilot, Graham, looking over maps of potential study areas. We showed him the location of my previous camp on the lower Wara Oo (*wara* means "water" or "river" or "stream" or "rain" or "wet"; Tok Pisin can be confusing) and the general area we had in mind for the station. The maps were old, so we wanted to do some overflights to look for gardens and bush houses. We wanted to be as far from people as we could get. With a full load, low reconnaissance flights were not prudent, but fortunately the weather cooperated and we were able to make higher passes with good visibility. From the aerial vantage we could see a fair number of gardens and houses along the lower Wara Oo.

The first-choice area looked a bit crowded for our tastes; a small bush house and garden appeared every few kilometers along the lower Oo and Pio. It was impossible to tell how many of these houses were in regular use. The semi-nomadic Pawai'ia come and go, sometimes staying an entire growing season, sometimes just a couple of weeks or days. But with so many houses, people would be traveling through the area fairly regularly, and the Pawai'ia always had bow and arrow at the ready. We wanted a place where hunters rarely stepped. Graham expanded the Cessna's circling and moved north toward the rugged headwaters and a large plateau that seemed uninhabited.

The Oo leaps from a plateau, formed when pressures blew out the side of the Crater volcano about ten thousand years ago and lava poured out in a giant moving wall. The lava fanned out and then cooled in what looks like a delta from above. With the heavy rains that fall on this side of the volcano, dozens of small streams spread across the plateau like the ribs of a fan and have eroded innumerable steep, but not deep, ravines and ridges. The spreading "delta" ends in a huge cliff along the south and west sides. All those streams throw themselves over the precipice in a series of stunning waterfalls. The lush vegetation of the plateau curls over the edge like a thick head of beer. Circumnavigating the plateau in the Cessna, we felt as if we'd circled back in time. The forest was thick with *Podocarpus*, an ancient gymnosperm that produces a fleshy fruit like a plum (very unlike the cones that fall from our familiar pines). The twisted arms of *Pandanus*, ending in palm-like fans of long narrow leaves, resembled an ancient plant usually seen in artists' portrayals of dinosaur habitat. We spied not a single sign of humanity on the entire plateau. The area looked ideal—to the north it abutted the wall of Crater Mountain and on the other three sides it ended in steep cliffs. No one would journey up there without a good reason—and what better reason than to study cassowaries?

We landed at Haia and unloaded our gear. After eighteen months I'm sure many of the locals had concluded that I would not return. Eighteen months prior I wasn't sure I'd be able to come back. The Pawai'ia were pleased to see us, and especially pleased to see the shovels and axes we'd brought along, as they spoke volumes about our intentions. It appeared we meant to stay awhile. The jockeying began among the elders, the *papa grauns*, to have us visit their particular territory. The cash cow had returned and everyone had the best pasture for him. Fortunately, we had already identified our target area, so the selection of guides was not completely up to the impenetrable village politics (though we learned in time just how little control over such decisions one has in rural PNG). Imagine being teleported from a sixteenth-century Cherokee village into contemporary North America: how poorly you would understand the culture and way of life! That's how it was for me, in reverse, in Pawai'ia country. My ignorance kept things interesting and kept us humble.

Jack and Isa Douglas, the missionaries at Haia, invited us to stay in their house. They took an instant liking to Deb and approved of the fact that we were married. But their values and priorities were quite different from mine and we never became close. Through the years we knew the Douglases, they were cordial and helpful. They often gave us good advice based on their decades of living among the Pawai'ia, and hosted us a few times for delicious meals. Later, when the research station began attracting more researchers, they became less supportive. We were seen as bringing change and a cash economy to their little corner of paradise. I would argue that these changes were coming regardless of a few scientists. Better us than a logging or gold mining company that wanted to denude the forest. Eventually the missionaries and the Pawai'ia would learn firsthand the stark difference between what prospectors and loggers brought to the culture and what we brought.

Many changes would come to the Pawai'ia that the missionaries disliked, particularly other churches they considered "false gospels." They blamed us for bringing in outside influences, though they did not seem to see themselves as "outside influences"—even though it was their presence and the airstrip they built that brought outsiders to this otherwise remote part of the country.

Jack had built his house in Haia by hand and it was an impressive structure, much more sophisticated than anything Deb and I had planned. He even had a mini hydro plant, outlets on the walls, and lights with twenty-four-hour power. On several occasions Jack gave us very good building advice. By then I'd spent hundreds of nights in rural homes in the tropics. It's easy to lie in bed and examine the construction of a house that has no interior walls, drywall, or ceilings; you can see where the diagonal braces go, for instance, and how the windows are framed. All those hot sleepless nights in the tropics, staring at the interiors of hand-made houses, I'd never realized I was collecting data on how to one day build one myself.

Our next step was making the trek to the plateau to reconnoiter for a research station site. As it turned out, few Pawai'ia had been there, and the young men who hung around the mission were not sure of the route. This was a promising sign! The plateau stood about five miles away in a straight line. But the terrain was so rugged, getting there meant extra miles to avoid vertical cliffs. The men sauntered off to find out who knew the way up to the plateau.

Later, they returned with a small man named Moai, who had gray hair and eyes that could switch from lively to flat, unrevealing, and a bit spooky when needed. He, like Batanimi, was old school and did not speak any Tok Pisin (or at least never revealed that he did). He had been around well before whites arrived in this remote part of PNG, and would most certainly have killed a few people and likely eaten them as a young man. If you push them the wrong way, such old warriors can reveal these credentials via the look they give you—as if you've passed some point and have become nothing more than an annoyance that can be eliminated. It is the same calm, calculating appraisal you get from a big cat or bear in the wild—it will size you up, know it can do whatever it wants with you, and then decide if it's worth the trouble to kill you. Moai's subtle facial expressions suggested he was not someone to screw around with; he commanded respect among the Pawai'ia. He would prove to be a great ally and lieutenant for our work forces. Years later, after he died and authority passed to his ebullient son, Joe, labor relations became a little more difficult.

We interviewed Moai through an interpreter. Yes, he said, he could take us up to the plateau, called Aedo. He conveyed this with a grunt, a short nod, and a sly smile. In his mind, he was reconstructing the way up, as it may have been a couple of decades since he'd taken the route. Pawai'ia have an uncanny ability to recall details of a forest they may have passed through only once many years earlier. A forty-year-old guide might point to a small scar in a tree trunk, saying he'd made that with his bushknife the last time he had traveled this route, as a small boy with his father. The people knew their way around their vast lands the way I might know my way around a two-bedroom apartment. All manner of details would be recalled on a patrol. So-and-so killed a pig here once; there used to be a garden here, tended by a family who all died; over there you will find a place where birds come to drink mineral water.

With a guide settled, we set about selecting a group of eight carriers. We would do a couple of weeks' reconnaissance, and if/when we found a suitable spot, I would pop back for the tools and the rest of the food and supplies. A crowd of men, none of whom I knew except for John, who was part of the crew from my last patrol, gathered seeking work. I chose John and then selected those who looked strong, enthusiastic, and honest. On this and many patrols to come, we would have to size up carriers and make on-the-spot decisions based on their demeanor and physique. One man in the crowd, Sima, was exceptional because he was about twice as wide as the average Pawai'ia. He looked like he could tear stumps out of the ground. I would not have been surprised if his name had been Mongo. He had one bad eye, but the other one looked straight into mine and I saw an honest man. I chose him to complete my promising-looking team of strong men.

That evening, while we sat chatting with Jack and Isa, Sima came by shyly to talk with us. He spoke at length in Pawai'ia with Jack, who translated for us. Jack said Sima worried that he might slow us down. Apparently he was nearly blind. He wanted to come and would work hard, but thought he should first explain his vision problems. Isa told us his story. Sima had been born a twin when the missionaries were new to the area. Twins were considered bad luck, so he was left in the forest to die. Isa found him, but by then ants had infested his eyes and nearly blinded him. Isa saved him and found a family to raise him. Jack and Isa said Sima was capable of going into the bush, and that he did so with others. This would be his first chance to earn some pay. We thought the other carriers would keep an eye on him and help him along. I figured a near-blind, barefoot Pawai'ia would probably move only marginally slower than me in my slippery shoes. We agreed to keep him as a carrier and said we would set out with him the next day as planned. He beamed with happiness. Sima would become a lifelong friend, though we could hire him only rarely due to his handicap, taking him on as a carrier when he wanted a few kina. He essentially felt his way barefoot through the forest, following the tracks and sounds of the carriers ahead of him.

Like slipping into bed for the first time with your lover, the anticipation and excitement the next morning was intoxicating. After years of effort, planning, red tape, and fundraising, my research was really under way! This was a short scouting trip, so we traveled light: food, a dry change of clothes, and a roll of plastic for building a camp. In paring down the load to what eight men could carry, we left the big first-aid kit behind in favor of a smaller kit. How much could go wrong on a short patrol? Unfortunately, we would find out. We set out in the morning as the usual nightly rain shower slowed to a drip and the clouds parted a bit. This part of the world typically offers a few hours of relative dryness in the morning before the afternoon rains—except for the times when it rains all day, that is.

We followed the trail I'd used on previous patrols, over a small mountain and across the Wara Hwalia (which can flood so quickly you can be swept away, we would one day discover). Then we trudged over a larger mountain, following a route that seemed uphill in every direction until it finally descended to the Wara Oo. Rather than turn downstream as I had before, we now turned upstream. After a short while, we came to a bush house that belonged to Moai, who indicated we would stay the night there.

I wanted to push on, and lobbied for us to do so. It was only lunchtime, the weather was holding, and we were wasting good time just for the sake of spending a night in a house rather than in a camp we could make at 4 p.m. Much discussion in Tok Pisin ensued, followed by even more in Pawai'ia, which probably ran along the lines of "This guy doesn't know jack; how do we get him to shut up?" Eventually, someone condescended to translate for Moai. If we kept walking, we'd find no place to camp and no water to drink. Reaching the next water and viable camp area would take a full day. Fair enough. We stayed at the house and I went to the river to savor a leisurely dip before the nighttime rain of cockroaches. Imagine: We were about to step into a trail-less wilderness, a place only one member of our team had ever been before. Deb and I were almost certainly the first white people, not to mention the first biologists, to visit this plateau. It is an intoxicating and addictive sensation.

The next day it did not take long to see what Moai meant. We moved up river a short distance, hopping from boulder to boulder. As always, even without a backpack or load heavier than my binoculars, I could not keep up with the heavily burdened carriers, who laughed, chatted, and smoked as they went. Looking back, I saw Sima, carrying his *bilum* (the traditional bag of woven bark fibers) and a 45-pound bale of rice, managing to keep within earshot. At least I moved faster than the blind guy. Upriver a few kilometers we turned left up the steep riverbank, using roots as handholds. The forest leveled briefly and then we ascended the base of a ridge that quickly grew steeper and sharper. Soon we were winding up a razor ridge that dropped off nearly vertically on both sides. Had we tried to camp here, we would have had to lie in a line along the crest. There was barely room to stand side by side in many places, and no indication of a foot trail, which you might expect on a ridge crest. Eventually the reason for this became clear. The ridge abruptly ended in a huge crevasse. We had absolutely no direction to go but right back the way we came. Here, Moai's experience came into play. The carriers all dropped their loads and wandered back along the ridge; some went carefully down its steep flanks. Moai and the men shouted back and forth. Deb and I sat and enjoyed the lush, mossy vegetation. Before long we heard the chop of axes.

One advantage of working in a big wilderness area, compared to the relatively small islands of forest that typically host mainstream research stations, is that when you need a tree, you cut down a tree. We did not risk disrupting someone's field study; we were the first biologists ever to walk this forest. Before long, six of the men dragged a long, narrow tree—though "pole" might be a better description—up the ridge crest, bringing the base right up to the edge of the precipice. I looked at the pole. I looked at the crevasse. I said to Deb, "I don't have a good feeling about this."

A couple more smiling carriers appeared, dragging yards of rattan behind them. Bush rope, they call it. They swung the pole/tree over the crevasse and let it fall across the opening. The tip found a purchase on the other side and the pole bounced up and down like a lethargic bowstring. Deb and I watched the proceedings, occasionally exchanging silent looks. I was the heaviest and clumsiest of our group.

Soon the crew arrived with another tree, plopping it across the chasm next to the first. Now two wobbly, tenuous stems spanned the void. The skinniest man eased onto the structure. A couple of others had prepared the rattan, splitting it and bending to make it more supple. The guy dangling over the crevasse used pieces of the tough vine to lash the two trees together, then inched forward, repeating the process again and again. This somewhat reduced the flex. He sat in the middle and helped position a third, heavier tree, pushing it hand-over-hand above his head until it bumped to the far edge. He then lashed this to the other two. The "bridge" was at least gaining rigidity and the skinny guy had made it across to the other side, where he immediately lashed that end of the contraption to some tree roots.

By now the men were walking across the crude balance beam, their large bare feet splayed, grasping with their big toes. Another look exchanged with Deb. We have to trust that these guys know what they're doing, I thought; after all, they'd just performed an impressive feat of engineering. And Moai was in no mood to lose us this early, so he instructed the crew to lash on a few more supporting pieces. By the time the Pawai'ia had carried all the cargo to the other side, Deb and I were ready to trust that it would hold us. One at a time, we made our way over the makeshift bridge. When I has halfway across the great divide, I looked down and flashed to a scene I had seen in a dozen Tarzan movies, where the hero eyes the ground, envisioning a certain death, from astride a swinging suspended bridge made of vines. Surreal for me; just another day for our guides. Once safe on the opposite side, we set out again with no further thought about the ravine. I made a mental note that should this end up being the best route to the research station we would need to construct a much better, permanent bridge.

Farther up the ridge we came to a vertical rock face. Again, with very little discussion, the men dropped their loads and spread out into the forest, returning later with the required construction materials. It was like living in the Home Depot megastore. The engineers went to work again, using the same construction materials of poles lashed with vines. They quickly tied together a bush ladder and secured it to shrubs clinging to the rock face. Again, convinced by the adroit passage of the carriers, Deb and I followed up the cliff. Clearly, if we found a good study area up on Aedo, we could be fairly certain that few hunters and passersby would be bothering us.

Cool air greeted us at the edge of the plateau and we felt a chill in our sweaty clothes. We'd spent the better part of the day just traveling the last kilometer. I understood now why we slept at the house rather than forging on as I had wanted. Deb and I began to scope out the area, seeking any sign of cassowaries or the fruits they eat. The vegetation had changed dramatically across the vertical boundary we had just scaled. Here the forest was much mossier, thanks to the mist in the air. We found shorter trees with smaller leaves and stronger wood, lower diversity, fewer trees with compound leaves—characteristics of montane forest. We had left hill forest and were in a very different forest from that of my initial camps on the lower Wara Oo. In many ways this forest was more like the one we had seen above Herowana, even though we were perhaps a thousand feet lower in elevation. We searched for a workable campsite. We told all the guys to keep their eyes peeled (Sima excluded) for *pekpek bilong muruk*, the all-important words in my Tok Pisin lexicon.

Moai took the lead, and we followed him over terrain that was confusing, to say the least. Every fifty meters seemed to bring us to another of the parallel streambeds stretching to the plateau's edge to form waterfalls into the jungle below. Often Moai stopped and squinted, dredging up long-buried memories, perhaps from hunting trips up here as a boy. Now and then we'd find the game trail of cassowaries, but these often peter out and resume elsewhere. We bushwhacked using Moai's dead reckoning. Each stream had a steep bank to descend and another to ascend. Working here would be a challenge and tedious, but with a good trail network it was potentially doable. We did not encounter big cliffs like those around Herowana, just lots of mini cliffs that could be negotiated with carefully positioned trails. But doing research here would be a constant struggle up or down. No place was level. Finding a site for the station would not even be easy. No one had ever thought it worth trying to put a garden up here. There were no telltale signs of people—no bushknife marks in a tree, no sapling cut off to indicate a hunting trail. We might have been the first people here in decades. But we were not finding many signs of cassowary, either.

Several times a carrier spotted a *pekpek*, but always it was quite old and populated with small seeds, not the big exclusively cassowary-dispersed seeds my research required. By the time we found a campsite, we were chilly, tired, and not encouraged by the indicators thus far. We cut a ridgepole and stretched plastic over it. You can make an amazingly comfortable camp with nothing more than an axe and a roll of heavy plastic sheet. Before the plastic was tightened down with vines, the carriers had a fire burning. Even in a forest where every surface is deeply shrouded in soaking moss, there is dry fuel wood to be had for those who know where to look.

The temperatures dropped as night fell. Deb and I huddled for warmth in our made-for-tropics sleeping bags, and the men stayed close to the smoky fire. By morning I was stiff and achy from sleeping on the cold ground, but ready to go. I had been working toward this for years. I had fantasies of coming upon the perfect place for a station, with a view, idyllic waterfalls and swimming holes, and cassowaries roaming the forest like squirrels in Central Park. Deb felt under the weather; she was coming down with something. But being tough field biologists, neither of us made much of it. In the rainforest it is almost a weekly event to have some challenge to the immune system, some unknown arbovirus, a fungus, or a parasite. You tough it out or you never get anything done.

Before setting out, Deb and I followed the stream down to the edge of the plateau. The water rushed over and disappeared into fog and mist below. Stretching out to the south was a magnificent view of jungle-clad hills poking out of the low fog that clung to the riverbeds. Beyond the hills, uncut lowland forest extended all the way to the Gulf of Papua. We might have been perched at the edge of an uninhabited world—though we knew there were Pawai'ia, and certainly a few cassowaries, hidden under that unbroken cloak of forest below. Such places spawn a profound sense of humility for me, a sense of the utter insignificance of my existence. Astronomers tell me they experience a similar sensation when staring into the cosmos. The water rushing over the edge so close by and the bottom so far below gave me an odd, queasy feeling, as if my eyes could not figure out how or where to focus. I felt the water's force as it roared and shot over the brink. I stepped back from the edge, thinking I'd probably return to this spot many times to take photographs, but I never did. We did not know then that we still had a long way to go to find our study site, or that we would ultimately establish the field station close to the bottom of that waterfall, now hidden in the mist. I would have many chances to stand below, among the wreckage of trees washed over that edge, and look up at water shooting out into space, like a leak sprung in the mountain. But I never would make it back to the top.

After conferring with Moai we agreed to traverse the plateau. Toward the end of the day we could reach a way back down that did not require so much engineering. Somehow climbing *up* a bush ladder seems preferable to pushing one over the edge of a cliff and going *down*. If we found good signs along the way, as I hoped, we could stay on the plateau. If not, we would descend to a lower elevation where camping would be easier and a little warmer. We set out in our straggly line, most of the gang ahead of us, Deb and I scanning the forest for fresh research potential and Sima and another carrier typically somewhere behind us. It was comforting to know we would not be left behind, hopelessly lost. A couple of times Deb, who thought she might be coming down with the flu, stopped to rest, something she rarely did. I started to worry a bit, but a more immediate issue quickly subsumed my concerns for her health. We caught up to the men, who were circled around one of the carriers, Samson. He had walked into a bamboo splinter, which had entered horizontally, piercing deep between his toes and snapping off inside his foot. There was not much blood, just a neat little hole, some swelling, and a strong, tough man in a great deal of pain. The bottoms of the men's feet are half-inch-thick callous that little can penetrate, but the skin between the toes is not thus armored and the splinter had found the soft spot.

Sima caught up to us and began to pray. He was quite religious, perhaps thanks to the missionaries having saved his life as a baby. Our forest cacophony: an injured man making sounds of agony, another praying loudly to the Big Papa Bilong Sky, Deb suffering quietly, and the rest all talking at once in Pawai'ia about what to do. I really had no clue what to do. I dug out our little first-aid kit, but found nothing useful. Samson did not need Band-Aids and antiseptic; he needed painkillers, local anesthesia, a scalpel to cut out the splinter, and sutures to close up the wound. I seriously regretted the decision not to have brought the substantial first-aid kit. Like that hike on my first visit to this area, I was caught in the middle of nowhere needing a better first-aid kit. You'd think I would have learned. You'd think I'd have known that even on a short patrol, things can go seriously wrong. What I didn't know was that even more troubles lay ahead.

Moai summoned a dirty razor from his *bilum*. The men gathered around and held Samson down. The consensus in the Pawai'ia discussion was that Moai would try to cut it out. The splinter was extremely deep, I did not think this was a good idea. Sima prayed louder and asked the Papa Sky to keep Moai's hand steady. Leaning forward, razor in hand, Moai paused and then said he could not do it. Perhaps his anatomy lessons as a young warrior gave him an idea of what he would encounter. My courses in anatomy told me that the splinter was planted deep among tendons and ligaments needed to walk and maintain balance. Slicing away at that part of his foot with a dirty Gillette straight razor was perhaps not such a good idea. We divided up Samson's loads among the other carriers, bandaged his foot, and cut a crutch for him. Lagging back with the blind Sima and the crippled Samson, Deb stumbled along, feeling sicker by the minute with a headache coming on. Given the way the patrol was shaping up, and the low number of cassowary droppings, we decided to get off the plateau. About a third of the team was incapacitated. At least the loads got a little lighter with each meal we ate.

We pushed down a steep ridge, the temperature climbing as we dropped and the landscape returning to more open and taller hill forest. We could hear the roar of fast-moving water far below. Moai indicated we were headed there. Often in the dense steep forest of PNG, you hear your destination long before you see it. It always lifts my spirits, on a long march, to hear my destination, even if reaching it will require what seems an impossible vertical drop. We began to see a few more signs that humans had once passed through, and were back on to Moai's main stomping grounds.

Arriving at the river, we found a level, dry spot on the bend—a good place to set up camp. Although the site sat eight feet above the stream, remembering my experience on the lower Oo, I asked if this spot would flood. Moai and the carriers said no; it was fine. I looked around and did not see the telltale marks of past high water. If it flooded there, it did not flood often. Perhaps we would get a break for a little while.

Yeah, right.

As the plastic went up and the camp formed, Deb quickly became sicker and sicker. She had stopped holding down food and water while descending the ridge. Usually full of energy and helping wherever needed, she sat on a bale of rice and leaned against a mossy tree trunk, too tired even to discourage the insects buzzing around her head. I knew the signs: a fever that comes on quickly in the late afternoon, chills, shivering, chattering teeth, sweating. It was classic malaria. Your first bout of malaria is usually the worst, and if it does not kill you quickly by "going cerebral," with proper medications you have a pretty good chance of recovery. I'd been through hell with my initial case because it developed in the US where physicians 1) did not know how to diagnose it and 2) refused to prescribe any medication without a diagnosis. I had gone through three clueless doctors while suffering killer fevers every forty-eight hours for two weeks. I was literally pissing blood by the time I found a specialist who diagnosed me in fifteen minutes and prescribed the appropriate medicine. You must draw blood *during* the fever if you are going to detect the parasites, not when it is *convenient* to the doctor's schedule. Otherwise the parasites are completely hidden away inside your red blood corpuscles.

I knew malaria well from that first experience and kept chloroquine to treat it in the first-aid kit. The first-aid kit we'd left back at Haia. All I could do was give Deb aspirin to combat the raging fever and sponge her with a wet cloth. If the *Plasmodium*—the parasites that cause malaria—do not kill you, the fever might, literally cooking your brain. We had a horrible night to look forward to, trying to keep the fever low and waiting out the cycle. If you make it through the outbreak, you usually have forty-eight hours until the next main outbreak (which will be worse). But I was optimistic we could get medicine for her in time for the next cycle. She just had to make it through this night.

After midnight the fever began to ease and Deb got a little sleep in fits punctuated with delirium. By dawn I had a note composed for the Douglases. Isa was a nurse and would know how to treat Deb. A runner was sent with firm instructions not to stop for anything. I stayed to keep my eye on Deb. No way could I even hope to keep up with a Pawai'ia moving in a hurry. If it was *vivax* malaria, we had forty-eight hours. If it was *falciparum*, it was less predictable and much more deadly. I didn't talk about this to Deb, just about my bouts with *vivax* so she would be reassured that the symptoms would diminish if we got the medicine to her before the fever set in.

For once we had luck on our side; the river did not flood. The rocks in the river literally are the stepping stones/highway Pawai'ia use for high-speed transit. If they are exposed and dry, a runner can rock hop at what I would call a sprint half the way to Haia. Our runner, Mayabe, glided back into camp the next morning at sunrise. He gave me an envelope with meds and a note from Isa. I promised myself from then on I would always keep malaria medication close at hand. Leaving it behind had been a stupid blunder.

We got a big dose of chloroquine into Deb right away, but she was still a bit delirious and running a high temperature. The parasites release a lot of toxins for which the chloroquine does nothing. You swallow lots of aspirin and suffer through it. Every forty-eight hours the parasites emerge from their concealment inside the corpuscles and swim by the millions through your blood stream. That's when the real misery occurs. Taking the medicine does not affect them while hidden in the corpuscles; only when out swimming are they vulnerable. Extremely clever, these parasites. The worst part is knowing a fever is coming, like watching a train come toward you in slow motion and being helpless to get off the tracks.

By now Deb was quite weak and just eating a bit of Ramen noodles along with weak sweet tea. I had to keep her hydrated and bathed her with a cool wet towel from the river when the fever climbed. The medicine helped, but did not act like the magic bullet it should have. It looked like this strain of the parasite might be resistant to chloroquine. She seemed somewhat stable at semi-comatose. Time for another runner to Haia, who again returned in record time with additional meds, this time quinine and fansidar. I felt like a pinned-down infantryman when air support comes in.

Because we had been in the Sepik earlier for a survey (another story for another book), Deb had contracted an unusual strain of malaria that was resistant to chloroquine. The Sepik, a huge wetlands on the north side of New Guinea, was a hotbed for new strains of drug-resistant malaria. She must have encountered some that were immune to the prophylaxis she'd taken.

Without better treatment, her condition would continue to erode. Weak and eating little, she endured what I had the previous year—repeated cycles of the parasite, each one worse as their populations multiply in the body. Ruptured blood cells and toxins accumulate faster than the overworked kidney, spleen, and liver can deal with them. Such malaria is extremely painful, bringing on a slow, total system failure as the blood becomes toxic and the patient grows increasingly anemic. Your head pounds and the fever rages dangerously high. Nonetheless, you feel so cold your body shivers uncontrollably. Your teeth clatter as you wrap every available blanket around you, only to become totally sweat-soaked within minutes. You slip in and out of delirium and vomit up anything you swallow. The next risk was that Deb would not be able to hold down the quinine long enough to absorb it into her bloodstream, where it could nail the chloroquine-resistant *Plasmodium*. If that happened, we'd have to get injectable quinine.

Fortunately, the drugs began to work. For more than a week Deb had been delirious or in agony. Meanwhile, I'd been pumping antibiotics into Samson and the swelling on his foot was diminishing. If he rested long enough and it did not become infected, the splinter would eventually either work its way out or dissolve. In bouts between fevers, when Deb rested, Moai and I walked around a bit, scoping out the area. I saw signs of cassowary and big fruits galore, and figured this was as good a spot as any. The men all eagerly agreed this would be a great place for our studies and the station. So while Deb began to recover, I looked around for a place to build a helipad, our first priority. If anyone was seriously injured or sick again, we would be able to evacuate them.

It took a little while for Deb to get her strength back, but she is very strong, and it was not long before she could cross the stream, called the Wara Sera, and climb the far side to check out the locations Moai had recommended for the helipad and the research station. I walked back to Haia to collect the rest of our supplies, including two really good Swedish axes. I hired a couple more men (with Moai's approval) and was very happy to have Dupa back on the team.

There is an indefinable feeling—a sense of optimism, adventure, energy, and promise—when you start swinging an axe to make a clearing for a new home in a big forest. I feel so lucky to have known this sensation, which perhaps a few of my ancestors felt when they arrived in North America fleeing an oppressive and stifling culture in Europe. I too was leaving a stifling culture; what lay ahead was entirely up to me. How often do we really feel that way anymore? Deb and I would spend the next four and a half years in this place, and many more months intermittently after that. It would become home. From that point on, I had a mission in life.

Thus we actually chose our study area randomly, an inadvertent way to add rigor to the statistical analyses we'd be undertaking. Many ecological studies need to be done in randomly selected sites to eliminate bias—the first lesson of a typical statistics course. But almost no one in my discipline selects their study area as we did, placing the camp where Deb got too sick to carry on. Most scientists select a field station for its logistics: terrain that is neither too rugged nor too steep, a minimum of rainfall, and so on. Then they walk out into their pre-selected forest and make "random" selections by choosing a plot within the easy-to-work site using a random number table. Such subtle non-randomness has led to much field ecology being done in nice, comfy, level sites with easy access to transportation. We, however, had chosen rugged terrain, folded with cliffs and waterfalls, where landslides are common and a tree can simply lose grip and slide downhill. Not only had we found a wonderful place to work, we'd found a place quite different from many sites where our colleagues work around the world.

A year or two later, when discussing some of the shortcomings of this site, Mayabe would tell me that he and his brother Luke (another soon-to-be favorite assistant) knew much better forests, with better populations of cassowaries and my focal plant species than this site. I asked why he had not mentioned those forests during that first camp when I was agonizing over whether this was the spot. Mayabe told me that on that first recon trip Moai had forbidden the carriers from suggesting any other place might be superior to Moai's ground at the Wara Sera. No matter how much I thought that I was in charge among the Pawai'ia, much of the time I was being played like a rainforest puppet. They controlled my movements and the information I received.

Chapter Ten

Building the station

Wokim haus

Our first priority: a helipad. If we learned anything from Deb's skirmish with malaria—besides *Bring the BIG first-aid kit, dummy*—it was to have an evacuation plan in place before any future medical emergencies. Mal had given me some pointers on how to make a good helipad. The safest and most cost-effective place to land helicopters would be a sharp ridge where we could cut the trees on the downslopes, providing a broad, level approach, which allows the pilot a little more margin, especially when carrying an external load in a sling.

I also wanted a place with a view. Rainforests are wonderful, but they are dark and dense. The canopy blocks up to 95 percent of sunlight, and you typically cannot see more than a couple hundred feet in any direction due to thick vegetation. The helipad offered the opportunity to build a place where I could stretch my eyes, see the sky, and look out on something other than columns of trees.

I talked with Moai about the kind of site I had in mind, and he squinted as if actually looking over his expansive lands from above, searching for the right spot. He scratched his gray stubble as do thinking bearded men the world over. He said he had two places in mind. We set off, climbed, and climbed some more, gaining over six hundred feet of elevation, finally arriving at the crest on top of a ridge with a good southern exposure—and an amazing view! Through a few gaps in the canopy, we could see all the way down the Oo valley to where it joined the Pio and bent to the west against a small mountain. Behind that mountain the vast lowlands of Gulf Province reached south to the sea. No signs of clearings, roads, or even smoke rising from a cook fire anywhere in view. To the west loomed the vertical wall of the plateau. Even though we had climbed quite a bit, the top of the plateau where I had stood gazing to the ocean was still far above. To the east sat more ridges of unbroken forest. A large human population could be found far over the mountain in the central valley, but on this side of the range, you could follow the entire length of New Guinea, some 1,200 miles east to west, and be in virgin, roadless forest the entire distance. Only in the far west, in Indonesia, did a road ascend these steep mountains to reach the world's richest gold and copper deposit in the Grasberg Massif. Nothing short of an actual gold mine could make it economically feasible to push a road through this terrain. You slogged on foot through mud that would stop a horse or you flew in by helicor' such an inaccessible spot made us feel safe from outside ild, much later, prove to be wrong.

 and a helicopter would have an easy approach,
l likely build the station. Shuttling loads up and
mpty-handed I had to stop to catch my wind.
which was closer, lower, and offered less of a
other side of the Wara Oo, but Moai did not
across the river was owned by another clan.
np and came to a little bluff where two small
lge. In deep forest with a level area not even
id not look feasible, so we headed back to
a second look because it was convenient
area. After wading across the Wara Sera
st clip, we scouted around the site with
, while a couple of other guys sat back
harp. We could clear a level approach
s would be the site of the helipad, and
sites for the station buildings.

way down to the river, where we had our camp, we'd found a less steep if not quite level bluff on the side of the mountain—the sort of place you stop to catch your wind when climbing. The riverbanks were very steep; this was the first quasi-level spot on this side of the Sera. It fit most of the requirements for the station site, which were critical and hard to come by. The station had to be reasonably close to the river, so we could bathe and fetch water if necessary, but not so close it could ever flood. It had to be large enough for at least two buildings, the station and the workers' house, with enough space between them to provide a sense of privacy. After being stared at for days on end at Rutanabi, I did not want anyone looking in our windows. It needed to have stable soil and be unlikely to fall prey to a landslip, a real concern here and one almost impossible to predict. This is one reason many highland villages are located on the tops of ridges, far from water, rather than at the bottom. But we wanted a place downhill from a water source so we could put in a gravity-fed water supply to supplement rainwater.

Other criteria were required. It shouldn't be so close to the river that conversation was hard; the water really roars in these steep, tight valleys. And we wanted a decent view from the verandah-to-be. The land tenure had to be 100 percent clear and unambiguous. Moai was a good future landlord because most of his clan had died; we would be dealing with fewer clan members than many other sites in Pawai'ia country. It had to be reasonably close to the helipad and close, but not in, the main study area. Finding a site that met all of these criteria in this rugged terrain was nearly impossible, but the bluff where we now stood, with the quiet rush of the Sera and Oo below us, pretty much had it all. We learned from Moai that his clan used to hide in this area when mixed up in tribal fighting. It would not be an easy place for anyone to sneak up on you if you had a few sentries in strategic places. Not that we anticipated warfare, but it indicated this area had never been steadily inhabited or substantially cleared for gardens.

When we laid out where the helipad would be, Moai took command. We had several axes, sharp bushknives, eight able-bodied men, and the ever-busy Dupa. The men were experienced at this kind of work: they frequently cleared land for gardens to replace those that had reverted to forest—a regular occurrence in those parts. During our years in Pawai'ia country we would watch gardens arrive under the axe and vanish under the rapid proliferation of young second growth. Around the station and helipad we would have a never-ending task of cutting back the regrowth. The record annual growth rate of a tropical tree in Borneo exceeded thirty-five feet in a year, about an inch a day. Sometimes on a sunny day you could almost hear the groan of wood and emerging leaves as trees strained for their place in the sun.

While I found this task far from easy or straightforward, Moai was in his element. I'd thought we would just cut down trees one by one until the landing zone was clear. But felling large rainforest trees with axes is really hard work. If you cut one, chances are it will fall partway and lodge against another, creating a dangerous situation if you subsequently want to cut down that second tree. So instead, the men went around and notched the downhill side of every tree, cutting deep enough to destabilize them but not so deep they would topple on their own. The idea was that later, when hit from uphill, they would all fall like dominoes. Careful attention was paid to the lianas linking the canopies of different trees. Some would help pull the neighboring trees down. Others would do the opposite, so someone, usually Dupa, would climb into the canopy with a bushknife and sever the connecting strands in strategic places. The depth of notches also depended on the expected force of the upstream strikers. There was no point in chopping more than needed. The less useful members of the team, Deb and I, helped clear the small growth with bushknives. I tried helping with the tiring work with the axes. But rather than the nice precise strokes that released large chunks of wood, my flailing loosened fragments barely larger than splinters and elicited robust laughter from the team. We were already establishing the divisions of labor. Through the rest of the project, I would leave the axe work to the Pawai'ia. If I tried to help I would most surely injure myself or someone nearby. They were so proficient that we decided a chainsaw would not really make us more efficient, and would certainly add a greater element of danger. These men grew up using axes and handled them well, but I would never put a chainsaw in their hands without weeks of training.

The construction team as we cleared the helipad.
Dupa is the boy second from left and Moai, the shrewd landowner (papa graun), is on the far right.

It took two days, but eventually the area was cleared with every standing tree neatly notched. One tree stood at the top. Moai scrutinized the entire layout one last time, then gave Pero the nod. I noticed he communicated a lot with a nod and grunt, even when talking with his clansmen. Pero went to the uphill side and started the last cut. We all drew back uphill, paying a lot of attention to make sure the trees would not pull any lianas and branches free overhead. This was not kid stuff. As Pero cut, we were in fully closed rainforest. The tree groaned and swung into its neighbor. The succeeding trees were notched so as to fan out and open a large circular landing zone, not just a linear downhill slash. In a matter of seconds the entire forest downhill from us was in motion. The falling trees actually pushed the air out like a huge fan and collapsed in one terrifying roar. Leaves and detritus blew up from the ground, mixing with leaves loosened from the canopy as it fell in a brief, swirling blizzard. The men hooted at the tops of their lungs as they did whenever funny or exciting things happened. We were now standing at the edge of a half-hectare opening only seconds old. In an instant, the first tangible step in the creation of the research station appeared, along with a spectacular view. We would spend many hours here in the years ahead, watching the weather change and the cockatoos and hornbills cruising above the canopy below. After hundreds of hours over fifteen years gazing over the forest from the helipad, I would still see new things. There is so much life and so much happening all the time in the rainforest that if you find a good place to sit and watch, you can sit forever without being bored. Try that with television.

With the trees felled we could really see the lay of the land, and it was clear our choice of site for the helipad was a good one. An arc spanning nearly 270 degrees had a steep drop-off permitting a horizontal approach. Even better, in taking off, a pilot would be able to lift up and away from the pad and then simply nose down, diving toward the river to pick up speed. The playful pilots would sometimes drop down until they were completely out of sight below us, the *whopwhop* of their rotors dulling behind the trees, then they would bank sharply out of the gorge, rising quickly and exploding over us with a roar. It never failed to thrill us.

I have always said the one thing possibly as gratifying as being a biologist in PNG is being a chopper pilot in PNG. Both carry certain risks, but the dividends are huge. Sometimes Mal, or one of his pilots, would thunder past so close to the ground that our eyes would meet, both of us grinning like monkeys, and we would connect in the way of two people who pass each other, each knowing they are exactly where they belong—one happy spirit to another. And then the moment would be over as the chopper roared up to the clouds, the noise of its rotors fading quickly in Doppler shift and the quiet sounds of the rainforest settling back in. I envied the fast freedom of the pilots, but knew they missed all the subtle nuances I so enjoyed that would be invisible and inaudible from within their machines.

Clearing the trees for the research station was not as difficult as the helipad had been, given the Pawai'ia's skill at dropping trees. We cut a hole in the forest large enough for a house. The site was on the edge of a ravine, so by strategically felling a few trees, we had a nice view over the Sera gorge to the opposing ridge. Later, we would find that someone standing on the opposing ridge could shout and be heard in the house; the gorge was that tight. We did our best to identify trees that posed a risk of falling on the planned house and felled them. We would later find in our research that any one spot in the forest has about a 1 to 2 percent chance of having a tree topple over it in any given year. This constitutes one of the biggest hazards in a rainforest. People scoff at me, but treefalls are scary things; I've had too many near misses with big trees and have been clobbered a couple of times just by falling branches. It doesn't take much wood falling from sixty feet up to knock you out. Sooner or later a tree will fall and hit any spot in the forest. Eventually, one did indeed tumble and hit the house, scaring the bejesus out of the people inside. Miraculously, the structure withstood the stress, though significant work was required to replace the buckled beams.

Clearing the site was necessary for another reason—the virtually futile hope that the tropical sun would dry the ground enough so we could actually begin construction. Our first order of business was digging out a level area the size of the building. The clay subsoil, now exposed to the daily rain, turned into a quagmire. We built drainage ditches around the "pad," but they had no drying effect. We shoveled out one side to make it somewhat lower. Then we dug parallel, downhill trenches every four feet. The gluey clay held water like a sponge. Even the slightest depression—a footprint, for example—filled with water that never drained.

We could not build on top of such a soft base, so in addition to the hopeless efforts at drainage, we carried rocks up from the river. I'd choose a soft spot, lay a heavy rock on it, and push it in until it submerged. Then we'd put another mini boulder on top and it would sink down, driving the other below it. We repeated this over and over until we had a nearly solid foundation of stone floating on clay.

We hefted tons of rocks from the river. Because we hiked up and down that steep trail so often, I tried to improve it by putting down flat stones to use as steps, strategically placing them in the muddy sections. Believe me, it's no fun slipping on mud with a fifty-pound rock balanced on one shoulder. But repeatedly one of the Pawai'ia, perhaps thinking I had accidentally dropped the flat stones in the middle of the trail and moved on unaware I was fifty pounds lighter, would pick the stepping stones up and carry them up to the foundation. Perhaps it was a matter of being too lazy to walk all the way to the river. This was classic Pawai'ia—rather than place stones to make every trip to the river easier, they would cannibalize those steps to make one trip easier. I had to gather everyone around and explain the reason for leaving stones on the trail, and still every now and then a step would disappear. Still, it was good, hard, dirty work we enjoyed. Every evening Deb and I would walk back to our camp on the bend of the river and take a bath in a beautiful pool around a bend in the Oo.

When building the station we had to cross the Sera every morning to get to work. Here Deb uses a tree we dropped to make a good bridge. But eventually the river rose and washed it away like a toothpick. In floods those boulders tumbled downstream, clunking together like giant bowling balls.

Rain fell every night. While building the station, our camp had two frames: one for the Pawai'ia men and one for Deb and I and the gear. The men liked to keep a fire going and we needed a little privacy. Usually they cooked what they wanted on their wood fire and we cooked separately on a small kerosene burner. The pole frames were draped with plastic sheeting pulled tight with ropes. In the night, water ran down the tarps and right through the camp. Our beds and gear were raised on platforms so the water could run under us. There was no escaping the mud except when we were actually in the river. A mosquito net covered our bed, making it the only relatively insect-free zone. If we sat and read at night with a headlamp, hundreds of wonderful moths and other night flyers would swirl around us. Their presence could become tedious when they bashed into our faces or danced across the page. We learned to place a candle outside the mosquito net and lie inside to read, watching the entomological diversity swarming on the other side of the sheer mesh. Every so often a moth would kamikaze into the flame and snuff it out, preserving itself in hot wax. After all the hard manual labor, it was easy to fall asleep at an early hour and rest the weary muscles. Tomorrow would be another full day of shoveling wet clay and carrying stones from the river up to the bottomless quagmire. Eventually, it became clear the earth would not dry until we got a roof over it. We started building.

We had a rough plan, just a sketch on some scrap paper that benefited from the advice of Jack, the missionary in Haia. Constructing a house isn't such a difficult task, especially with no building codes to meet other than those of common sense and utility. The "blueprint" called for a big wooden box with a metal lid sitting upon posts that sit upon flat rocks that sit upon the clay and river stone substrate. The Pawai'ia men were accomplished builders, having all built their own homes as well as those of others. They'd done this many times before. Unlike houses in the US, ours didn't need insulation, electrical outlets in every wall, or air conditioners. It wouldn't pose a risk to neighbors if it caught on fire, or drive down area property values with a less-than-desirable design. The nearest neighbors were miles away and this was the only house in the entire region, other than Jack's, with a metal roof or nails. What we were creating was a mansion by Pawai'ia standards.

Imagine building a house with no access to a lumberyard or power tools. The men provided raw timber and split planks with the axes. We planed floor boards and notched every joint in beam and joists with chisels so round timbers met snugly. The sheer number of hours required was daunting. We worked every day from sunup to sundown, often in the rain. On sunny days we sweated. Salt being in short supply in the rainforest, perspiration is a highly prized resource among the six-legged community. So when the sun shone, several kinds of trigonid stingless bees grazed on us as we worked. Hundreds would swarm around us, and dozens of the boldest ones clambered all over us—through our hair, up our noses—licking up the salty perspiration. Most annoying were those hovering inches from our faces watching for the perfect bead of sweat. Unfortunately, the site also hosted European honeybees. This introduction from Europe has colonized pretty much all of the world, even the remotest areas in New Guinea. I was sorry to see them because no one knows how they have altered natural pollination systems. Do they outcompete native bees? Do they move pollen differently and thus affect seed production?

Honeybees are particularly annoying because, unlike the native trigonids, they carry a painful sting. Several times a day I'd squat and find the bee on the back of my knee was a honeybee, which would sting me to register its displeasure at being squeezed in my soft skin behind the joint. Several times a day, on sunny days, Deb or I would punctuate our work with a loud string of expletives. Perhaps the biggest key to success as a rainforest ecologist is developing a very high tolerance for discomfort. This capacity is probably the one attribute that has helped my career the most. (It certainly isn't my smarts or good looks.) I can deal with constant itching, chiggers, leeches, stings, typhoid, and so forth, while others might be driven out of the forest.

Before starting work on the building itself, we hired one of Mal's helicopters to fly in the roofing iron. We calculated what we would need for our buildings—a house for the workers and a larger building that combined living quarters and workspace, plus enough extra to build another house in case of future expansion. Like all our manufactured supplies, we had the metal sheets flown from Goroka to Haia in the Cessna. It took several charters, at 850 pounds per trip. These loads were then divided into several smaller piles, according to the lifting capacity of the chopper. When we had the iron positioned and ready in Haia, the chopper came. Deb connected the loads in Haia and I unloaded them at Sera. The chopper carried a long cable under the belly, ending in a pin and clevis. The pilot would lower the chopper so the cable could be attached to the load by Deb, who would then quickly scurry away and signal to the pilot so he could gently ease the load up and fly away to Sera. At Sera he would deftly lower the load through the forest gap we had cut for the station and ease the load onto the ground. I would run in and disconnect the cable while the pilot held the chopper in place just above the treetops, which would whip wildly in the rotor downwash. The pilot had to make sure the cable did not swing and brush against any branches or the helicopter could quickly be thrown out of control. It's tricky maneuvering. A year later, a pilot we knew made an error with the long line when delivering a load in another province, causing him to crash and die. But our roofing iron arrived without incident, along with a few other supplies that were carried inside the chopper and dropped off on the helipad. Deb flew back to Sera on the last run—in the passenger compartment; not on the end of the long line. It sure beat hiring seventy-five carriers and hiking two days in to the station. We had a foundation, crates of nails, and roofing iron. We were ready to build.

We placed flat stones on a grid every six feet and set stout posts on them. People often think you need to sink the posts into the ground so they do not wobble, but this is the biggest mistake you can make, because they'll rot underground and in a couple of years your house will topple. The Pawai'ia did not know this until Jack demonstrated it with his house in Haia. Now all the houses around the airstrip were built with posts atop stones rather than buried. Just a simple technological innovation like this probably saved the Pawai'ia thousands of man-hours in rebuilding houses and certainly saved hundreds of trees a year. With cross bracing, the posts stand rigidly. Once they were up and plumb, we topped them using a line level so the floor would be horizontal. The site was about four feet lower at the verandah than at the back, which was on the uphill side. No two posts were the same height. It was much easier to level the heights of the posts than to attempt to level the entire foundation.

After getting the site cleared, roughly leveled, and making a "foundation" of river rocks, we positioned the posts on which the building would sit.

Once the posts were up, it was just a matter of measuring, cutting, notching, and nailing to layer on bearers and joists, frame the walls, raise the ridge pole, and lay on the roof beams and slats. When the ridge pole went up, I climbed to the top and balanced there, nailing down the roof beams one by one as they were handed up. I was more than twenty-five feet above the ground, supported by joints we had notched and nailed—something I tried not to dwell on as this was the first real test of my carpentry skills since seventh-grade wood shop, where the teacher gave me a C out of compassion. Sitting up there, I had a clear view across the Sera gorge to the basin that would be the core study area. I paused a moment, lost in reverie as I pictured living here for the next few years—then quickly snapped out it. The bees found me up there and I had to concentrate to keep from falling while I put the roof beams in place.

The station going up. The bearers and joists are down and we are putting up the side walls.

Once the roof was up, the work became much easier and more comfortable, as we were protected from the hot sun and frequent rain. The quagmire slowly began to harden. Eventually, it would become like concrete and would crack, raising new concerns for how that would affect the posts as the foundation shifted. A year later we'd have to shore up the front of the verandah where it perched at the edge of a ravine by making gabions (wire boxes filled with tons of rocks, carried up one by one from the river). Maintaining the station would prove to be a never-ending chore that demanded more and more time as the years progressed. In the rainforest everything rots. As we built the station we made sure the men brought strong wood for the structural beams, wood that would not rot. But since their houses rarely lasted more than five years, and soft wood is easier to cut than hard, they brought us lots of soon-to-rot timber with the assurances that it was all "*strongpela tru na no inap kisim stink.*" Really strong and won't rot. "Yeah, right," I would mutter dozens of times later when I had to jack up beams to replace them and wedge new timbers beside rotting ones.

A team of about eight men was tasked only with cutting wood. We would specify what sort of timber we needed next, and they would go and find it, cut it, and carry it back to the site. We were adamant about where they cut, confining this disturbance to an area on the periphery and outside the future main study area. With a few exceptions, the crew stuck with this mandate.

The exceptions were a few of the "cedar" trees cut for the floors and walls. These trees, which grow quite large, have two excellent features: they do not rot, and they can be readily split by axe into relatively straight planks. The guys spent a large portion of their time splitting planks—thin ones for the walls and thicker ones for the roughly 1,400-square-foot floor. My two prerequisites for living comfortably in the rainforest, a sturdy floor and a reliable roof, were coming together. As each hand-hewn plank was unique, a different width, length, and depth, we spent considerable time planing each one by hand so the edges in the floor met tightly. Each plank was custom notched so it would rest level and at the same height on the uneven floor joists, which were not exactly level either. This was the most time-consuming part of the construction, but it made the house very livable. There were few gaps between boards, though a couple appeared after the green timber thoroughly dried. The walls, much thinner planks, went up quickly in clapboard-fashion. Installing the floors and walls gave stability and strength to the whole structure. We'd occasionally get earthquakes, and the house would flex and sway, but it always held.

The camp Deb and I lived in for about four months as we built the station at Wara Sera. Kerosene stove on the right, bales of rice and other supplies on the left, and bed in the rear. Everything is raised on decking because every level place floods during the heavy rains at Sera.

Deb and I had moved our camp up from the bend in the river once the roof was on and work had started on the floors. We'd been living under a plastic tarp for about four months, and we found living under a metal roof to be much more comfortable, even if the floors would take another two months or so to complete. We were happy to escape the mud of the campsite and the roar of the river as it bent around us in the tight gorge—especially after the night the river rose quickly with the afternoon rains, then roared louder and louder into the night. . . . Our idyllic bathing pool disappeared under an extra six feet of raging water. Huge boulders clacked and thunked together as they rolled in the current just a few feet away; the ground shook with their impacts while we tried to rest our weary bodies. Moai, savvy guy that he is, pointed out that if the water undercut a big tree on the other side of the torrent, not only would the tree drop on us but it would divert the torrent directly over us. By then the edge of the water lapped within a few inches of swamping the bank and raging through our camp. We all stood in the rain with a flashlight, staring at the water level. Had it risen another centimeter? The crew had packed all their possessions in their *bilums* and slung them over their shoulders. If the river topped the bank, they were ready to run for it. Deb and I, laden with supplies for the years ahead plus all our tools and research equipment, could not quite fit all our possessions in one *bilum*. Resigned to the fact that if the river rose a few more inches we could quite likely lose it all, I packed the smallest and most valuable items—camera, notebooks, and binoculars—in my Pelican case, and prepared to run. Just as I had been two years earlier on the lower Oo, I was again close to losing my camp to the wild and unpredictable fluctuations in river level and flow. It would not be the last time. Hence, Deb and I were quite delighted when at last we could move our camp and all our gear high above the river and under the metal roof.

With the station taking form, step one of the grand plan came into place. The real proof would come from pulling off top-quality research there. We felt that if we built it AND proved it worked, we could eventually attract researchers not only to PNG but to the Pawai'ia's lands, which would be a win for everyone. Scientists would have a suitable place to work, and Pawai'ia would have a nice income without having to sell their timber to the Malaysian loggers who had concessions to log all across PNG; with this arrangement we could learn things important for conservation in New Guinea, and we'd have the first truly protected lands in PNG. Eventually our station could become a place where PNG university students could work alongside international scientists and become scientists themselves. We could catalyze science and conservation. These thoughts drove our hands every day. Each hand-hewn plank and every nail was part of this grand, long-term plan.

The year: 1990. The drop-dead day: May 1. No matter what state the station was in, I would start fieldwork by then. I could work out the finishing touches on the house as we went. By May 1 we had been working on construction all day, every day for nearly five months. The station was up, the walls almost complete, the windows screened, the floor mostly installed. We'd made counters for the kitchen with Formica tops. The kitchen boasted a sink and the bathroom a flush toilet. A solar panel on the roof provided enough current to power a VHF transceiver (which was, alas, nearly always broken). I was particularly proud of the door, which was stout and swung perfectly for years until the ground under the front of the station settled a bit. On May 1st we could get down to the real fun and start studying cassowaries.

The work room inside the station. We carried in a few sheets of plywood to make good work surfaces and some plastic chairs for the long hours of lab work. It was very comfortable and tranquil.

The completed station as seen from the air. The main house on the right and the workers' house on the left. We would later build an enclosure for two cassowaries we raised in the forest between the two houses.

Chapter Eleven

Blazing trails and exploring

Klinim rot na wokabaut

The only trails in the area were those we made from the station to the helipad and from the camp to the station, and an old path of sorts coming from Haia that disappeared where it met the Oo a few miles from the station. In order to develop a study area, we would need trails. Trails give you quick access and save precious research time otherwise spent navigating from place to place. They keep you from getting lost, saving even more research time that would have been wasted trying to figure out where the hell you are. Trails can also provide a reference for geographical position to assist the research. Much of ecology deals with spatial relationships. How far are male from female trees? How far are seeds being moved? How far do cassowaries move when foraging? Determining these things without established points of reference could waste many hours of valuable field time.

We faced the challenge of mapping the forest at a time long before affordable and accurate GPS units were an option. It was mid-1990 and it would be another year until President Clinton directed the US military to turn off GPS systems' "selective availability" that deliberately made GPS inaccurate for non-military users. This presumably prevented the Russians from guiding their missiles using the US GPS system. But it also meant we were stuck mapping our area in basically the same way as Lewis and Clark crossing North America—using a compass and tape measure.

With Moai and two other guides to lightly cut the way, we set out from the station. We followed the existing trail up to the helipad and then extended beyond it, ascending to the ridgetop once considered as a candidate for the helipad; then we moved along the ridge, bending toward the plateau with a view of the Wara Sera, and back through some lovely forest until we ended up at a small pond. Located in the middle of the rainforest, it had the look of a dark swamp from which some horrid beast must surely emerge at night. The water was black, reflecting only the dark shadow of the rainforest leaning over it. The pond had formed a long time ago when a landslide closed off a small basin. We generously called it "the lake." The ground around it was deep mud and the trees growing around it eventually grew heavy and leaned in, drowning in the still, black, anaerobic water and seeming never to rot. I did not ever swim in it. It was just a little too creepy.

As the trail extended behind our bushknife-wielding guides, we systematically measured and marked the distances, using a fifty-meter tape measure. Deb stood still and held the end while I unreeled the tape, whooping when it was fully extended. She then followed along the tape, taking a bearing at each bend and recording the meter mark, gathering up the tape as she went. When she caught up to me, I placed a numbered metal tag in the nearest tree. Then we repeated this process until the A-Trail, which led to the helipad and from there up to the lake, was complete. Each numbered tag, multiplied by fifty, indicated how far we had come from the trail head at the station. Deb's notebook contained a series of distances and bearings that, with a bit of simple trigonometry, we converted to an x-y plot of the trail.

We used this system in laying out trails A through C and F through H. There was no D-Trail because we would use the letter D to label droppings; no E so we could tag epiphytes; no L because we'd want liana tags, and so forth. Eventually, we would add trails where needed up to P. But the first six trails were the main arteries of the study area. Each had a unique character and the forests each traversed were distinctive in their own way. People often imagine the rainforest as homogenous, but as you spend more time in one, you begin to see subtle differences due to terrain, past disturbances, drainage, etc. Each acre has its own character.

The A-Trail climbed steeply with a break for the helipad, then leveled in a bowl that ended at the lake. Beyond the lake came the base of the plateau and the best view from the study area. On a clear day you could see the Gulf of Papua. We especially appreciated A-Trail because we did not have to cross a river to get to it. All the other trails entailed crossing the Oo, the Sera, or both, which could pose a problem when the rivers flooded. We often worked along the A-Trail on flood days.

B-Trail crossed the Sera to the old camp at the bend of the Oo, then ascended the ridge we had come down that first time when Deb had malaria. It climbed and then skirted the side of the mountain, crossing the Oo again at a much higher elevation. Then it climbed almost vertically to the top of the plateau and went on to wind for miles to Herowana. This trail had existed as a faint track when we arrived, occasionally used by people on their way to and from the village. Once we established the study area, passersby were under orders to leash their dogs and to refrain from hunting. Some complied, others probably did not. We later initiated a policy, per suggestion from Moai, that anyone who killed a dog in the study area earned a twenty-five kina bonus. We never had to pay out, but people were a lot more cooperative about keeping their dogs at home or restraining them while passing through the study area.

C-Trail left the station and paralleled the Oo for about a quarter mile of undulating hills and ravines, then dropped steeply to the place where the next small river, the Wara Sana, and the Oo converged. Nearby stood a magnificent waterfall and deep swimming hole that was always shady and cool. On the many hikes coming in from Haia, the appearance of the first tag of the C-Trail a kilometer from the station was always a very welcome sight. That last climb past the Sana often required my last bit of strength after eight hours of constant ascent, descent, or hopping boulders in the riverbed. We had cut most of the trees for the station along the C-Trail, so we did the least research there. In my later banding studies I would show that clearing smaller trees for the station (we cut nothing larger than what several men could carry) affected bird densities, even though the canopy was intact and closed.

F, on the other side of the Oo, climbed without relent for three kilometers. It took forever to reach the end of F. One of our future assistants would joke that he expected to find the giant's castle from "Jack and the Beanstalk" at the top of the trail. At times ascending it was like going up a ladder. The forest on this steep slope had a different character. With better drainage, it was somewhat drier, and it was exposed to a slight breeze at times when air shifted up or down the Oo Valley as the lowlands heated up and cooled each day and night. There was less moss and epiphytic growth than in other parts of the study area, except at the top of F, which was true montane forest like that around Herowana. One of the tree species that interested me was mostly found high on the F-Trail, though I disliked the days designated for work there because it was so steep.

The G-Trail traversed both the Sera and the Oo. We either took off shoes and pants and waded, or we just got wet. Usually it hardly mattered because most mornings at the station we put on yesterday's wet shoes and clothes. Daintily trying to keep pants and shoes dry made no sense when we could expect an inch of rain and would be walking in ankle deep mud or streams much of the day. G was my favorite trail because it was the most level. It climbed gently, so I could actually stroll and, being mostly unconstrained by cliffs and ravines, it allowed for wandering off in any direction. G also led to many of the *Aglaia* trees that would become the focus of much of my research.

H, a simple loop that diverged from G at the G8 marker and returned at the G27 marker, circled first through a nice level stretch, then sharply up to a boggy basin occupied almost exclusively by *Pandanus* trees, which gained stability from widely spreading stilt roots.

When we blazed the G-Trail, we crossed a faint track near G60. I realized this was the track I had followed in 1987 when I hiked from my camp on the lower Oo to Herowana.

At that time I thought it a beautiful forest I would almost certainly never see again. Now we had built the research station three kilometers away. I'm not superstitious, but sometimes I felt like something else, some might call it fate, was at work. I've always felt this was where I belonged, a sensation I've not experienced elsewhere.

You had to go all the way to G60 or F50 to leave behind the sound of the roaring Wara Oo. Those high forests had a hushed feeling of vastness missing in lower areas where the river noise always bore testimony to how close you were to the station. Away from the river, with the clinging mosses absorbing every sound, I could sometimes find the kind of stillness felt in the desert or above treeline. In mid-day, when the birds and insects took a break from their singing and moved silently, I felt like a tourist visiting a great cathedral in that high forest. I could close my eyes and feel the calm, with the only audible reminder of the surrounding rainforest an occasional inquisitive peep from a microhylid frog safely buried in the leaf litter. The standard movie jungle, teeming with raucous animals, is far from reality.

After two weeks or so of mapping, we had the core trails laid out. Orange flagging tape marked the 50-meter tags and another flag marked the 25-meter midpoint between tags. It was June 1990. The first call from Don Bruning had come in 1986. Everything until this moment had been preparatory. After nearly four years of what most graduate committees would consider unproductive effort, I could finally begin my research on cassowaries in earnest—the research that would ultimately make or break my career and make or break the dream of a research station in PNG. If I could not pull off some good science now, it would mean all that aggravation and pain was for nothing; the dour skeptics who counseled against such an ambitious risk would be proven correct. It was time to get started. Fortunately, as we were about to discover, June is primetime for cassowaries. Their scat and the fruits they eat abound in this season. Had I begun work in February, I would have been frustrated by the relative absence of large fruit, cassowaries, and their *pekpek*. Instead, I found a bounty, and the possibilities seemed endless.

Chapter Twelve

Cassowaries, chiggers and conservation

Muruk, liklik binatang na lukautim bus

The answers to some of my key questions stemmed from learning how well seeds fared after being dispersed by cassowaries. This required many months 1990 to mid-1993 of wandering through the forest looking for cassowary *pekpek*. I cannot imagine a better activity; nothing beats roaming the forest, beholding everything it has to offer, and being awed a dozen times a day. I saw colonial spider webs ten feet across dotted with hundreds of spiders that teamed up to subdue large prey. I saw birds of paradise that cleared immaculate display courts on the forest floor. I saw eight-inch-long stick insects, birdwing butterflies, and spiders that mimicked ants. Every day I found something new while searching the forest for *pekpek*.

I'd tear myself away from such wonders and move on in my quest for droppings. If I had a Pawai'ia assistant with me, he would roam more widely and then direct me right to whatever we were looking for. The Pawai'ia had great faculties of recall when it came to spatial details in their forest. I could work up a dropping *en situ* with a guide and then two years later, when trying to relocate it, that guide could take me straight to it. I, on the other hand, with my notebooks of directions and compass, sometimes expended hours searching for a long-lost *pekpek*. But there was no guarantee I'd have the same guide again, or when that guide might be available. I could not count on a particular assistant to help me remember specific places. This was one of the downsides of our employment strategy. We rotated work as widely as we could. We did not want half a dozen men earning a handsome income and the rest of the tribe getting only temporary work as carriers. We would have been spared considerable time and aggravation were we not training a new worker every few weeks. We could have delegated much more autonomy to our field assistants had we kept a small staff of well-trained Pawai'ia rather than training new helpers dozens of times. But in PNG societies new to the cash economy, with no other source of income, seeming to favor a few while others feel they have missed out often leads to resentments and hostility, both within the community and directed, possibly, toward us. We meted out work to hundreds of people over the years.

If a guide, particularly a new one, accompanied me, he would watch with mild interest as I processed a *pekpek*, and I would explain again the purpose of my research and the important role of cassowaries in the ecosystem. I spent hundreds of hours in the field engaged in one-on-one chats about conservation. The usual conservation organization modus operandi back then (and still to some extent) was to send a staff person to a village, convene a village meeting, and tell everyone how important their resources are. Having met the terms of the organization's grant, the staff person would then fly out. These in-and-out "workshops" had virtually no effect, and often served only to irritate the indigenous people.

Conservationists, though well-intentioned, have been cultivating reputations as white people full of talk who often can't spend even a single night in a village, much less out in the bush. An important aspect of our research and program was that we did more than talk. Both Deb and I spent hundreds of days out in the rain, sharing food with the Pawai'ia, swatting the same biting flies, and having prolonged conversations about conservation. To build a conservation ethos, we had to be out there, in the forest, working side by side with the forest's owners. When I came upon the den of a wallaby or hornbill nest, I took the opportunity to ask the Pawai'ia workers questions and to talk with them, not at them, about wildlife management. I listened to their stories and told them my own, describing, for instance, how the water where I grew up was undrinkable and much of it too polluted even for swimming. This always amazed them because we drank from every stream and bathed anywhere we liked. They told me about how they hunted or knew where to put a trap. This was another advantage of using a research station as the core of a conservation project. Researchers tend to stay longer and spend more time with rural people than do typical professional conservationists.

I carried a day pack with all my *pekpek* supplies. For every fresh *pekpek* I found, I recorded a number of site variables so I could statistically describe where cassowaries defecate. I would measure ground slope, distance to nearest tree, litter depth, and more. One of the most important measures was the canopy photo. For this I had a Nikon camera with a fisheye lens that I'd set up, lens pointed upward, on a small tripod nestled directly over the *pekpek*. This would provide a 360-degree panorama of everything above the dropping. By leveling the camera and orienting it to north with a compass, I could later use software that plotted the sun's path across the image and generated detailed scientific information, including a value for how much direct sunlight reached that spot and how much reflected light would reach it.

On a randomized basis, some *pekpek* were collected in plastic bags and given to Deb for her detailed analysis of just what comes out of a cassowary.

The canopy photos were a key component of my research and provided good, reliable numbers. But keeping film at Sera, with its constant 90-plus percent humidity, was fraught with risks. Even when I stored the camera in the heated "dry" box, where we dried our plant specimens and fruit pulp samples, the film came out sticky and wet. Such dampness, I learned early on, damaged the emulsion and rendered the film useless. The solution was to develop it myself. I got the needed chemicals and a developing can, and on a dark night (and in Sera, almost all nights are dark; you hardly ever see the moon) I'd huddle under heavy blankets and transfer the film from its canister to the developer. Using this system, I knew right away if my photographs were workable, as compared to the anxiety of sending film off every three months to a developing lab. We were becoming very self-reliant. If we wanted a chair or bookshelf, we built it ourselves from wood cut from the forest. If something broke, we either fixed it or went without.

Because the camera sat low above the *pekpek*, I used a long cable release to snap the shutter from behind a large tree or downhill to avoid catching myself in the image. But early on, the cable release broke and I couldn't fix it. My only option was to lie flat in the mud beside the *pekpek* and manually trigger the shutter. This was a great way to increase the density of chigger bites over my entire body. Chiggers itch, sometimes a lot. Often we could not sleep at night thanks to the itching. I'd learned in Costa Rica to swab the bites with rubbing alcohol, which temporarily soothes the problem, and then try to fall asleep before the effect wears off. We kept a gallon jug of medical spirits by the bed so we could wipe down the itching when necessary, sometimes several times a night.

One day, on my back in the mud preparing to take another canopy picture, I burst out laughing. My guide thought I had lost it. But I'd just realized that my camera had a timed release—the feature people use to include themselves in a group photo. I could set that and have a leisurely fifteen seconds to amble behind a tree. My chigger loads above the ankles diminished significantly after I started this.

For a while, one of my guides was an old man who did not speak any Tok Pisin. He watched me scoot behind a tree whenever I took a picture, and I guess he thought I was hiding so I would not see the camera, rather than so the camera would not "see" me. So when I snapped photographs, he would cover his eyes with his hands. I explained and demonstrated to him that he should get behind a tree as well, and he learned to do so. But he still covered his eyes. God only knows what he thought I was doing. We would explain and explain and explain our activities, and when we thought we had discussed things with everyone in the clan, intensively and one-on-one, someone would come up to us and ask, "Is it true you are going to build a road to Goroka?"

Years later a mainstream-thinking conservationist would find that some Pawai'ia did not understand our work there. This conservationist would upbraid us for "not having done enough awareness-building and workshops." I countered that we spent years one-on-one with nearly all the men of the community, that we had demonstrated our work in person, and been observed in the field by Pawai'ia for years. Deb even took three dozen Pawai'ia on their first trip out of the forest to Lae and Port Moresby for the express purpose of showing them the specimens from their forest on deposit in the National Museum and National Herbarium.

I really do not think a workshop with diagrams and flowcharts would have been a better method of conservation education than spending months with someone in the forest and talking casually as we shared leeches, rain, and other discomforts. But the workshop/flow-chart mode of outreach is still very popular in many organizations. Living in the bush and talking with the Pawai'ia taught us vital lessons about conservation that would help us develop a more effective program years later. We were bucking the conventional model of foreign white experts disseminating information (or, in conservation jargon, "empowering stakehold-ers"). After all the communicating we'd done, we realized that some of the misunderstandings stemmed from great cultural differences and the preconceived expectations the Pawai'ia have for white people. Even after we'd been spent years out there, people would still think we were 1) going to build a road; 2) looking for gold or oil; or 3) somehow making money by selling our plant vouchers. These expectations were set the moment they saw our skin color.

Sometime in the 1980s and '90s conservation organizations, desperate for an economic justification to preserve biodiversity, came up with the strategy of promoting rain-forests as wellsprings of untold priceless drugs waiting to be discovered. Soon the propaganda spread, with rainforests advertised as sources of bazillion-dollar cures sitting there for the taking. This in fact is not really true, and it had the undesirable side effect of convincing people around the world that foreign researchers are in it to make money. All this talk about studying cassowary scat could be a ruse. Why would anyone work so hard for no pay and some *pekpek bilong muruk*?

I believe the conservation movement did a great disservice and set back rainforest research with this sort of talk. Even if a drug was found, it would soon be more cheaply produced in a factory in Germany than by sustainably harvesting some berry, leaf, or bark in the forest. Fears were aroused in PNG of pharmaceutical companies stealing information and the complex issues of intellectual property rights were distorted out of proportion. The concept emerged that if a tree growing in a New Guinea forest has a chemical in its bark that cures a disease, then the people of that forest should be compensated with ongoing royalties for the sale of the resulting drug. Legitimate non-commercial research became even more difficult—except, of course, for the researchers with "deep pockets" from a pharmaceutical company.

One irony: everyone in PNG uses quinine and quinine derivatives to treat malaria. First found in the bark of the cinchona tree in Colombia, quinine could be considered the intellectual property of the people indigenous to that country. No one in PNG, as far as I am aware, has called for paying royalties to the indigenous people of Colombia. Many self-congratulatory white do-gooders advocate for intellectual property rights, but they do not cut the cloth in both directions. No one argues for sending money to indigenes of Brazil for giving us rubber, or to the Quechua for potatoes, and so forth. PNG's largest agricultural export is coffee, a plant most definitely not native. There's a lot of hypocrisy in the conservation racket. For some, any means that achieves the end result of biodiversity conservation is justified. Bioprospecting, largely discredited as a conservation panacea, has now been followed by the notion of cash from carbon credits for rainforests *not* cut down. Many executives in "corporate conservation" now embrace various carbon credit big money schemes. Such lack of vision can impede conservation more than it helps.

Slowly we began to realize, much to our disappointment, that as foreigners we were more limited in our capacity to affect conservation than we had realized. Rainforest conservation or management concepts would best take hold when Papua New Guineans spoke to Papua New Guineans. Despite our best intentions and our years of living out our beliefs, we would find that the conservation ethos we had hoped to develop still fell short.

These important larger conservation lessons arose as we undertook our long-term research and extended residency with the Pawai'ia. In gaining an understanding and perspective quite different from that of the "conservation leaders" back in the United States, we were slowly diverging from the standard wisdom about "how to do conservation" that had been integral to our coursework and education.

In the forest, after collecting the data I needed at the site of a *pekpek*, I'd number the dropping with a metal tag and put up a piece of flagging tape nearby so I could relocate it. Then I would use my compass and pace off the distance to the nearest point on the trail. Eventually I had a list of several hundred droppings *en situ*, the location of each noted with a vector such as "120 m 80 degrees from G17.5." I returned to each *pekpek* monthly for the first three months, then less frequently as the scat aged and matured, like fine wine. On each return I tagged and measured the seedlings emerging from the *pekpek*. I paid particular attention to the seeds of a few targeted tree species to study how they performed after dispersal by cassowaries. This information could be compared to data on seeds not dispersed (i.e., those that fall under the maternal tree and germinate there). It might take years, but I hoped to get some idea of how trees benefited by having their seeds eaten and voided by cassowaries. As I learned how things work in the PNG forest, I was also learning how to work in the PNG forest.

Chapter Thirteen

Two cassowaries, Huey and Louie

Tupela muruk, nam bilong em Huey na Louie

Even in the middle of a remote rainforest in PNG, people occasionally pass by. The station was just a few hundred yards from B-Trail that connected on the Aedo Plateau with the faint trail to Herowana, to me a difficult one-and-a-half-day hike away. To those of us accustomed to the immaculate trails reticulating US parks, the link to Herowana was virtually invisible. Calling both the Appalachian Trail and the track to Herowana "trails" is like calling both Interstate 95 and the Appalachian Trail "highways." In Tok Pisin there are no words distinguishing quality of "trails;" both the faintest track and largest highway are called a *rot* or "road."

Every so often, someone practically naked carrying just a *bilum* and a bushknife would glide out of the forest at the edge of the tiny station clearing, chat a few moments, and then disappear en route between distant villages. I found such feats impressive given that for me making such a trip meant bringing along a substantial crew to carry food, bedding, a tarp, cookpots, and so forth. Both Pawai'ia and Gimi travelers usually carried no more than a few pounds of personal effects, even when "going bush" for weeks.

One day in March 1990 while still building the station, two travelers passed through bearing two recently captured cassowary chicks. They wondered if we wanted to purchase the chicks; if not, they'd take them to Haia and export them on the MAF Cessna to the Simbu people in Kundiawa or Karimui, who paid a hefty price (by Pawai'ia standards) for cassowaries. In many parts of PNG, cassowaries could no longer be found, but they retained their cultural significance. People still use them in ceremonies (like our Thanksgiving turkeys only about ten times larger) or for brideprice. People without local cassowaries will purchase them for a good price from more rural landowners like the Pawai'ia, whose forests are still home to cassowaries. It's great to maintain cultural traditions, but not all traditions are sustainable when human populations grow and forests shrink. Because small fixed-wing planes, like the MAF Cessnas, connected large villages and rural outposts like Haia, the "urban" demand for cassowaries reached some of the remotest corners of the country.

We wanted captive cassowaries for a variety of experimental trials we planned to conduct over the next few years, so we negotiated a price with the hunters and purchased the two chicks. We made sure everyone knew that we now had all the cassowaries we needed, and would refuse to buy more. Knowing how rumors fly through Pawai'ia country, we could expect to be inundated with cassowary chicks within a week if word leaked out that we were paying for them. The price for the pair we bought was thirty kina each (about thirty US dollars at the time)—a tremendous windfall for the hunters. At the time I was anxious to get started on research, but we had a long way to go on the station, which still lacked floors and walls. Deb and I still slept on the ground under the building's frame; every morning we climbed up on the joists to work and every evening we climbed back down to rest. Buying the chicks was a good way to get started on our research while continuing construction. We had no idea whether it would be easy or difficult to acquire more chicks, or whether we'd have another chance to do so.

The hunters were delighted, and two fine young cassowaries were ours. The chicks were crammed in spindle-shaped cages made from bamboo strips lashed with split rattan and lined with a few banana leaves; they could not even stand up. We immediately freed our new goggle-eyed wards and they stumbled unsteadily to their feet, looking a bit stunned and confused, much as would anyone who was captured by giants, caged a couple days, and then let loose to wander among the giants' feet. Cassowary chicks do not have smooth plumage. Every bristly feather stands straight up, making a rough coiffure that resembles a striped brown Brillo pad. Like adult cassowaries, their weight is centered over their legs, well back on the body, and their long necks stick far out in front. They look perpetually, awkwardly unbalanced; so much so that when they lean too far forward, you get the idea that if they don't run forward to stay upright they'll fall on their chests.

The young chicks are especially awkward, wobbling like drunks emerging from a bar. Tilting forwards, they run a few steps, stop, stand up straight, and teeter a bit before repeating again with a few more steps in another direction. Most birds balance with subtle movements of the wings and tail, similar to the way humans use their arms for balance. But wings and tail are essentially nonexistent on cassowaries. Instead they adjust their center of balance by shifting their body mass and long neck. Unpracticed chicks go too far one way and then too far the other, making them sway and stagger.

Huey and Louie shortly after they became our wards.

Our new chicks emitted soft, up-slurred peeping whistles, the sound they use to contact the daddy cassowary. From what little we know about cassowaries, adult females lay their eggs in the nests of the males (and possibly in nests of several males in any one season), and then take off. Deadbeat moms! The males do all the incubation and parental care, though it's unclear how often the attending males are actually the real fathers. Without some form of mate-guarding (like the constant hand-holding of happy newlyweds), there's ample chance for a female to mate with more than one male and then give her mate some other male's egg to incubate. Perhaps that explains why I saw two cassowaries fighting at Varirata on my first trip to PNG—one male may have been keeping another away from his mate.

The chicks spend an unknown amount of time with the male—certainly at least nine months—learning where and how to find edible food. While they travel with father, they keep in touch with whistled notes. We made a point of moving around and whistling back to them, and the chicks almost immediately imprinted on us as their parents. Any large biped nearby would do.

We christened them Huey and Louie. Like all cassowary chicks, they were a light ochre brown with dark stripes and spots: a pattern that is perfectly cryptic when they hunker down on the leaf litter. Camouflage is their defense in early life, the only time they are vulnerable to predators. At any sign of danger, the male runs away, issuing an alarm note. When the chick hears this alarm it crouches, blending in to the mottled leaf litter on the forest floor. The defense obviously works well against animal predators, but not so well against humans. Papuan hunters simply search for a crouching chick when they hear an adult give the alarm note. They speed the process along by whistling like an adult cassowary, which elicits the chick to respond with its own whistled contact note, thereby revealing itself and sealing its fate.

Chicks grow quickly. Within a few months they're big enough to discourage or escape from most of their native predators—snakes, eagles, and varanid (monitor) lizards. But they also grow too big to nestle under a parent's feathers for warmth and protection from the elements. They also lose their cryptic spotted fuzz, acquiring a waterproof plumage much like that of a full-grown cassowary, but dull brown in color. It takes a few more years before they fully develop the glossy, jet black plumage and brilliant blue neck skin of an adult.

During their first six to seven months, Huey and Louie followed us around, hugging our feet and whistling the cassowary equivalent of "here I am." The safest place for a vulnerable chick to stand in the Papuan forest is directly beneath a fifty-pound cassowary—or in this case, two human cassowary stand-ins. We found this clinging both amusing and annoying. One ill-placed footstep could have easily reduced our experimental population by 50 percent.

We found it nearly impossible to photograph our two youngsters. As soon as we got close enough to do so, they'd run to us and stand on our feet, whistling contentedly. If I squatted down to snap a picture, they'd try to snuggle in beneath me. The best option was to ask Deb to hold Huey or Louie about six feet from me while I focused on a midway point to the chick, then when Deb let go the chick would dash to get underneath me as I snapped the shutter. This produced many pictures of brown blurs.

We built a small enclosure of chicken wire, including a rain shelter, where Huey and Louie would be safe from my muddy size twelve boots. One risk of domesticating cassowaries is that if you feed them too well (they normally have very little protein and calcium in their diet), they gain more weight than their legs can support. We kept them on a modest diet, but even so, the birds were growing quickly and would obviously be too large for their little pen within a few weeks. So while they could still be contained by chicken wire, we built a larger enclosure, one sturdy enough to withstand the forces of the inmates' powerful kicks. The onslaughts of said kicks, combined with the rapid decomposition of wooden posts and rails turned soggy by our daily inch of rain, made fence maintenance a constant chore for the next three years.

There is no way to tell the sex of cassowary chicks. Even in adult cassowaries the genders are essentially indistinguishable. But some scientists wrote a paper describing a technique for distinguishing the boy cassowaries and the girl cassowaries: you simply insert a finger into the cloaca—the single avian orifice that combines excretory and reproductive tracts—and feel around for a penis-like "intromittent organ" found only in males. Now, I'm not sure I want to know who first figured this out, and how he or she happened upon it, but this technique obviously has to wait for maturity (the birds' maturity, not mine) as chicks are too small for digital intrusion. But by the time our birds were mature, and presumably big enough to have fingers stuck inside them, they also each had a dagger-like claw on each foot and the kicking strength of Bruce Lee. One does not scoff at such formidable weaponry when planning to probe a cassowary's cloaca. We'd never learn their gender (they were both females) until much later when they met their traditional fate as PNG's version of Thanksgiving turkey.

We constructed a pen for the rapidly growing duo that consisted of an oval enclosing a T-shaped divider, creating two large enclosures on each side of the "T" with a smaller enclosure above the top of the "T." We built a gate into each side of the cross arm, so the birds could move freely among the enclosure's three subdivisions. Not knowing how the cassowaries would behave as they aged, we designed the enclosure so we could easily segregate them if they began to fight, without necessitating the adventure of having to add a divider in a pen occupied by two ornery, battling cassowaries. The design also allowed us to isolate a bird in the smaller sub-pen while we conducted experiments. A small stream passed through the enclosure, which contained enough trees to fully shade the cassowaries. Our two little darlings quickly kicked the life out of all the smaller saplings and undergrowth. Nothing smaller than ten inches in diameter survived.

The enclosure for Huey and Louie made of stout timbers they still managed to kick through now and then.]

The pen design challenged the limited mental capacities of Huey and Louie, who epitomized the expression "bird-brained." The divider between the enclosures was made of parallel strands of fencing wire running between posts implanted every few feet. Even after living in the pen for two years, these two rocket scientists of the bird world did not know enough to walk around to the open gate when I brought their food to one side of the pen. Instead, they would try to run straight to me, despite the wire fence between us. Not realizing the divider was a barrier to forward movement, they would poke their head and neck through the wire strands, push, decide they couldn't get through, move about two feet, try again. . . .

Eventually they'd arrive at the open gate, whereupon they'd act as if this opening had just appeared miraculously for the first time, and then dash to the waiting food. Huey and Louie consistently failed the sort of simple maze that a planarian—those flatworms you observe in high-school biology class—can learn. They never figured out that seeing food didn't necessarily mean they could walk straight to it. In fact, they had this problem all day long, not just at feeding time. While patrolling their fenced domain, they poked through the dividing wire hundreds of times a day, each time eliciting the same "oops, can't go there" response. Their reaction demonstrated that, although well adapted to the rigors of the rainforest dating back to early in the evolution of birds, cassowaries might not cope well with the modifications that humans bring to their world. Australia's cassowaries are disappearing due to the novel introductions of automobiles and dogs. Both take a heavy toll because the birds are not highly adaptable and have no hard wiring to help them cope with such hazards.

Cassowaries need places without people.

Because the birds were constantly kicking any convenient target, we frequently mended their fences. But we had many things to do, and checking every post and rail was not always the highest priority. Eventually Huey or Louie would identify a rotted timber before we could replace it, and set to work kicking it to smithereens. Once a post was converted to a pile of soggy splinters, they would abandon it, contented. Sometime later, as they poked along the fence, they'd poke near the ex-post and find the barrier gone.

"Hey! I'm out!"

Now, you'd think that after trying to get outside the fence for so long, they'd make a break for the endless forest just a few steps away. Not so. Once outside the fence, the stunned escapee would stop and look around, as if she'd just passed through some portal in the time-space fabric and landed in a bizarre alien world. Rather than running free, she'd immediately set to tasting all the bits of detritus in front of her. She'd bend over, pick up a piece of twig or a dead leaf, raise her head, chew on it a bit, and drop it:

"I wonder if this is food. . . . Nope [drop]; I wonder if this is food. . . . Nope [drop]; hey, that looks good. . . . Nope, just a leaf [drop]. . . ."

They might slip through the fence while everyone was in the field, potentially giving them hours to make good an escape, but still we'd return to find them ten feet from the pen having tasted every possible bit on the surrounding ground. A few times, and I swear I'm not making this up, the ever-inquisitive cassowary would be outside the pen trying to poke through the wire to pick up some twig *inside* the pen that she had certainly tested for edibility one thousand times already.

If wild birds acted like this, they could never forage among widely spaced fruiting trees as they do; they would die of starvation as they tasted every leaf on the forest floor before randomly coming across a fruit. I suspect that the months that the chick spends with the father are critical for learning what is and what is not food as well as where to look for food. Huey and Louie never had that experience, so to them, the forest floor was littered with millions of potentially edible items. We often fed them fruits that we'd bring back after a day in the field, so they had seen and tasted many species of fruit. But I suspect something crucial was lacking in their upbringing, as they'd never followed their father as he made the rounds of fruiting trees. Having a bucket of fruit appear at your feet is not the same as spending a day seeking it out.

Maintenance is not a well-embraced concept in rural PNG and among tribes like the Pawai'ia. We grow up learning the need to lubricate moving parts, to paint or keep electronics out of the rain, et cetera. The Pawai'ia build a house and when it rots, build another; they have no paint. The philosophy of our Pawai'ia assistants, tasked with care of the birds, was to wait until something broke—which in this case meant neglecting the fence until a cassowary got out. Then they'd try to find the breach and mend it. If several candidates for a cassowary-passable gap were presented, much discussion and argument would ensue among the workers regarding which hole to fix; no one advocated fixing *all* the potential escape holes. They saw little reason to repair a gap if it was not the one the cassowary had actually escaped through. It required repeated and explicit direction from senior management to induce the affable Pawai'ia assistants to repair potential weak points *before* Huey or Louie found their way through the fence.

Great excitement ensued whenever a bird escaped. All the workers would participate in the recapture, and particularly in extensive discussions on how to respond. All the men would talk loudly and feverishly in Pawai'ia for several minutes, growing extremely animated. They'd point and argue, apparently refining a clever plan to get the ornery fifty-pound bird that had just kicked through a ten-inch post back into the enclosure. I'd wait patiently for their counsel. After all, they've been raising cassowaries all their lives. When they reached a conclusion, I'd ask in Tok Pisin what they had decided, and their response would be along the lines of:

"The cassowary is out of the pen."

The first time this happened, the initial attempted strategy was to have the men quietly encircle the escaped bird and guide it gently toward the gate leading back into the enclosure. The problem with this strategy was the bit about doing it quietly and gently. Pawai'ia with a loose cassowary are like dogs with a cat. I'd firmly instruct them not to make any sudden movements or loud noises, and we would get into position, the men practically quivering with restraint. But each time we coaxed the bird toward the gate, it would make some slight move-ment that would prove too much for the keepers. One of the men would shout and lunge, terrifying the formerly placid bird and causing it to bolt through our phalanx, whereupon all the other men would join in pursuit, alarming the poor bird to no end. I'd have to holler to get the men to stop, sometimes grabbing and holding a man, not the bird.

Calm would return eventually and the cassowary, now even farther from the enclo-sure, would resume sampling items from the forest floor, keeping a wary eye on us. Having tried yelling and screaming and found it ineffective, we could move on to a new strategy. One favorite trick was to lead the cassowary with a brightly colored item, like a red Frisbee.

"Wow, looks delicious . . . must peck. . . . Hey! It moved! [step forward]. . . . Must peck. . . . Hey! It moved [step forward]. . . ."

Such a bright thing was almost irresistible; it just *had* to be edible. You could lead them right back to the pen this way by not letting them really taste it—if they didn't become distracted by some tantalizing dead leaf or stick along the way.

Sometimes a piece of canned fish, something that was actually edible, could be used as bait. During one frustrating escape attempt, we'd finally lured Huey back to the fence. Deb was just inside, holding a fish she was straining to reach. Victory was nearly ours, but there was one last hurdle: Huey had to step over the small log that formed the base of the gate. Wild cassowaries step over logs every day, but Huey acted like the log was a coiled cobra or a hair-triggered landmine.

"Hey, that fish looks good [step forward]. . . . Oops, there's a log in the way [step back]. . . . Hey, that fish looks good [step forward]. . . . Oops [step back]. . . ."

After some thirty repetitions, my patience gave out. I crept up behind Huey, who was transfixed on the slab of mackerel in Deb's hand. I grabbed Huey from behind, wrapping my arms around her chest to lift and shove her through the opening—something akin to grab-bing a racehorse as the gate opens at the Kentucky Derby. She launched through, taking me with her, neither of us even touching the log. I landed face-first in the mud, stunned at the power and speed of Huey's reaction. She had pulled me, at three times her weight, as though I were nothing more than a gnat on her back. But at least she was in the pen, and Deb and the Pawai'ia had seen the funniest comedy routine of their lives.

Our main purpose for keeping Huey and Louie was to undertake a number of feeding experiments and to learn what we could from up-close observation of this secretive species. Huey and Louie saw their purpose for existence somewhat differently, and they had just one feeding experiment in mind: to determine how much they could possibly eat every day. Keep-ing them fed meant paying men to carry *kaukau* (a local variety of sweet potato), bananas, *pawpaw* (papaya), and squash from the village gardens to Sera. No sooner did a load arrive than it completely disappeared into our two feather-coated digestive tracts.

Initially we paid the men a fixed amount, nine kina, for a "load" of *kaukau*. After some months we began to observe an interesting phenomenon. The size of a "load" was slowly diminishing despite assurances and loud protestations from the carriers that their loads were as heavy as ever. More and more carriers were needed. At this rate, before long half the able-bodied men in the province would be in our employ, each carrying a single potato once a week to the station.

Executive decision time. We changed our policy and unilaterally declared that carriers would be paid by the weight of a load. I expected lots of resistance to this new policy and prepared for considerable negotiation and heated discussion. However, there were no protests, no lengthy diatribes about the difficulty of the work and how badly the money is needed, and no indignant protestations that they were good Christians. There was only the usual initial unintelligible discussion among the men in Pawai'ia, which typically proceeded hours of discussion. But this time it simply ended with an "okay," the men displaying sly grins as they left. I knew something was up.

New loads of *kaukau* began to arrive, brimming over the army duffel bags used to carry them. Loads doubled in size. A few came in over fifty kilograms, roughly the weight of the men carrying them. Now, carriers could earn more with a single load than they could earn in a week on salary. No wonder they grinned. The supply of *kaukau* piled up to hitherto unimaginable dimensions. The simple shift in policy pleased everyone. The men earned a nice stipend quickly, we no longer had to negotiate about load size and pay, and the birds had a steady supply of food. Even though the men could not read the scales, they never questioned the pay they received. It was easy to see how unscrupulous people, from their own government officials to expatriate businessmen, had bilked many Papuans as they learned, often the hard way, how a cash economy works.

The big supply of *kaukau* was a staple not only for the birds but for all the people at the station. It was nutritious and tasty. Despite the extra cost of carrying in the heavy *kaukau* (relative to carrying in bales of rice, our other staple), it avoided the expense of transporting it in the MAF Cessna. The bonus was that it provided a nice income to the community, especially the women. Carrying the vegetables to the station became the work of the women, who did most of the gardening in Pawai'ia society. We would pay them a set price for the produce and a price for the weight. This way we could get leafy greens, not just heavy items like *kaukau*. Some of the families planted extra gardens just to supply everyone at the research station. This type of win-win arrangement made a permanent research station a good asset to the community. Women earned a decent income (they were not allowed to work as research assistants for cultural reasons we could not violate) and everyone got fresh produce to eat. In exchange, the traditional landowners honored the voluntary moratorium on hunting and clearing—making Sera an effective conservation area, of which there were very few in PNG at the time.

The huge larder of *kaukau* and produce attracted a less welcome component of the Papuan biodiversity: rats. Rats could chew through pounds of *kaukau* in a night, especially the *Uromys caudimaculatus*, otherwise known in Australia as the giant white-tailed rat or, as we sometimes called it in Tok Pisin, *bigpela rat no gut tru* ("the big, really big rat"). The *bigpela* rat weighs in at two pounds and measures over half a yard long. The hunting moratorium did not extend to things inside the station buildings eating our food.

Kaukau and squash were Huey and Louie's staples, but we supplemented their diet with a variety of fruits brought in from the forest. We wanted to learn if the birds exhibited any preference for certain kinds of fruits. The gluttons would gulp down almost anything we brought them, but they did reject fruits that were even just slightly rotted. The microbes of New Guinea must put out some fairly nasty toxins, as cassowaries do eat fruits that contain all sorts of toxic compounds highly poisonous to humans. Indeed, the fruit flora of New Guinea has remarkably little that is not toxic to humans. Huey, Louie, and their wild brethren relished fruits of the *Gnetum* genus, which are so densely laced with glass-like splinters that we wore gloves when handling them. Deb even found that the splinters would remain in the droppings she sieved, and had to wear gloves when handling *pekpek* of birds that had recently eaten *Gnetum*. Cassowaries seem able to consume almost all the fruits in the forest, but only fresh ones; a bit of decay and they'll pick it up and reject it. Of course, one attempt was not enough for Huey or Louie.

Eventually it would sink in that it was not edible and they'd walk away, only to spot the fruit from a couple meters away with their acute avian vision and dash back to give it a taste. One bruised fruit would keep Huey or Louie occupied for hours until they accidentally stepped on it a few times and drove it out of sight into the mud.

The treat that really drove them to a frenzy was fresh rat. Living on a diet of carbohydrates, we assumed "the kids" needed a shot of protein now and then. We frequently trapped and removed rats from the station in our never-ending battle to protect our fresh food. They destroyed everything edible and many things inedible as well. The rats especially liked insulation on electric wires; our only electrical device, which they frequently damaged, was a critical one: the emergency VHF radio.

Thus, we had a ready source of protein for our "kids." When we plopped a dead rat in front of the birds, the fastest and closest would grab it and run around, relentlessly pursued by the other bird in an effort to steal it away, sometimes successfully, in which case the roles would reverse. Just finding a moment to stop and position the rat for a smooth head-first slide down the gullet was tricky. Cassowaries are not good at eating on the run. To avoid these squabbles and ensure both birds got some meat, I began chopping rats into bite-sized chunks, using the bushknife on a large stump at the base of the stairs. The birds quickly learned to associate rat meat with the sound of the heavy knife whunking onto the stump. With the first chop, Huey and Louie would go nuts trying to run through the wall of the pen. It made for a pretty macabre scene, me chopping rats into chunks with a bushknife and two cassowaries going berserk a few meters away. Sometimes when things got a little slow around the station

I'd whack the stump with a bushknife just to watch the Pavlovian frenzy it inspired. Who needs television?

We undertook a series of experiments that would be impossible to perform with free-ranging cassowaries. Deb was particularly interested in fruit preferences and conducted numerous replicated trials with balls of rice tinted differently with food coloring or with different-sized rice balls. Huey and Louie did not prefer one color more than another, but did prefer larger rice balls over smaller ones. But there were no hard rules; they'd try anything. My job was keeping the two away from Deb while she laid out the experiment. A human with its back turned was an invitation to be kicked! When a bird ventured too close, a gentle whump on the chest with a broom discouraged mischief.

I used the two captive birds to study seed dispersal, especially for measuring gut transit times. We humans are accustomed to slow gut passage times and reach for some form of medical cork if food moves through us too quickly. But among birds, transit times of fifteen minutes are not uncommon. Because (most) birds fly, they want to jettison excess baggage (i.e., indigestible seeds) as quickly as possible. Fortunately for plants, birds aren't particular about where they do so, which provides for good seed dispersal. Seeds are deposited wherever the bird might be in the elapsed gut transit time after swallowing a fruit.

I performed a number of trials by feeding fruits to the birds and then monitoring them until the seeds came out. I found that transit time can vary widely. Sometimes a seed would exit forty-five minutes after being swallowed; other times seeds stayed in the gut most of the day, only to be voided that night. How much and what the birds ate after swallowing the marker seeds appeared to influence transit rate. When the birds had lots to eat, seeds tended to come out sooner, but this was not a hard and fast rule. For the sake of my work, it would have been easier if all seeds came out in some consistent transit time—then I might have been able to figure out what a bird does in that post-feeding time, giving me an idea of where and how far seeds are moved. The fact that cassowaries retain some of the things they've eaten until night, when they completely clear their guts, was important to my research.

We learned a good deal from watching Huey and Louie up close. Wild cassowaries are so elusive that one usually only gets a glimpse. If you surprise them, they thunder off through the undergrowth. More typically, they steal into the shadows and disappear like a Hollywood special effect. Birdwatching tour guides in New Guinea count themselves very lucky if a few participants get a decent look at a cassowary. We were fortunate to have two under constant observation. The manner in which they handled the various fruits we gave them told us things we never would have observed in the wild. For example, when feeding on a large number of small fruits, a bird will sit down on its tarsi (lower legs) with its chest on the ground and pick all the fruits within reach. This probably requires less effort than feeding from a standing position, which calls for bending over for each little fruit and then raising the head high to let gravity help it down the esophagus.

We also learned that really large fruits were difficult for cassowaries to consume. Once Huey or Louie had properly positioned such a fruit in her bill, she would move her head backwards then jerk it forward, using the fruit's backward momentum to force it into the esophagus. Large fruits acted like a wedge that, with repeated lunging, forced the mouth open wider. Imagine trying to swallow a whole orange without using your tongue (like most birds, cassowaries have small, non-muscular tongues). Once the fruit started into the esophagus, a few more up-and-down head jerks with the bill raised would send it sliding down the throat nicely. You can see the large protruding bulge of such a fruit sliding down a cassowary's neck like something out of a cartoon. They undulated the neck in sinusoidal waves to encourage the fruit to descend to the gut. Swallowing is mostly done by gravity, as their throats are not very muscular.

Most large fruits have a layer of pulp that is stripped off in the gut, so the seed that comes out is smaller than what went in. This is not the case with *Pandanus* trees, which have very woody nuts that come out virtually identical to their pre-ingestion condition and size. I was amused one day by Huey's antics in swallowing a particularly large *Pandanus* fruit I'd given her. Once she had it started down the top of the esophagus, she rose up vertically to tip-toes, as if pointing to the sun with her bill, and undulated like a sheet hanging in a gentle breeze. She walked a few steps, the bulge still protruding like a huge goiter that moved from side to side of her neck. When she realized it was still working its way down her neck, she stretched and undulated more, seeming a bit startled. After a fair amount of bobbing and undulating, only half the seed's journey was complete.

The next day Huey acted very strangely, slowly walking about in a very unusual, upright posture and squirming her body back and forth sideways. She'd rise vertically and raise her rump feathers, as cassowaries do when defecating, but nothing would come out. Then she'd step away and look behind her, checking to see if she'd left a deposit. Cassowaries don't have expressive faces; birds have few facial muscles. But today Huey definitely looked perplexed and a little concerned. I suspected that the large *Pandanus* nut that she'd eaten was now plugging her up.

When I got a good look at her from directly behind, I could see her cloaca was greatly distended, a huge pink ring with the *Pandanus* seed firmly lodged and partially protruding, like a champagne cork. I wasn't going to stand directly in that line of fire. Every now and then something back there seemed to shift and Huey would leap forward and quickly turn around to look behind her, as if some invisible being had kicked her in the butt. She was totally baffled that something was causing a sensation back there. She once again rose up on tip-toes and rocked her entire body back and forth. After many minutes of prancing and squirming, to no effect, Huey decided an up-close inspection was required. I never would have guessed a bird could do what Huey did, and I never would have guessed I could laugh so hard. She stretched her head down through her legs, so it looked like she'd been neatly decapitated at the chest, and then stretched it so far back that her bill was just a couple of inches from her swollen, plugged arse.

"Hey, what's going on back there?"

For a moment I thought she'd grasp the offending seed in her bill and pull it free. But unable to stretch the last few centimeters, all she could do was inspect the situation. The cloaca became more distended, and with every change in status Huey closely scrutinized what was happening.

Despite the hilarity of Huey's predicament, I began to worry. Could I have seriously injured her by feeding her something too large? Could a bird actually die of constipation? Would she continue eating and eventually explode? As an evolutionary biologist I knew there must be strong selection to ensure animals cannot swallow things larger than they can void, but with Huey I was not too sure. Perhaps her regular diet of mostly *kaukau* and soft fruit made it hard for her to expel such a large seed. It had been more than twenty-four hours—a very long gut retention time—since she had swallowed it. I mentally considered a plan to get into the pen with her to assist with the channel-locks.

Fortunately, the seed finally popped free on its own, followed by a high-pressure stream of partially digested *kaukau* and pumpkin. I was greatly relieved for Huey, and happy that I did not have to uncork her myself. Huey's normally inert face exhibited every sign of relief and perhaps a touch of the pride that comes from a difficult task performed well. She relaxed and preened, acting nonchalant in her quest to recover whatever shred of dignity remained.

Having captive cassowaries right next to the station was a nice perk for more than strict research purposes. Being able to start observing cassowaries up close while we finished construction of the station helped temper our frustration at not being able to be out in the forest. The economics of keeping them fed benefitted many Pawai'ia women. But perhaps most of all I simply enjoyed watching them up close. These birds are in many ways the closest things, in form and evolutionary descent, to dinosaurs. Nearly everyone is fascinated by dinosaurs. They are the biggest attraction in natural history museums, and innumerable cinematic iterations of Godzilla capitalize on our fascination with dinosaurs. I had two dinosaurs as my nearest neighbors.

Chapter Fourteen

Big Reds and radio-tracking dung

Wanpela kainkain diwai i gat redpela prut na painim pekpek i gat liklik radio insait

Some of the first *pekpek* we found contained massive seeds, roughly the size and shape of a mid-sized baking potato—certainly too large for anything other than a cassowary to disperse. Most weighed more than a quarter pound. I also soon observed that they germinated quickly and produced vigorous seedlings. There were many other species with large seeds that took a long time to germinate, a trait that would make them harder to study. I wanted to study a species with germination rates I could measure. Some seeds incorporate into the leaf litter as part of the buried "seed bank," remaining dormant for years until conditions are right for germination. I could not afford to wait months, let alone years, to see if a seed germinated.

In the manner I had started in 1987, I gave the massive seed a number, AM 257. I was up to two hundred and fifty-seven unidentified seeds and trees. Before you can talk or even really think about something, you have to have a word for it. We couldn't keep calling it "that really big brown seed that sort of looks like a fat potato," though "AM 257" did not exactly roll off the tongue either. When we found the fresh seed, we discovered it was about three-quarters covered with a brilliant glossy scarlet pulp (called the aril), and about one-quarter covered with a lustrous creamy white tissue (called the funicle). It became "Big Red." As was the case for nearly every tree in the forest, there was also a Pawai'ia name for it, *Orei*. So in my notes I would write AM 257, in English conversation it was "Big Red," and with the Pawai'ia I called it *Orei*. Typical of our work, such multiple naming demonstrates the importance of scientific names that are consistent and uniform around the world. With the eight hundred languages in PNG, there could well be a hundred local names for a widespread species and very similar names for completely unrelated species. I would spend considerable effort in the coming years trying to find the scientific name for Big Red.

After we found the Big Red fruit-bearing tree, I became convinced it would make an ideal species for study. The magnificent tree, part of the mahogany family, can grow to the top of the canopy and emerge above the other trees. The fruits resemble cantaloupes, with brown husks that split along three sutures and reveal one to three of the scarlet aril-covered seeds inside. Often, the fruit fell before opening and on impact the husk burst, exposing the bright red and white seeds (technically called diaspores—the seed plus the pulp that the frugivore eats). The inside of the husk is bright white too, so the entire "presentation" is conspicuous and clearly meant for cassowaries since the fruits are closed, cryptic, and brown when high in the tree. Later, Big Red would be the archetype in a publication describing this sort of presentation as a "cassowary dispersal syndrome." This is a very distinctive syndrome, and one that is quite specialized, since cassowaries live only on New Guinea and in the remnants of rainforest in Australia. This particular mahogany species had evolved a fruit adapted specifically for cassowaries to disperse. It had not, like other close relatives, retained small fruits that could be dispersed by birds of paradise and hornbills. Big Red was betting on cassowaries for dispersal and I had bet on Big Red for my dissertation.

With a hammered, flaky texture, Big Red's distinctive bark is light brown to pinkish white. Because the bark flakes, few epiphytes or vines grow on Big Red trees. Almost every other tree in the Sera forest was shrouded in mosses, vines, algae, and other climbing plants, thanks to the very wet conditions. These epiphytes could get all the water they needed from the rain and had no need to send roots into the ground. Without this green covering, Big Red trees stood out conspicuously in the forest. You could spot an *Orei*'s luminous whitish brown trunk against the uniform green background of the forest from fifty yards, making it a good candidate for study. Once I knew what to look for, I could walk through the forest and spot the Big Reds without having to tediously inspect every single tree for some obscure defining character. I was confident that I would eventually figure out its scientific name, as it was one of the most spectacular trees in the forest, a mahogany, with one of the most distinctive fruits I had seen in New Guinea.

Deb and I intended to get a broad study of the cassowary-fruiting plant and seed dispersal system. She quantified the amount of fruit produced per hectare in the forest and she came up with very detailed tallies of what the cassowaries ate by counting every seed in fresh *pekpek*. By the end of the study she would have sieved through nearly a thousand droppings, using the gravity-fed water hose to wash bits of undigested pulp from the seeds. Real shit work. From that broad perspective we hoped to get an overall picture of the ecology of cassowaries. At the other end of that spectrum was my detailed look at the seed dispersal by cassowaries, and especially of one species—Big Red's seeds.

I took some big gambles on Big Red, so I tried to make sure I always had backup plans B, C, and D. One major thrust of my study was to be the first to really measure how far birds move seeds. To do this I mapped all the fruit-bearing Big Reds in the 400-hectare (just shy of a thousand acres) study area. This took weeks. Big Red occurs in low densities, about one mature tree for every four hectares, which meant searching nine acres of dense forest to find one tree. By the end of the study in 1993 I had tagged and mapped fewer than seventy mature trees. A bonus of this system was that Big Red is dioecious, meaning the sexes are separate plants; so while I couldn't tell a male cassowary from a female cassowary, I could differentiate the genders of Big Red trees.

To begin, I followed two strategies to measure dispersal distance. The first was to implant a small transmitter in a freshly fallen fruit, hope a wild cassowary would eat it, then radio-track the seed to its new location in the *pekpek*. I thought I would be the first person to radio-track scat, and that this would make a nice title for papers and presentations; e.g., "Direct quantification of diaspore dispersal vectors via radio telemetry of avian excretia." Now that would win a standing ovation at the National Academy of Sciences. The other strategy was a little less dramatic, but would yield the same information. I would implant in the freshly fallen seeds a tag with a code identifying the source tree. I would then discover tagged seeds in *pekpek* and know their origin. Between these two methods I would be able to construct, not surmise, a map of where and how far seeds are dispersed. This would be the eye-catching new aspect of my study.

Deb, who had learned to make transmitters when she radio-tracked opossums back in Florida, made a few prototypes for me. My fine motor skills were seriously lacking so soldering capacitors slightly larger than dust on a circuit board smaller than my little fingernail was out of the question. But if I could prove the technique worked, Deb promised to make as many transmitters as I needed. Because I anticipated that a proper study would require dozens, I had to prove the concept before asking her to spend days on such a difficult task. She had come prepared with all the necessary components and supplies "just in case."

I collected Big Red seeds, minimizing the human odor I might leave by wearing gloves and smearing my hands in Big Red fruit pulp. I smelled like a fruit, though we had no evidence cassowaries had either a good or a poor sense of smell. Implanting the transmitters in the field was difficult, so I carried seeds back to the station. With a scalpel I carefully exca-vated a place for the transmitter, inserted it, and replugged the seed with the seed coat and aril. I would do this and immediately take the seed back to the tree where, by reading their tracks, I knew cassowaries were visiting and eating fruits. I'd set down the shiny yummy-looking radio-tagged fruits away from my tracks and not return for several days. By then the fruits would begin to spoil and the birds would be going for the fresh fallen ones. So after three to four days I would return to see if a cassowary had taken the bait; if not, I'd retrieve the transmitter for reuse. I approached each deployment with growing anticipation. Would the fruit be gone? Had a cassowary taken it? Was I on my way to fame?

Every time the answers were no, and it looked like I was on the much more crowded path to obscurity. I tried everything I could think of to increase the chance of success. I did not linger at trees, but quickly picked up the old baits and carried them back to the station where I carefully extracted the precious transmitters and implanted them into fresh new fruits. I tried placing them in different ways, locating them differently under trees—all under one tree, one each under several trees. I tried removing other fresh fruits so the only choice (until more fell) was the transmitter-loaded fruit. I increased my speed and the amount of red pulp I slathered on myself. I muttered incantations in the middle of the night. Nothing worked. All I could surmise was that the birds avoided fruits with even the slightest bruise. Every day in mid-1990 I spent hours retrieving old fruits and collecting new ones to deploy from trees scattered across the large study area. After extracting their transmitters, I heaved the old, uneaten fruit in disgust off the verandah and into the ravine below. I knew the fruiting season would soon come to an end because there were not many more fruits in the canopy waiting to drop. I was sleeping less and muttering more.

Then one day, now long accustomed to finding the most-recently implanted fruit untouched by cassowaries, I could not locate the implanted seed. Newly fallen fruit lay scattered beneath the tree, but the fruit containing my radio transmitter was nowhere to be found. I looked again to be sure, and in a moment my pessimism disappeared. Maybe this plan could work! Maybe I'd just have to put out fifty transmitters a day. But the big questions now were: Would the transmitter work? Could I relocate it? What if it broke during gut transit? What if the bird took the seed miles away? I imagined its batteries running out as it silently beckoned its location to a desperate biologist scouring the wrong valley for the signal.

Best to get started right away.

I dashed back down the G-Trail, crossed the Oo hip deep in rapids, raced through our old camp, waded, knee deep, across the Sera, and ran up to the station, where I breathlessly gathered the receiver (check the battery—Yay! fully charged, for once), and grabbed an antenna and headphones. The *pekpek* trek was afoot, I told Deb, whose excitement matched mine; then I shot out of the station. Down the trail, across the Sera, across the Oo (keeping the equipment high and dry) and up the trail, and I was back at Big Red source tree T 547.

I got to the tree, dialed in the frequency, and listened. Nothing. That was good. At least it hadn't just rolled downhill a bit. I circled around the tree and listened some more. Nothing. Larger radius. Still nothing. This was all good. Because the transmitters were small and weak, probably close to the ground, and certainly surrounded by wet mossy forest (and possibly wet soggy *pekpek*), I knew the signal would be faint and I might be looking for weeks. The idea was to get as many transmitters out there as possible so I could search for them all simultaneously. My first strategy would be to work ridge tops where the signal reception would be best. I moved along one of the spines that graded from the G-Trail up to F, listening constantly. I stopped every fifteen meters, slowly rotating the antenna 360 degrees and straining to hear the "bip, bip, bip" through the roaring static.

Then I heard it. *Bip, bip*: the faint signal from the transmitter. I had the gain turned all the way up and radio snow roared in my ears, but the barely audible *bip bip* was there. It was just a matter of slowly turning the directional antenna 360 degrees, deciding which direction offered the strongest signal, and moving in that direction. Stop, repeat. Move a few yards, stop, repeat. Move some more . . . and eventually the signal strengthens. Eventually, when you are right on top of it, the signal screams *BLIRP BLIRP* in your headphones, even with the gain turned down. Well, in nice open country it works that way. But in the rainforest of Sera, with its gorges and ridges, the signal bounced around in confusing ways. Sometimes it sounded stronger to the east, but when I walked twenty yards east the signal would be loudest from the north. I spent a couple of hours chasing it, working down a steep hillside until I nearly slid into the river. The bird that had swallowed the seed that contained the transmitter had crossed the river; now the sound came from somewhere along the B-trail. I went up B and listened. The signal was off to the west, across the Sera. I bushwhacked through some dense riparian growth and crossed the Sera myself. Now the blips led me in the direction of the crew's house at the station. The bird must have passed nearby—interesting. Then the strengthening signal shifted, coming from the north, then the west. I moved up a ravine.

Taking note of the ravine's exceptionally thick vegetation, I realized I was traversing the area where we'd cleared some trees to enhance the view from the station verandah. I was beginning to get a bad feeling about this. I continued to follow the signal until I heard that loud *BLIRP* sound. And there it was. In my haste to switch transmitters, I had heaved a loaded fruit off the verandah and placed an unloaded one under T 547. I looked up and saw Deb on the verandah looking down at me.

"What are you doing down there in the ravine, honey? Did you find the transmitter?"

I don't think my reply was very polite. By the time I scrambled back up to the station through the thick second growth and cat-clawed lawyer vines, I'd given up on radio tracking. Instead of determining how far a cassowary disperses a seed, I had determined how far a moron can throw a seed. I saw my career options diminishing.

On to Plan B: tagging the seeds. I had put out tags at half a dozen trees during the 1990 fruiting season, though most of my energy went into radio tagging and various other aspects of research, not to mention working on the interior details of the station, like building beds and other furniture. I had not noted any removals from my small pilot sample of tagged seeds by the end of Big Red fruiting in August. The advantage of this technique was that I could make lots of tags and deploy them quickly. The tags were made by filing notches in a three-quarter-inch wire nail using a triangular file. A code like 1-2 would mean the nail had one notch on one side and two on the other. I could make a huge number of codes, limited only by the number of notches I could make down the nail. I spent many evenings filing notches in small nails by candlelight so I could be ready for the fruiting season in '91.

Meanwhile, I focused on a variety of other projects. For instance, I wanted to learn what happened to Big Red seeds once they germinate. I tagged and monitored hundreds of Big Red seedlings that had sprouted from both dispersed seeds (old *pekpek*) and undispersed seeds (under the maternal tree). I also monitored *pekpek en situ* to see what survived and what perished. I started several experiments in the shade house I built (and rebuilt several times as wood rotted over the years) in the small clearing where our original camp had been. It provided a place to perform controlled seed germination experiments where treatments had a more uniform light environment than the varied conditions of the forest interior.

A cluster of Big Red (*Aglaia mackiana*) seedlings emerging from an old pekpek.
These seedlings have been tagged to monitor growth.

In March of '91 I started to get nervous. The previous year, we'd begun to find fruits in May. Such a large fruit, it seemed to me, should have been apparent in the crowns of Big Reds by March. April came and still the big mother trees were barren, devoid of anything resembling fruit. By May it was obvious. The Big Red population was not going to produce fruit that season. Coming from the temperate zone, I carried certain expectations about seasonality. Things happen on an annual cycle, right? Spring and summer bring flowers and fruit. But not so in Papua New Guinea. Seasonal plant activity, or phenology, is not so simple in the tropics, and especially along the south flank of PNG's central cordillera. This is a zone of very high and aseasonal rainfall, a pattern we had not yet fully documented but suspected after eighteen months of nearly incessant rain. Certainly in the first year we experienced nothing that remotely resembled a dry season. We checked the rain gauge every day at 6 a.m. and 6 p.m. It always held some water, usually more in the morning than the evening. Through the years of continued monitoring we'd learn that there was no dry season. We documented about six and a half meters (over twenty-one feet) of rainfall per year—more than four times the annual rainfall of Louisiana, the wettest state in the US.

Every day Deb collected fruit production and phenology data from her many plots. Whether Big Reds fruited or not had no bearing on her research. She was watching what the forest did and how the cassowaries responded. Did they eat a random subset of what is available, or search out preferred fruit? If some were preferred, why? Did availability vary by month or year?

Her data were not yet complete, so we could only guess when my tagged population of Big Reds would fruit again. By the end of the study, after completing her data analysis, Deb could discern some patterns in species and the overall forest. Some species fruited seasonally on an annual or biannual basis, some fruited aseasonally with individual trees in fruit at almost any time, and some fruited only once in the course of her study, leaving us with no idea when they would fruit again. Even with three full years of fieldwork, the data provided too little information for us to discern what pattern those species might be exhibiting. As it would turn out, Big Red fruited biannually. I would have another crack at them in 1992. But in June 1991, after a year of work with the species, I had no way of knowing if I would ever see those red and white fruits again. I had vials of nails filed and ready to go. If they began to drop fruit, I would be ready.

Chapter Fifteen

Some extraordinary help

Sampela lain i givim bigpela halp

There were a number of things we could not rely on our Pawai'ia assistants to handle, chief among them tasks that involved numbers. Some of them counted the way a four-year-old does ("one, two, three, nine, five, twenty, twenty twelve . . .") and had even less of a grasp of even the simplest mathematical concepts. Teaching them to read rulers or other measuring tools took considerable time, time we'd have to invest again and again as new workers rotated in (as mentioned earlier, we chose to rotate work widely so many shared the benefit of an income). When we went to town for supplies every three months, we would train a member of the crew to record the rain gauge data the week we were away. The easiest way to track the data was to put the gauge beside a pre-dated page and make a mark next to the water level. Sometimes the designated assistant managed this nicely, but then forgot to dump the water out of the gauge after each reading. Sometimes the assistant would take readings until the gauge was full, and then dump the water. For the most part, we couldn't use these data. So much that we took for granted was totally alien to our Pawai'ia helpers. Once, for instance, I assigned a worker to paint the posts under the house with sump oil, a preservative. He painted right over the min-max thermometer attached to one of the posts. I had failed to specifically tell him not to paint over the thermometer.

We needed literate help.

Bringing in qualified assistants would also serve to diversify our social life. Imagine living alone in a vast wilderness with no one for miles other than a few people who don't speak English. Now imagine sharing your small house—a house with no real internal walls, I might add—with another person. Said person is your spouse—and also your research collaborator. Imagine the issues that can arise from that relationship. "I need that *pekpek* for my study." "No, I need it for mine. . . ." People really do fight over dumb shit sometimes. Along with needing competent literate help with the research, we also needed a more varied social life.

Because PNG is such an exotic and wonderful place, we knew if we got the word out that we needed research assistants we would get some applications. We advertised with the proviso that candidates had to pay their own way to Goroka and we would cover field expenses. The fieldwork would be split between Deb's and my research, and the assistant would share equally with maintenance work like cooking. We expected fieldwork six days a week, but we'd reduce that to five for someone who wanted to pursue his or her own field study: a great opportunity for the right person. For us, it was also a strategy to get students invested in their own research in PNG and use their preliminary data to solicit funding to come back, much as I had used my first pilot trip to leverage funds. Our plan worked and did yield outstanding results. Mostly.

Our first solicitation in late 1990 brought an immediate response from an older woman who sounded very keen, and claimed field experience in Mexico and Alaska. She included a letter from her physician citing her excellent physical condition. She could come right away and stay for an indefinite period of time. The few other applicants were students available for only short periods during breaks in their studies, so we decided to give the older woman a try. I pictured a strong, independent woman, perhaps with slightly graying hair, who had a rich life history to draw from. Someone ready to step out and try new things now that she was free of children and recently widowed. Someone with spirit who could add a capable, mature perspective.

I couldn't have been further from the truth.

We timed her arrival to coincide with our next resupply trip, and waited for her in the usual crush of humanity by the gate at the small Goroka airport. First-time newcomers to Goroka tended to be conspicuous because of their inappropriate dress and shocked, bewildered expressions. We spotted Barb among the new arrivals instantly. Deb and I locked eyes across the crowd and exchanged similar telepathic thoughts: *Oh, no!* This was not going to be like anything either of us had imagined.

We put on our best faces and greeted a sixtyish woman who looked to be a bit overweight and very out of shape, dressed in the style that can only be described as retired eager birdwatcher: a vest with field guide in the pocket, sensible L.L. Bean shoes, and a sun hat cap replete with patches from famous birding locations. We introduced ourselves and took her back to the Lutheran Guest House, where we sat and talked.

As it turned out, Barb had a slight problem. She'd recently had a hip replacement and was not in shape to walk. We asked, almost plaintively, if she had not read in our description of the position that we required a strong hiker in great physical condition. Somewhat defensively, she countered that she thought she was in good shape, that she had successfully bird-watched all over North America. But she had never imagined we meant an *all-day* hike over mountains and through swift rivers. This woman had hardly ever left a sidewalk or ventured more than a kilometer from a road.

We learned our first lesson about prepping potential visitors. We had to exaggerate the rigors of life at the research station for Americans unfamiliar with PNG. Nearly everyone overestimated their capabilities; nearly everyone had no concept of the difficulty of fieldwork in the PNG rainforest. From then on, we insisted that new research assistants be verifiably fit (as in having hiked the Appalachian Trail as a warm-up to joining us). We pretty much stuck to people younger than ourselves from then on. Of the many people who visited us over the years, almost all who were older struggled and suffered more than the younger ones. One still calls it the "Death March" to this day. We learned to talk up the mud and leeches, the raging rapids, the millions of chiggers, the relentless malarial mosquitoes, and various other hazards and discomforts, and if people were still eager to work with us, they'd make the first cut. We'd grown used to the trials and travails of daily life at Sera, and saw the conditions as typical of wilderness rainforests. To us, a difficult hike was an all-day trek on either of two substrates— slippery mud or slick round river rocks—and included pushing through fast waist-deep rivers a dozen times, crossing two large mountains, and teetering across ravines on fallen trees, all conducted under a steady drizzle. But Barb's preconceptions about wilderness, rainforests, and difficult hiking bore no resemblance to what these words meant to us. With Barb, we had miserably erred in our decision-making. She assured us brightly, however, that she would be very helpful if we could get her out to the station.

Deb and I conferred in private. Barb felt we had misled her by calling for someone in "great physical condition;" she thought we should have advertised instead for someone along the lines of "a superhuman triathlete." We, on the other hand, felt we had been sold a bill of goods, and I would still like to meet the doctor who wrote that glowing letter. She clearly couldn't make the grueling hike in to the research station, but once there she could hopefully handle tasks like measuring seedlings, counting fallen fruits, or checking the rain gauge. So we decided to move up the date of a rare and expensive helicopter supply run and had her flown in. She agreed to chip in for a chopper trip out at the end of her stay—a promise she would stiff us on later.

Turns out we were wrong about Barb's ability to help out with our research—or with anything else, for that matter. When she arrived, it took her over an hour to walk two hundred and fifty meters *downhill* from the helipad to the station. Flustered, she said she'd never imagined the area would be so steep and muddy. I thought to myself, *Just what did you think our ad meant when it described "rugged, muddy terrain?"* She worried that she might slip and damage her artificial hip. While I certainly did not want that kind of injury to deal with, my compassion for Barb had subsided to nearly zero. In damage-control mode, Deb and I focused first on keeping her alive (including not strangling her ourselves) and second on trying to get some utility out of her. Awed that we had built this place ourselves, Barb kept calling us "pioneers," which irritated us both. All around PNG were millions of people, like the Pawai'ia, who built their own houses with far fewer tools than we had.

Barb was capable of walking a short distance from the station with a folding chair and then sitting and watching for birds. She could not run a mist net or drag a tape measure through the woods. I referred her to the helipad for the best birdwatching, but she was not going to brave that 250-meter trip until it was time to catch a chopper back to civilization! We thought, Okay, you can cook. That will save Deb and I time, as we shared that duty equally. If Barbed cooked every night, that would be a big help. Well it turned out—and I am not making this up—Barb did not even know how to light a match. She had one of those electronic striker things that lit with the pull of a trigger. Working our temperamental kerosene stove was beyond her. One moment she'd have yellow flames licking nearly two feet into the air, the next black soot billowing out and coating the kitchen. She had no idea how to make a meal from the supplies on hand. What did she cook at home? Well, she told me, she always started with fresh meat. We had no fresh meat, so she did not know how to start. As it turned out, her experience "all across North America" had taken place in the passenger seat of a Winnebago. Her husband had handled practicalities like lighting matches. I shouldn't pick on her. But her two-month stay with us provided a sobering demonstration of how far Deb and I had already diverged from mainstream America. Barb saw us as pioneers, and we saw her as helpless and soft as a baby. She had no idea of what it meant to walk any farther than the mailbox, how to cook her own food, how to make a fire, how to wash clothes in a river, how to fix anything that broke, or how to sharpen a knife. Even cooking beans not from a can was a revelation for her. She was completely unable to adapt to life as experienced by most people outside the US and Europe.

Barb made one significant contribution, however. Sometime back in the Winnebago days, her husband had been seriously burned. His injuries deeply upset her, so she always carried a couple of large tubes of an expensive and very effective cream made especially for severe burns. She gave them to us when she left. The station had become a small health post, and we found ourselves patching cuts and treating malaria every week. For people who'd never had access to even an aspirin, getting some of our over-the-counter painkillers was worth a day or more of walking. The relief we provided ran the gamut from comforting to life-saving. Sometimes people came from great distances and then we'd never see them again. We regularly bought canisters of pills, including antibiotics and anti-malarials, with five hundred or a thousand doses at the Goroka Pharmacy—something that would be impossible or extremely costly to do in the US. Many useful medicines are cheaper in PNG than in the US, and don't require an expensive visit to a doctor for a prescription.

One day Nei, one of the Pawai'ia we knew, showed up with his young wife and a screaming baby. The baby's head was covered in dried mud. It had rolled into the cook fire when the mother was not watching and had very severe burns. The mother had coated the burns in mud as first aid and it appeared the poor thing had not stopped howling since. We used bottles of sterile saline, originally intended to clean contact lenses, to wash off the mud and then gingerly applied the special cream Barb had left us. It was one of the more difficult ministrations we ever did. Adult Pawai'ia are stoic and take a lot of pain without flinching, but this baby wailed louder with the slightest touch. Removing the caked mud and ashes from the burn was agonizing.

We kept them nearby for about a week to refresh the salve dressing, watch for infection, and monitor progress until the burns seemed a little less angry. We could administer a baby dose of painkiller, but did not trust the parents to provide proper treatments. We also wanted to keep an eye on them because we feared the husband would give his wife a very harsh beating for her errors. When they arrived it appeared she had already suffered from his wrath. Such beatings were common among the Pawai'ia. More than one woman died in the village during our years there due to beatings from her husband. The mother could not have been more than thirteen or fourteen. There weren't any courses or resources for pre- or post-natal care in Pawai'ia country. Among young, first-time mothers, who often spent much of their time alone in isolated forest huts with their babies, it was shockingly common for babies to die.

After the debacle of Barb, we never had a bad assistant again. The next great assistant, Wayne Crill, arrived before Barb left, easing the work and tension, and possibly saved Barb from me throttling her out of frustration. Barb used us as a way to do some birdwatching in PNG without having to shell out for a guided tour. After she stiffed us on the helicopter bill, she managed to travel around PNG on her own and add to her birding "life list." All the assistants after her were more in the model of what we wanted—students who could benefit from the field experience and hopefully go on to develop careers in PNG.

The next assistant we had certainly fit this model. Chris Filardi came out with his girlfriend Phillipa. Both super fit, they had hiked some of the tougher trails in the Cascades and Sierra Nevadas. Chris said the hike from Haia to the station had been the toughest one he'd done so far, and for that reason loved it. The always-cheerful pair worked tirelessly, even helping with some of the remaining construction details. They knew how to use a plane and chisel and worked on finishing the floor in the assistants' bedroom.

Chris went on to do more research in PNG, publishing a paper relating to Palm Cockatoos and seeds they take from cassowary droppings—something I also observed at Sera. Later, when Deb and I were in Miami writing our theses, he did key work expanding the conservation program in the Crater Mountain area. His ability to hike the vast area and talk with people in their remote huts remains legendary, and it's something few white visitors have replicated. He is now the top expert on the birds of the Solomon Islands, and I rank him as one of the finest people I know. I think he would agree the Sera experience was transformative for him. It was for nearly everyone who made it there.

The list of student research assistants we had in this period is not huge, but all were exceptional young biologists who have done well since. Among them, Chris (mentioned above) is an ornithologist at the American Museum of Natural History, Peter Burke is a top bird artist who recently illustrated a field guide to the birds of Chile, Eben Paxton ran a federal program to conserve the endangered Arizona Willow Flycatcher, Brian Kennedy is a leading limnologist at the University of Idaho, Heinrich Jessen has spearheaded a major corporate green shift in Singapore, Hector de Garza Silva is a leading Mexican ornithologist, Wayne Crill is a virologist, and Kalan Ickes is a rainforest ecologist at Clemson. We eventually stopped advertising when the reputation of the station grew. Many people contacted us and offered to volunteer as assistants just for the chance to be at the field station.

Later in the saga, we would sponsor even more researchers at Sera and elsewhere in PNG. The tally of people we subsidized partially or fully, mentored, or merely provided with a research site eventually rose to the hundreds. Research at the station and surrounding areas would yield at least six PhDs, eight master's degrees, and over a dozen honors degrees. Many outstanding scientists from around the world visited, and the list of peer-reviewed publications coming out of Sera and nearby Crater Mountain sites topped sixty (and still climbing) by the time of this writing. The station was able to compete with US field stations and receive one of a handful of prestigious Field Station grants from the National Science Foundation in 2002. If you could put together at one place and time all the biologists who made it out to Sera, I think you would have a most extraordinary gathering of strong, independent, and well-rounded people. The Sera experience attracted the exceptional and, I think, helped to make them even more exceptional. Landing there offered the genesis of something profound.

Chapter Sixteen

Big Reds and the last contributions of Huey and Louie

Stori long studi bilong diwai i gat redpela prut na lastpela taim Huey na Louie helvim mipela

Early in 1992 I was relieved to see plum-sized young fruits maturing high in the canopies of some of my tagged Big Red trees. Hopeful that fruiting would occur again, I had spent much of the year working with Big Reds in other capacities. One key step was to ascertain the identity for the species, as it would be hard to publish papers about "Big Reds," "Oreis," or "AM 257s."

I'd had some help from a botanist, Matthew Jebb, then living in Madang, on PNG's northern coast, at the new Christensen Research Institute (CRI). Matt and the Institute became important in our lives. For the first time, we had friends who not only understood what we were doing, but did not consider our work some sort of big joke the way most pilots did, or a misguided road to hell as many missionaries did. Matt, the director of the new institute, was a top-notch biologist with a great sense of humor. We'd visit the institute for some R & R in the sun and for the opportunity to stretch our eyes on the ocean. We looked forward to evenings with Matt and his family, usually roaring with laughter and sampling his home brew.

Located near a great reef system, the CRI focused primarily on marine research. Someone else, Diane Christensen, had also seen the necessity of starting a research station in PNG. But unlike our operation at Sera, the institute had money. The Christensen Fund is one of the only significant foundations with an emphasis on PNG. In the world of conservation donors, most of the attention goes to endangered species and last-ditch efforts to save the _____ (fill in the blank, preferably with a charismatic or cute mammal). Places like PNG with healthy ecosystems and robust animal populations get less attention, even though support at this stage might help prevent the inevitable degradation to the more desperate scenario typical of those other tropical rainforests that need last-ditch efforts. The Christensen Fund had invested wisely, and its research station proved what I'd said all along—that a good research facility could transform the status of science in PNG.

Sadly, in a few years the CRI would fold, due not to lack of support by the Fund but to petty politics and misunderstandings. CRI closed because of a disconnect between the field program and "the bosses" back in the US—a hazard almost all international field programs encounter when decisions are made by people in control but far from the program. Deb and I would run up against this same problem in the years ahead. CRI, a very productive research station with excellent facilities, sat on the grounds of a hotel owned by Mal, so it had a supportive landlord. And only one other marine station, financed by the Belgians, existed on the island of New Guinea, home to the richest reef ecosystems in the world. CRI could and should have been saved, but I think personal issues clouded some judgments, and what might have been salvaged was abandoned. It was a tragic loss for PNG, and would highlight for us how critical the right people are for success. This wonderful station with real financial backing failed largely due to personnel issues and poor management.

We did not have strong financial backing, but were deeply committed to the research station at Sera and our Pawai'ia friends. Even later, after Deb and I had divorced, and to this day we have continued to work together for the sake of the programs we established. We'd already seen how frequently terrific programs collapsed when their founders left. CRI failed after Matt's departure, as did Wau Ecology Institute and the Baiyer River Sanctuary when their key leaders moved on. Without fully trained and competent people in place and functioning before the transition of leadership, programs tended to founder in PNG. Deb and I developed two strategies to avoid this common problem: first, we would commit our lives to Sera, and second, we would build a fully competent national staff to carry on management long before we retired or moved back to the US.

But in the early 1990s, CRI thrived. Matt helped us begin to identify our many dried leaf and fruit vouchers of cassowary food plants that we knew only by Pawai'ia names or numbers we'd assigned. Big Red was a member of the genus *Aglaia*; this we could be certain of because of the stellate (star-shaped) hairs on the leaf. Getting it identified to species would take a few more years and another expert who specialized in *Aglaia*. When working with birds, I had relatively little trouble identifying even the minor subspecies, most of which had names and were easy to distinguish. But when delving into the plants of New Guinea I was frustrated, and at the same time stimulated, by the bewildering diversity of poorly defined species. I was studying the ecology of New Guinean plants, many of which were not even cataloged by science, much less be readily identified.

Finally in early 1992 the fruits began to swell so I knew they would be dropping soon. I readied the tags, assigning a code to each of twenty-six female trees. Heinrich, our research assistant at the time, had Danish origins but was quite cosmopolitan—one of those people I envy for their ability to switch with ease among a handful of languages. After his first few days with us, he was speaking Tok Pisin like a native. When fruits started falling we'd split up to visit as many trees as possible. Heinrich was one of the most competent and no-nonsense fieldworkers I have ever had the pleasure to work with. I remember sitting with him lamenting about how hard it would be to visit all twenty-six trees scattered over 400 hectare of rough terrain bisected by the raging Wara Oo on a schedule that would maximize our success. After patiently listening to my complaining, he said, "Andy, let's just do it." And I realized he was right. I stopped thinking about the difficulty of the task and instead focused on getting it done. It was hard work, but we were able to divide the sample and make our rounds, tagging the seeds and returning to the station in time to avoid the worst of the afternoon downpours and the rise of the river.

One day he'd take the trees located along B-Trail, and I would take those on F, and so forth. They were too spread out to cover them all every day, and on the days Heinrich worked with Deb on her projects I was on my own tagging fruits. We had no margin for error. If I found a tag in a dispersed seed I had to be 100 percent certain of which tree had produced that seed. I could not screw up like I had with the transmitter. As the season began, my prospects looked good. Some of the tagged fruits were disappearing. If I could locate them later in *pekpek*, I would have the holy grail I sought.

I had tested marked fruits with Huey and Louie. Like most seeds, the experimental ones passed through their guts in fifty to two hundred and forty minutes. Tracking wild cassowaries suggested to me they normally moved at a fairly laid-back pace, meandering through the forest from fruiting tree to fruiting tree. Based on the figure of one to four hours in gut transit, I suspected I'd find most tagged seeds within a mile of their source tree. By tagging seeds at widely scattered Big Red trees, when I later searched any section of the study area I had the possibility of finding seeds from both faraway and nearby trees.

The living conditions at Sera could be tough on health. I put in many hours of hard work and was wet for long periods every day; close contact with sick Pawai'ia seeking medicine at our pseudo-clinic exposed me to their illnesses; and my immune system constantly battled God-knows-what in the way of arboviruses and parasites. All these onslaughts led to frequent days of feeling lousy. Early on in the study I'd contracted something that often made me extremely weary. I might get up in the morning, hike one kilometer, and return to the station exhausted. My head ached and my body temperature dropped below normal (my typical response rather than fever). This pervasive malaise eluded diagnosis.

The only tangible evidence of something not quite right was very cloudy urine. Our dog-eared manual, *Where There Is No Doctor* (note: one of the most useful books ever produced, this has probably saved tens of thousands of lives worldwide), listed a way to diagnose protein in the urine. You simply boil the urine and any proteins congeal. When I tried it, my piss turned to the consistency of egg-drop soup. My response to Deb's question, "What are you cooking?" caused a bit of amusement, but whatever bug I'd picked up wasn't much fun. Still, for over a year I just lived with the exhaustion and headaches. Then Deb came down with it, too.

Eventually we traveled all the way back to Miami to see Caroline, the tropical disease specialist who had probably saved my life the first time I had malaria. Caroline took us seriously even though our symptoms were nothing more definitive than exhaustion, persistent low-grade headaches, and malaise. She started with a list of possible illnesses based on where we'd been living, and then she worked through test after test. She enjoyed the detective work. "Did you drink any unpasteurized milk? Let's check for strongyloidiasis. Maybe anthrax." She checked us for things I'd never heard of and hope never to encounter. Her persistence paid off and eventually she diagnosed filariasis, a tropical disease caused by parasitic round worms. One test for this is to visit an eye doctor after midnight, when the worms are most active, rest with your face down for fifteen minutes, then sit up and have the doc quickly look inside your eyes for the worms—they can invade the vitriolic fluid and will sink to the front of the eye and become more readily visible if you leave your head facedown after midnight. Fortunately, we did not yet have worms in our eyes. But we did have filariasis—along with the tremendous sense of relief that comes when something that has made you sick for years is finally diagnosed.

Every tropical biologist develops a real and somewhat morbid interest in parasitology. It was sobering to think that every single Pawai'ia likely dealt with the same filarial fatigue, malaise, and headaches for their entire life. No doctor existed to treat them as Caroline had treated us. I was a new man within days of my first de-worming pills. The Pawai'ia, and millions of rural poor in the tropics, spend their whole lives coping with debilitating sublethal parasite loads, a condition some colonial administrators might have interpreted as lassitude.

Just as the 1992 Big Red tagging season was in full swing, I had some particularly strong bouts of filariasis. I rested in bed for a couple of days, but to my dismay, I was not improving. I came down with a fever, which suggested a different illness. Then my lungs started to feel heavy and I developed a slight gurgle in my breathing. The fatigue turned to weakness; just making it across the room to the toilet became arduous. Right at the start of the crucial experiment I had been preparing for two years, I was incapacitated.

Deb grew increasingly alarmed as my condition worsened. She got on the radio and managed to find a mission emergency health service. She explained my symptoms and her concerns. The doctor there replied by asking our church affiliation, saying that the service was only for "believers" in their missions. She wanted only answers to a few questions, but help was denied because we did not worship at the altars of their missions. They asked her to clear the frequency for their believers. The next day, my condition further deteriorated; Deb soothed my fever with a damp cloth and noticed I was breaking out in spots. I had measles! Our medical references indicated this could be serious in adults, and my other symptoms suggested complications with pneumonia were setting in. After toughing through some really debilitating filariasis and malaria, I was now coming down with my most serious illness, measles. My health did not improve, and my lungs gurgled in a disturbing way. Deb and Heinrich decided to evacuate me. I was a bit feverish and mainly concerned with my research. All I could do was count on Heinrich, who performed this key phase of my research for me as if it were his own dissertation on the line. He doubled his efforts and made the rounds to tag fruits at as many trees as the weather and river allowed.

Rain and clouds often prevented helicopters from landing at Sera, and this was one of those borderline days when we normally wouldn't risk bringing in a flight. Because we couldn't see enough sky from the station to judge the weather, our routine was to run up to the helipad, scope out the conditions, then run back to the radio in the station to update Mal's dispatcher in Goroka. On that day, visibility was poor and the ceiling was low—in other circumstances we would not have given the go-ahead to the dispatcher in weather like this. But for med evacs, the pilots will push the margin a little.

Deb called in a chopper and helped me struggle up to the helipad, taking half an hour to cover the 250-yard hike. I nearly beat Barb's record for slowest ever to the helipad. We emerged from the forest to find a sinking, opaque ceiling and light rain. The only approach would have to be low over the treetops coming up the valley; the exit would require following the same path. If the chopper did not get in very soon, landing would be impossible once the clouds pressed down into the valley below us. Sometimes the weather stayed at near zero visibility for days. Do we tell the pilot to turn back and hope for better weather the next day? Or do we take a chance that the gap will stay clear until the chopper arrives? A bad decision could put the pilot in jeopardy, or leave me stuck for a few more days with no chance at all to get out. Clouds were everywhere, but the pilot wanted to try.

The chopper arrived with Dave Earhly, the chief pilot, at the controls. Only Mal had more experience in PNG than this guy. He urged us to hurry. We lifted off and ducked under the sinking cloud as soon as my feet were in the chopper. I buckled in the back, shrouded in a blanket. Deb sat up front and peered into the mist, hoping to spot one of the ephemeral gaps that sometimes open up and let a plane pass through. The weather worsened. Dave reported that he'd barely made it over the mountain under the settling ceiling of clouds. Once the clouds overtook the lowest passes in the mountain, there would be no getting back to Goroka, and now our helipad was closed in, too. You never, never, never fly into clouds in PNG. Hundreds of airmen met their deaths in World War II trying to guide their planes through these clouds.

Dave nosed the chopper up one valley only to find the pass closed, and had to carefully retreat before it closed behind us. Pushing into a valley tight under cloud posed serious danger, because if the way out closed behind you, you could either hit the hard center or creep along so slowly at treetop level that you ran out of fuel before ever finding a place to put down in that endless sea of forest. With no view, even the best pilots became disoriented. We nosed up two more valleys and retreated, just barely above the trees. Dave announced that we were nearly out of fuel. We had two options: go all the way around Mt. Michael and risk running out of gas, or gamble on flying high over the cloud. If you went above cloud and did not find clear sky to descend through, you were screwed. We went up. As you ascend the air thins, and thus the thrust of the rotors diminishes. You can go only so high in a chopper. Finding it incredibly hard to breathe at the higher altitude, I huddled in the back, gasping, as the chopper labored forward above a sea of cushiony cloud. When you get above in the sun, the sky is so blue and the clouds look so bright, it is hard to imagine their undersides are dark, gray, and raining.

Fortunately, after some time Dave spotted a hole in the cloud and descended through it. We were over the mountain and had a clear straight shot into Goroka. He took the chopper directly in to the hospital backyard and rather unceremoniously kicked us out, barely feathering the rotors before lifting and turning to the hangar a kilometer away. In the hospital yard, hundreds of surprised onlookers gawked at the huddled white guy wrapped in a blanket and the woman leading him to the entrance. At last, something interesting had happened! Later, Dave told us that the chopper had been essentially on vapors when he dropped us there. We had eaten up all the margin of error and he barely made it back to the hangar.

In the hospital, I sat on an examining table eyeing the unsanitary conditions some might call filth. While waiting for a doctor, I looked at a sign that read "No Spitting." It appeared a lot of visitors ignored that sign. Also in the room was an EKG machine, possibly the first model ever made. A few hospital staffers brought in a very worried-looking older man and made a big show of plastering electrodes all over his torso. Once they finished hooking him up, they proceeded to unhook him. No one had even turned the machine on. One of the orderlies told me the machine was *bagarup,* or "broken." The poor patient had no idea what was going on; I suspected this was his first time in Goroka, much less in a hospital. I wondered what they would tell him the fancy machine said about his condition. I wondered what the doctors would tell me.

We decided that no matter what they said, I would not stay long in this hospital. I was sure in my weakened condition I would only contract something worse. A doctor showed up, and after a fairly perfunctory examination said he would put me on an IV and keep me under examination for a day or two. Deb and I protested this plan, Deb more vehemently than I was able. Just tell us what medicines we need and we'll be going, we told him. In the midst of this argument with the doctor, the head physician and surgeon came by, took one look at my polka-dotted skin, diagnosed measles, ordered some strong antibiotics, and sent me away. He said I must protect my eyes from the sun. Like me, he did not want me occupying a bed in his ward.

So I bedded down in Goroka while Heinrich carried on. It was also a key time for Deb's research. A lot more than Big Reds were fruiting now. She needed to get out on her plots and measure fruit production, so she got a plane back to Haia after I began to improve. I stayed to fully recuperate at a friend's house.

Eventually I made it back to the station, but it took a while because the MAF plane was being serviced and pilots were on leave. Fewer Big Red fruits were dropping, but we continued tagging them until every tree was finished fruiting.

Then began the task of looking for tagged seeds in *pekpek*. I hired a few extra Pawai'ia to assist, and every day we scoured different parts of the study area. Whenever we found a dropping, my hopes soared. I would cut into the seeds with a knife to expose any buried tags. Every time, my hopes sank to frustration and then despair. I'd cut the seeds into tiny bits just to make sure I missed nothing. Days passed and then weeks. Nothing. At one point, I told Heinrich I was ready to make a deal with the devil. After years of preparation, this was my last chance. I did not even know when the Big Reds would fruit again. The transmitters did not work. I was out of ideas. I hired more Pawai'ia and our team of a dozen men searched and searched the Sera forest for cassowary droppings.

I imagined finding a tag so frequently that when it actually happened, it was anti-climatic. One by one we found tagged seeds. In order to make any conclusions with a modicum of statistical rigor, I needed at least twenty. The tally crept toward that number. The excitement at the research station grew palpable. The Pawai'ia were gleeful when we found a new tag. I mapped the position of each using the compass and tape measure technique. One by one I plotted the locations on a graph paper chart. The sample size finally grew large enough that I could run some simple statistical tests on my calculator. I had a result! After that, each new tagged seed was gravy and added confidence to my conclusions.

By the time I was back in Miami eighteen months later to write my dissertation, these data—good, solid stats on some very hard-to-answer questions—were sufficient for publication in a good journal. The short and essential point was that cassowaries disperse seeds in a non-random fashion. They do not often cross the rivers and steep ravines taking seeds with them. They disproportionately move seeds uphill. They do this because many seeds are voided when the birds sit down to rest or sleep for the night, and they tend to spend their nights in upslope, comparatively dry places. Like me, they don't like to sit and sleep in mud. The resting habits of the birds create a demonstrable non-random distribution, an important finding in order to understand the overall ecology of this rainforest.

There is considerable scientific literature, some of it speculative, on what plants gain by having their seeds dispersed. Some studies show dispersal avoids competition around the mother, others that it prevents seedlings from being lethally infected by pathogens from the mother. Still others indicate that dispersed seeds are less likely to be found by seed-eating insects and rodents that hone in on the mother plant and the fallen seeds beneath it. A whole slew of complicated explanations strive to account for seed dispersal, and every species stud-ied has its own complex ecology. Yet very similar dispersal mechanisms are found in almost every plant. Was the phenomenon really this complicated? I thought not. All plants share the physical realities of gravity. I would show in my study that most seeds fall and land downhill. If undeterred, in succeeding generations the population of Big Reds would simply march down-hill, the speed of this descent would be dictated by the steepness of the terrain. Dispersal, by cassowaries or other means, takes some seeds uphill. This action sustains a population's distri-bution on non-level ground; without it, populations would shrink downhill.

Scientists like "elegant" answers. Ecologists especially like untangling a bit of the bewildering complexity that surrounds us. In so doing, they sometimes overlook the more obvious and simpler answers that might be staring them in the face. You do not need complex pathogen and seed predator relationships to provide an advantage to dispersal. These certainly do exist. But the effect of gravity is uniform across the globe, and across the globe plants have dispersal mechanisms. My research highlighted this commonsense explanation. I think one reason gravity has not figured strongly in the literature about seed dispersal is that most field biologists actively or subconsciously avoid study sites with steep terrain. Deliberately choos-ing study areas for their benign terrain might add hidden bias to all subsequent sampling done at those sites.

About six months before we were slated to return to the US, the men started asking what we planned to do with Huey and Louie when we left. They told us these birds had *plenti gris* (abundant fat), a thinly veiled suggestion regarding the fate of the pair. I think they were a bit concerned about to whom such spoils would go, like contentious heirs to a fortune when the patriarch is given a few months to live. The men worried that we would release Huey and Louie to the wild, as we had with the Vulturine Parrots we'd raised from chicks. Letting two such fat cassowaries go would be akin to burning the inheritance rather than passing it on to the rightful heirs. Normally the Pawai'ia sell their captive cassowaries before they reach adult size, or eat them once they are adult sized. There is little point in wasting food on a bird that won't grow any larger. We had kept ours for years, letting them gorge to their hearts' content. Huey and Louie were the biggest, fattest cassowaries they had ever seen.

Many nights in the station Deb and I discussed this dilemma. The captive birds had none of the skills needed to survive in the forest; they could get lost in their own pen. More importantly, they were completely habituated to humans. If we released them to the forest we knew that within a few days after we left they would walk up to a person who, like everyone in these parts, would be carrying a bow and arrow, and that would be the end of them. An easy shot at such a large piece of meat would be an irresistible temptation for even our most dedicated workers. Once we had already "gone finish," who would ever know? No matter how we looked at it, Huey and Louie were doomed.

Our discussions were not bereft of feeling. Deb shed a lot of tears and I still have bad dreams about it. With us for three years, the two big birds had been a source not just of data, but of daily entertainment. They had earned a place in our hearts. True, they were not cuddly and would have disemboweled us given the chance, but they were like pets and the decision to eat them was difficult. But it was the inevitable result after many nights of discussion and angst. We were certain they did not have what it takes to fend for themselves, to find food and compete with wild cassowaries. Also, the Pawai'ia who had worked with us all those years might have seen letting them go as selfish, or even as an insensitive snub. They had asked to eat them and if we had no further use for the birds, refusing that request would only weaken the bridge we had made between their culture and ours. Imagine being someone's reliable chauffeur for years, only for them to burn the Mercedes rather than give it to you when they move away.

We decided to have a *mumu*, a traditional feast. We would invite any and all Pawai'ia, particularly those who had worked so hard for us, helped us in innumerable ways, and made us feel so welcome in their midst. It seemed an appropriate way to give something back to them after all they had given us. Furthermore, I was interested in examining the birds' gastro-intestinal tracts.

Great advances have been made in telecommunications, linking the world in a single community. But I would contend that Twitter does not spread news any faster than the Pawai'ia rumor mill. We told the five men working for us about our decision to hold a *mumu* with Huey and Louie as guests of honor. Within minutes the word had spread to the farthest reaches of Pawai'ia territory. Between then and the day of departure, we confirmed and re-extended our invitation many times with Pawai'ia who "just happened to be passing by."

On our next-to-last day at the station in June 1993, about seventy-five people showed up to join the feast and then help us move out the next day. Rain sprayed down on us, as usual, and the dismal weather matched everyone's mood, despite the prospect of the *mumu*. A great deal of discussion arose over how best to kill our two birds. I left that to the men, who could complete the task without the emotional attachment I had. We hid in the station and let them follow their traditions; this was one I did not want to observe. Coupled with the knowledge we were leaving, possibly for good, it was a very unhappy time.

As the birds were dressed for cooking, I removed the guts and took a number of measurements and photographs. Deb stayed inside not wanting this memory. For such large birds, their gastro-intestinal tracts were very short, reflecting their diet of easily digested fruit. I wanted to see the size of the ceca, two diverticula of the hindgut where digestion aided by bacteria might occur. If they were digesting cellulose or other complex carbohydrates through fermentation, it would probably be indicated through the presence of large ceca. Somewhat to my surprise, the ceca were quite small, adding to my puzzlement over how such large birds supply their nutritional needs through a diet of fruit that often comes out of the bird looking much as it did going in. The small ceca eliminated one potential complication for my seed dispersal studies. Emus, the sister group to cassowaries, have large ceca and seeds can remain in them for months—thus opening the possibility of very long-distance dispersal. Cassowaries don't seem to have this potential. They probably do not carry seeds more than one day or deposit them more than a day's travel from their source.

A pit was dug and a fire had been roaring in it for hours despite the drizzle. Rocks were brought up from the river and heated in the inferno. The birds were sliced into strips, which, true to expectation, swelled with fat. One of the men leaned toward me and quietly said, "You know, their fat is very yellow, much like human fat"—an interesting comment in an area where cannibalism had been practiced within the lifespan of the old men like Moai. The fire was allowed to die down and the meat and vegetables were wrapped in banana leaves and laid on top of the hot rocks, then the whole pit was covered over and allowed to roast. Jets of savory-smelling steam vented from the ground, and everyone's mouth watered when the time came to reopen the pit.

Huey and Louie provided a surprising amount of meat and fat (the latter especially coveted by the Pawai'ia); everyone, even the smallest children, received generous helpings. The meat was delicious—very dark and sweet tasting, more like beef than any other bird I've sampled. Unlike beef, the fat was not marbled throughout, but appeared in separate layers, particularly on the back. This is one of the reasons the meat of ostrich and emu (cousins to the cassowary) is sometimes available at fancy restaurants. It tastes great and, because the fat is easily removed, it's low in cholesterol. Seeing how much everyone enjoyed the feast and knowing how rarely they get to eat meat, I was glad we had this chance to give something back to the people who had given us so much over the years. Despite having studied a wide range of topics in great detail, one of the most common questions I'm asked back in the US is, "What do cassowaries taste like?" On our last day at Sera we had obtained useful data and managed to please the Pawai'ia. Not a bad way to wrap things up, even if it was emotionally distressing.

Chapter Seventeen

Back to Miami and life in the US

Go bek long Miami na pasin laip long Amerika

Americans tend to think of culture shock as what happens when one leaves the US and lands in a place with entirely different traditions, customs, and ways of life. As cultures around the globe homogenize, the differences become less and less significant. You can now fly to 111 countries and eat at MacDonald's—and, while you're there, chat with the locals about the latest Hollywood movie. Often, new releases appear overseas on bootleg DVDs before they've even made it to your local theater. One time, in a hut in Borneo, I met two German backpackers who admired my Philadelphia roots—we talked about Eugene Ormandy and the Philadelphia Philharmonic by dim candlelight. What passes for US culture has insinuated itself in places around the world, but the soft and easy lifestyle in the States is not as widespread, and that is what people really want.

The contrast between life in PNG and in the US is in many ways as enormous a difference between two nations as you can imagine. PNG has no fast-food franchises. "Fast food" comes in the form of *kai* bars with dubious and greasy fish and chips or boiled sheep hearts sweating under heat lamps. The *kai* bars open only for lunch, as everything pretty much shuts down at night in urban areas when the raskols come out seeking opportunity. Restaurants cater to a small number of the wealthier citizens and foreigners.

There are not any fast food outlets along the highlands highway.
But there are plenty of small businesses like this one that provide food to hungry travelers.

I was in Goroka when the first traffic light in the highlands was installed there. Tellingly, it was placed not at a crossroad, but at a crosswalk. Generally many times more people travel on foot on any given road in PNG than in vehicles; sidewalks are rare, even in town centers. The traffic light worked for a while. Pedestrians learned to wait for the walk signal and drivers learned to stop for the red light. But because of the device's poor timing, huge crowds would pile up on each side of the street waiting for the go-ahead to cross the road, and with so few cars passing it was ridiculous to wait. Before long, walkers ignored the light, milling back and forth across the street at will, causing cars to back up as they had in the pre-traffic signal days. Soon, the signal broke, and now, years later, it still stands outside the Provincial Offices, lights out and slightly askew, the mute monument of a failed experiment in modernization.

But the culture shock experienced when arriving in PNG from the US is mild compared to that of arriving in the US after living in PNG. The descent into LA alone is a visual slap. Something in my mind says "danger" when coming in for a landing at LAX, whereas I hear "welcome" when dropping onto a grass strip in a rainforest. One quick glimpse of Los Angeles from the air contains more buildings, more concrete, more cars, and more people than exist in all of PNG. And bigger people: I'm always amazed, when I re-enter the States, at how fat and out of shape people are. There are very few overweight people in PNG (except a handful of politicians—people joke about measuring the success of a politician by the number of folds in his neck).

In the US, the noise, the pace, the lights all assault you. But what really shocked me, returning in 1993 after nearly four years in the rainforest, was the rampant commercialism. Advertising was ubiquitous. Not just on television, but everywhere. Billboards along the roadsides, on buildings, on the sides of trucks, even on cars. People wearing T-shirts and baseball caps emblazoned with logos. Drivers making statements about themselves with their vehicles. In the PNG highlands, people opt for one of just a handful of available four-wheel drive truck models if they want to travel anywhere other than on the one paved highway. In the US, people pay a premium for SUVs just to portray themselves as gutsy outdoorsmen, though most wouldn't have the guts to drive them on the standard dirt road in PNG.

What we Americans place such importance upon seemed trivial and ridiculous after living without it. The world does not end if no one applies chemicals to their armpits. One brand of toilet paper is enough. As for air fresheners, how can petrochemicals make the atmosphere more pure? After living in clean, open air for so long, I felt I was practically choking on fumes and pollution. No one else seemed to notice. See a nice yellow flower called a dandelion? Spray the yard with herbicide. The entire economy and society is based on people buying totally unnecessary things. The average middle-class American family wastes more money in a week than a Pawai'ia makes in a year.

Such was the culture shock I faced when I came back to the US. The incredible waste—which would have been incredible wealth to a Pawai'ia—took much more getting used to than did the simple life at Sera.

Chapter Eighteen

Data analysis in Miami and Big Red becomes "my" tree

Wokim numba bilong studi na diwai kisim nem bilong mi

I had completed the coursework, passed the comprehensive exam, designed and executed the research. . . . To earn my PhD, all that was left was analyzing the data and writing a dissertation. I found this step of the process exhilarating. I had made a clean break—no more fieldwork, no slipping back to the rainforest for some additional research. Students who work in university labs or in study areas near their university have to resist the constant temptation to get more data, to test one more hypothesis, to build a better sample size. I did not have this option.

But I had plenty to keep me occupied. I'd used pen on paper to record all the data I'd collected at Sera. Now I had to extract the information from my notebooks and data sheets and input it into a computer, where it could be organized and analyzed.

I also had the canopy photos that I took at the sites of a few hundred cassowary *pekpek* to quantify the light environment of the droppings and of Big Red seedlings—along with similar photos taken at random points for comparison. With these data I could determine if cassowaries dispersed seeds randomly in relation to the canopy above, or if they somehow directed seeds to a particular type of site. Did non-random dispersal present seeds with an advantage?

One of my dissertation committee advisors, Carol Horvitz, was using image analysis hardware and software in her research. I arranged to use the equipment when she and her research assistants were not—usually late at night. Progress was very slow; the software was primitive compared to what is now available. I had to make corrections by hand and re-analyze every image multiple times. Most people would find it tedious. But sitting in a comfortable chair, in an air-conditioned lab with electric lights and a radio playing my favorite music was a total cakewalk. I didn't itch. No one came to the door asking for medicine or a bar of soap. I worked on the analyses almost every night for months.

If you were a seedling on the forest floor, you'd want to be located in a sunny gap, where you'd have sufficient sunlight to generate new leaves, stretch your roots, and grow tall. So if seed dispersal presented an advantage in terms of the propagation of the tree species, then ideally cassowaries would move seeds to sunny gaps. Even if they defecate at random, some scats would land in gaps since treefalls are frequent in the rainforest. But it was obvious to me, from my experience searching for *pekpek*, that cassowaries did not defecate in existing treefall gaps very often. But being a scientist rather than a television pundit, I could not just assert this without proof. I had to have the numbers. Comparing the light environment from random points and from cassowary dropping sites, I confirmed statistically that fresh casso- wary *pekpek* is not often found in gaps and indeed is found less frequently in gaps than would occur if cassowaries defecated randomly. After all the time I'd put in tracking seeds, even trac- ing back to what Batanimi taught me in my first weeks of looking for cassowaries, I under- stood why. Cassowaries, like humans, are large bipeds that walk upright. Their large bodies require space to move around in. New treefalls are a tangle of branches and vines that is hard to penetrate—the fallen canopy mashed to ground level. Often the trunk itself is a barrier too large to step over. Older treefall gaps have dense vegetation growing up in them, often making them impenetrable without a bushknife. Cassowaries, lacking bushknives or arms to swing them, find it much easier to just go around a gap.

Like the woods-savvy hunter Batanimi, or even a less experienced rainforest denizen like me, cassowaries know enough to follow the path of least resistance through the forest. In movies, and now on reality television, stars slash through the "impenetrable jungle." These are scenes contrived to portray jungles as dense and dangerous. Or, as is likely the case in reality TV, the stars just don't know how to walk in the forest. Because the rainforest canopy blocks 90 to 95 percent of the sunlight from reaching the forest floor, the interiors of rainforests are often rather open and relatively easy to walk through. I rarely carried a bushknife in PNG or a machete in Latin America or a parang in Borneo unless I had a specific reason to. The places with thick, impenetrable vegetation occur where sunlight reaches the forest floor—in older treefall gaps and landslips, along river edges, or in disturbed (e.g., logged) forest. While survival/reality TV adventurers hack through jungle, any person as smart as a cassowary knows to simply walk around the gap in the untangled, cool shade of the surrounding closed forest.

The analyses of canopy photos also quantified and verified some other general impressions I'd formed about rainforest ecology. Although cassowaries avoided gaps, chances were good that eventually a gap would form over any given dropping. We'd often have to divert our trails—tedious work—where trees fell across them. Trees we tagged and studied fell surprisingly often. Sitting on the station verandah or out in the forest on calm days with no wind or rain, we often heard trees just give it up and collapse with a crash. You can't tell from a short snapshot, but rainforests are very dynamic. Spend some time in one and you realize trees and branches drop disturbingly often. I even have a dent on the top of my head where a falling branch clobbered me. What are the odds of that? I have a great appreciation for the dynamic nature of the forest and a unique set of data with which to quantify it.

The photos taken at the same spot over several years showed that any point in the forest has a 1 to 2 percent chance per year of having a gap form over it. Later, when training Papua New Guinean researchers, there were students whose work verified mine. Miriam Supuma would find 1 to 3 percent tree mortality per year on Deb's permanent plots. Arison Arihafa would study gap dynamics and find a 1 to 2 percent new gap formation rate per year. Three different metrics, the same result: for a field ecologist, it doesn't get much better than that.

I knew from monitoring Big Red seedlings that they could survive in a dormant state, just sitting there, for more than a decade. That starts to add up to pretty good odds. So although cassowaries do not move seeds to a gap, they do move them to many points around the forest, up to a kilometer away from the mother tree. All of those points have a 1 to 2 percent chance of becoming a gap, and many of the seedlings can live ten to fifteen years "waiting" for that moment. Big Reds definitely benefit by having cassowaries disperse their seeds, and the reason why was becoming clearer. If cassowaries deposit the seeds of one maternal tree in one hundred random spots, then in one year the odds of at least one tree dying above one of those spots and creating a gap to provide sun for the seed are considerably better than fifty-fifty. I'd buy one hundred lottery tickets with such odds for winning. This is one reason trees invest in fruit pulp and nourish seed-dispersing frugivores like cassowaries.

Not having any fancy technology, like a photocopier, at the station, I (with help from assistants like Brian, Eben, Ross, Heinrich, Hector, and Peter) had painstakingly traced hundreds of leaflets from Big Red seedlings. (Imagine coming all the way to PNG at your own expense to volunteer as a field assistant and end up being asked to draw the outlines of leaves! These guys were very patient.) We traced not only the outlines, but also every little hole in the blades. I did this to study whether herbivores chewed up more seedlings found under the parent tree (not dispersed) than seedlings found at a distance from the tree (dispersed by cassowaries), and to test whether herbivores chewed new leaves more than old leaves, big leaves more than small leaves, or leaves in gaps more than leaves in shade. Just as ecologists had theorized that seed dispersal helps seeds escape seed eaters near the mother tree, it was also proposed that dispersal helped seedlings escape herbivores near the mother. The caterpillar that barely damages the mother by eating three of its leaves could fall to the ground, climb up a seedling and kill it by eating all three of its leaves.

At Sera I tried placing a clear two by two millimeter grid over a leaflet and counting squares over the leaf to measure leaf area. But I found the task too tedious; every leaflet was a different shape, and often peppered with small holes. Because rainforest plants don't grow a new set of leaves every year, some leaves persist for years, being nibbled and rotting bit by bit. Lots of things chew and attack leaves in the rainforest. It was much faster to trace those leaves at Sera and use a machine to measure them back in Miami. After outlining the leaves, I dried them to measure their dry mass and then threw them off the verandah—a couple of years of work reduced to a few numbers and tracings. In a lab at Florida International University, using an image analysis camera and software, I analyzed the tracings as fast as I could flip them in and out of a scanner. With the images scanned and the statistics calculated, it was evident that Big Red seedlings dispersed away from their parent by cassowaries do not experience substantially less damage from herbivores or pathogens than those that put down roots under mother. Clearly, "escape" was not an advantage to dispersal for this species. My findings are contrary to those of many other studies in the Neotropics, where seedlings near the parent tree did not fare as well as the dispersed seedlings.

The story of Big Reds, cassowaries, and seed dispersal came together nicely. Finishing the dissertation was not particularly stressful, even though the senior professor in the department would stick his head in my office at least once a day and shout, "Aren't you done yet?"

Still, the matter of finances loomed. Deb and I had both been fortunate to have some of our doctoral studies subsidized by Maytag Fellowships, but we'd spent that money and were surviving on teaching stipends. But financial support from the university would soon run out, as would my deferral on repaying undergraduate student loans. I needed to find a job soon after graduating. After four years in PNG I knew I could happily live on almost nothing. But paying back my loans would take a little more than almost nothing.

My research was unorthodox and not very sexy. Many scientists buy into the mentality that something complicated, hard to understand, and requiring highly sophisticated statistics is inherently more interesting and "better" science. Good old-fashioned fieldwork using simple tools had gone out of vogue in academic biology by the mid-1990s, and hardly anyone completes a PhD these days without using some sort of technology requiring more than a couple of AA batteries. Starting a field research station in New Guinea, establishing one of the best conservation projects in PNG, and laying the foundations for fieldwork by dozens of researchers was fine. But it was not a good strategy for landing an academic position. University search committees don't really care what you have done; they care about how much you will publish in high-impact journals and how successful you will be at bringing in grants bearing overhead for the university. How much teaching ability factors as a priority varies widely among universities and positions; many care less about teaching if the candidate's publications and earning potential are strong.

My prospects for finding work were not great. Being out in the field for years and not "playing the game" in professional meetings meant I had dropped off any prospective employer's radar, if indeed I had ever been on the screen. I knew these liabilities and the only way to compensate for them was to publish. I had managed to place a few articles in scholarly journals in the past years despite the isolation at Sera. While at the station I wrote using an ancient typewriter we bought from a shopkeeper in Goroka. I suspect I might have been among the last authors to submit a manuscript typed on a manual typewriter with hand-drawn graphs and get it published in *American Naturalist*. Submitting manuscripts from Sera was very slow—our carriers delivered mail to the airstrip, where it waited with the missionaries for the next MAF plane, and we picked up incoming letters every three months when we went to town.

Although I had explained my circumstances, one clueless journal editor upbraided me for not including the required three photocopies with the original manuscript. He said that any student at the university with the nation's top-rated football team certainly should be able to afford Xeroxing. Sure, but I could not afford the five days and six hundred dollars it would cost to reach the nearest photocopier. I can understand why so many "normal folk" disparage academics for living in ivory towers; many of them do.

A job, paying my loans, and professional credibility all depended on publishing, and I still faced one big problem on that count: I did not have a proper name for Big Red. While in the field, Caroline Pannell, the expert on *Aglaia*, had told me she could not place my specimens unambiguously to a species. To do so would require samples of the trees' flowers. I had spent many months in my last year at Sera desperately scanning the canopies of *Aglaia* for flowers. I was so relieved when I finally did find flowering trees, but that relief quickly gave way to further stress. Remember, Big Reds have no vines on them because they cannot grip the tree's flaking bark. With their tall smooth trunks and absence of vines to offer handholds, they are too difficult for Pawai'ia men to climb. Moreover, the ones I found in flower were the largest individuals in my population and the flowers, out at the tips of the canopy, were inaccessible even if you could climb up the tree. When inflorescences—complete flowerheads including stems and stalks—fell to the ground, they were already too rotted to make useful specimens.

Eventually I found a female *Aglaia* with a flowering branch reaching out to within a dozen feet of a smaller tree, maybe twenty inches in diameter. We had a set of climbing spurs I sometimes used to collect voucher specimens. With these and a belt I could climb trees. It sounds easier than it was. Getting around the lianas and climbers on many trees and moving past branches took time and a lot of muscle. Reaching the tips of twigs to obtain fruits or flowers was often impossible. Using the extended pruning pole needed to reach those far flowers took even more muscle. Try holding an eighteen-foot pole horizontally with one hand and pulling the rope that closes the clipper jaw with the other hand. Now try it fifteen meters up in a tree, held up by two spurs and leaning back in a belt encircling the trunk. Pray there aren't bees.

Collecting vouchers this way was tough work, but I had done it fairly often in situations when a Pawai'ia could not just scamper up and grab the sample by hand. Near the end of our time at Sera, I finally managed to secure Big Red flowers. At Miami I nervously awaited the arrival of some twenty boxes of plant specimens we had mailed to ourselves. When they showed up, I quickly pulled the precious fertile Big Red vouchers and sent them off to Dr. Pannell. All this took time, and I could not hold off on publishing. So my first articles use the name *Aglaia* aff. *flavida*, which means affinity to *flavida*. In other words, this species, whatever it was, was similar to *flavida*, but was not *flavida*. This was sufficient for journals, but it was not ideal. Imagine saying you had studied something similar to a chimpanzee, but not a chimpanzee.

Eventually Dr. Pannell solved the problem. Big Red had fruits quite different from any other member of the genus, and its flowers were also distinctive. She named it as a new species, *Aglaia mackiana*—the "mack" coming from my last name. To have a magnificent tree in the mahogany family named after me was extraordinarily thrilling, and it reinforced the vision that great things could happen for anyone willing to take the chance of bypassing the "safe" mainstream research sites. Taking the risk of establishing a study station at Sera was beginning to yield some nice dividends. I hoped I could convince other young biologists that such risks paid off. It would be a hard sell in the years ahead, with surprisingly few Westerners willing to tackle PNG. But once I began teaching and mentoring PNG students, it would no longer be hard to find people amenable to working at Sera. They saw Sera as a great facility and an even greater opportunity; many Western scientists saw it as too much of a hardship or risk.

Chapter Nineteen

Finishing the dissertation and searching for a job

Pinisim bigpela buk bilong universiti, painim nupela wok

After two semesters of working day and night, by the summer of '94 my facts and figures had come together nicely. I could begin to tell the story, even if the dissertation was not completely written. Rather than produce one long, tedious document, my committee agreed I should configure each chapter as a stand-alone paper. That way I could easily format and submit chapters individually to journals, potentially placing an article for publication before actually defending the dissertation. The work clipped along.

I presented my findings at several meetings that year. My talks were generally well received, and at the largest annual gathering of ornithologists—the American Ornithologist's Union—I won an award for best student paper. That led to a job interview at Chicago's Field Museum. In the meantime, I successfully defended my dissertation, which included a hastily written new chapter, as requested by my advisor, that tied together the various aspects of cassowary seed dispersal and linked all my new knowledge to what was known in the field at the time.

I enjoyed the thesis defense, even the probing questions. Delivering my presentation at various academic meetings and conferences had prepared me for being challenged. Nothing had prepared me, however, for the kind of hostile, aggressive questioning I faced when I interviewed at the Field Museum—from a former colleague, no less. I was dismayed to learn later that this tactic was designed to see how well candidates could "stand up to the heat."

The museum did not extend an offer to me, nor did a rural university where I spent two days interviewing, only to learn that the dean would veto any prospects who could not add to the school's quota of minority faculty. But my former boss at the Academy of Natural Sciences in Philadelphia, Frank Gill, invited me to submit a proposal through the museum for United Nations grant money slated for a project in Guyana. I'd worked with Frank 1979 to 1982 and knew we could build something together. I gratefully accepted a temporary post-doctoral fellowship at the Academy, and Deb and I packed up and moved to Philadelphia. Unfortunately for me, Frank moved on to another job shortly after we arrived in Philadelphia, so we would not be building anything together. The postdoc funding was only a temporary option that was quickly running out.

During that time, Deb and I met with Mary Pearl of the Wildlife Conservation Society (formerly WCI), Megan Hill of Conservation International (CI), and Bruce Beehler, who served as PNG expert for both those organizations, to talk about Papua New Guinea. Big money from the US government-funded Biodiversity Conservation Network program was flowing into PNG, so the country had risen in importance for both WCS and CI. Despite all the talk about the big conservation organizations using science to set priorities, available cash frequently speaks louder. Deb convinced WCS to fund biodiversity surveys and training in the Crater area. This would produce data useful for the planning of the larger Crater Mountain project. In designing the surveys, she included participation of national landowners, conservation professionals, and university students, part of our changing emphasis from pure research to training. We did more than "our" research; we involved nationals as essential partners.

The surveys interested CI, as its Rapid Assessment Program (RAP) had begun as quick surveys by top experts to help identify conservation priority areas—and had grown to include a significant training component. CI agreed that putting these teams of experts in the field offered a superb opportunity to train national field biologists. The organization had a hefty US Agency for International Development (USAID) grant to fund RAP surveys and training in Peru, Bolivia, and the island of New Guinea.

Meanwhile the Sera model, using research as a form of "science tourism" income, was proving itself. Our station had been in place for more than five years and a protected area, the Crater Mountain Wildlife Management Area, was taking form around it. Indigenous people saw some new benefits coming to them through employment by researchers. In fact, the model had enough promise that CI had included the construction of a research station in its grant proposal to the Biodiversity Conservation Network (BCN), asking for funding to build a research station in the Lakekamu Basin. Some who'd considered a research station non-viable and likely to attract hunters changed their minds when 1) we showed that the station benefited the Pawai'ia, and 2) significant conservation outcomes arose from the hunting ban and research. The fact that CI could derive hefty overheads to support the headquarters in the

US from a grant to build in PNG did not hurt either.

So even though I was still awaiting word on the Guyana grant, I accepted a job offer to fill an unexpected opening at CI. Bruce Beehler had left the organization, and CI needed someone to replace him to meet the specific timelines on the USAID and BCN grants that needed ecological expertise in New Guinea. I could not believe my good fortune. This would keep me in PNG and I'd be working for one of the four big international conservation organizations. CI had a reputation for being more lean and efficient than the other "Big Conservation" groups, namely Wildlife Conservation Society (WCS), World Wildlife Fund (WWF), and The Nature Conservancy (TNC). You need to learn the acronyms to function in conservation, just as you do in the military or other huge bureaucracies. At the time, CI was considered a bit renegade, having formed when frustrated conservationists split off from the two largest organizations—WWF and TNC. Early in its gestation, the lean CI promised to operate differently, more science-based and community-oriented, than the other three. But by the time I was hired, I would discover CI was starting to grow larger, and had taken on such cumbersome grants (such as the USAID funding) that it was about to become just as inefficient as its counterparts. CI still did good work, though, and I was keen to join the organization.

Just two weeks after landing the CI job, the word came in on the Guyana program. My proposal would be funded! But despite the possibility of running a new program in a place I'd wanted to visit for years, I felt committed to CI and also to the Pawai'ia and PNG. But I stayed on at the Academy long enough to help hire a coordinator for the Guyana project. We settled on Graham Watkins, a recent PhD from Penn who had actually lived in Guyana at one time. Years later, I would bump into Graham at a professional meeting and exchange stories with him about his time in Guyana and mine in PNG. Our experiences bore a surprising similarity. We met similar roadblocks from our US-based employers. We both strived to build national capacity in poor, underdeveloped nations to help their people run their own conservation and research programs. Often we found the mindset prevalent back home was that US experts were needed for an almost indefinite period to guide conservation in these poor countries. There was too little investment in training the local people.

But those experiences were in the future. Right now, I was taking up a job where I would bounce back and forth between the US and PNG. It was like a dream come true. I was actually being paid to promote research and conservation in PNG. The work did not allow me to spend time at Sera. I finished my dissertation (from '94 to '95) and then I worked for CI and Deb did some more fieldwork in PNG and wrapped up her dissertation (from '96 to '98). Luckily we had reliable friends keeping things rolling at Sera.

Chapter Twenty

Meanwhile, back at Sera

Wanam samting kamap long Wara Sera taim mi stop long Amerika

The move back to Miami had been nerve-wracking. What would happen to the station? Who would look after it? How quickly would it start to rot and collapse? Would the Pawai'ia lose interest in the project? Maybe they would start hunting after we left, or worse, ransack the building. We felt pretty confident the Pawai'ia would stick with their side of the bargain for a good while. They'd look after the place and maintain the hunting prohibition, but that would not hold indefinitely. Our side of the deal was to find researchers to go work there, and in the process provide an income to the Pawai'ia as field assistants, carriers, guides, and gardeners. They had thousands of hectares on which to hunt and extract their livelihoods. But at that time, the Sera station was the only chance for an income. Only chance, that is, unless loggers or miners moved into their territory. Both seemed unlikely. In lower Pawai'ia country, loggers could operate by floating trees down the Purari to barges that would take the raw logs to the insatiable Asian markets. But most of Pawai'ia land was farther inland. Theoretically, timber could be floated down the Pio to the Purari and thence to the sea. But the Pio joined the Purari above the Hathor Gorge. In this incredibly narrow gorge, the entire Purari narrows to a tight gap between sheer walls—a churning hell through which few trees could pass and remain marketable.

The remoteness and terrain of Sera made it likely we would never have to directly confront loggers as we would at lowland sites. We also thought it unlikely miners would pose a problem. True, if there is enough oil or gold, miners will build a road anywhere. The $175 million (1972 dollars) investment to mine the Erstberg lode at 4100 m above sea level on the Indonesian side of New Guinea proved this. The lode of copper and gold there is so rich that access was created despite its being one of the most remote places imaginable. The access road is an engineering feat, including a kilometer long tunnel. To get to the mine, workers travel the last mile in a gondola; each car holding one hundred–plus workmen and spanning the longest gondola reach between pylons in the world. In PNG's Lakekamu Basin, the Allies had built a road all the way across the mountains to Wau in less than a year during WWII. The route was designed as a second approach to reach the Japanese on the north side of the island in case the Allied assault by sea did not work. When there is gold, oil, or war involved, roads can be constructed anywhere.

One day very early in our stay at Sera, when we were still camping on the bend of the Oo, George Carmen, one of the leading petroleum exploration geologists in PNG, came through. He said he thought it highly unlikely the area around Sera contained any oil, at least in sufficient volume to make it worth drilling, adding that gold miners wouldn't be interested in Sera, either. We considered the site safe for developing the research station and conservation program because it seemed unlikely we would ever have to lock horns with loggers or miners. So long as we could keep our side of the deal and supply the locals with a modest income from science tourism, the forest would remain pristine and the wildlife safe from hunting.

But when Deb and I first got back to Miami in '93, we did not have anyone based at Sera to keep the overall project rolling. Deb went back the summer of '94 to wrap up her research. Fortunately, one of our earlier field assistants came back late 1994 through 1995 to continue a project he started with us for his master's degree. A Kiwi named Ross Sinclair, he had quickly proven himself a very tough fieldworker. With farming experience, a very good sense of practicality, and competence at taking care of himself and things around the station, he was the polar opposite of our first assistant, who could not light a match. Ross could fix the plumbing, replace rotting floor joists, and build a bush camp.

When Ross first arrived at Sera, we helped him launch a study of primitive birds called megapodes on days he was not assisting the cassowary research. I'd found a number of megapode mounds during my searches for *pekpek* and was very curious about them. Three species of megapodes inhabit the area around Sera, which is as many or more than occur together anywhere else. According to the Pawai'ia hunters, more than one species would lay its eggs in the same mound, an aspect that warranted investigation.

Megapodes are windows to the evolution of modern birds. At Sera they scratch together huge piles of decomposing leaf litter with their strong legs (hence the name, megapodes). The female lays her eggs inside a hole in the mound; then the male covers the hole. The heat generated by the decomposition of the amassed leaf litter warms the buried eggs. Megapodes are the only birds to use environmental heat to incubate their eggs (as alligators do and dinosaurs presumably did). They are the only bird eggs that will properly develop without being turned periodically by the parent. They have the highest yolk-to-white ratio and the richest yolk. Indeed, they are quite yummy and eagerly sought by the Pawai'ia and all PNG landowners blessed with mounds on their lands. The eggs incubate deep in the litter with the male tending the mound to keep the temperature at the appropriate level. When the eggs hatch, the chicks dig their way out and run off on their own, able to fly within a day. The most precocial—the biological term for maturity at birth—species of bird anywhere, they make fascinating academic subjects as well as being important for peoples' livelihoods and a conservation issue. Ross quickly recognized the potential and latched on to them as his individual project. He conducted a pilot study that he hoped would enable him to return for more research on his own. He worked out a lot of the kinks in how to study the megapodes, mapped the mound locations, and began training local Pawai'ia to assist in the research. He then went off to be a field assistant with some friends of ours in Indonesia and while there he continued his interest and research with megapodes. This experience helped enable him to come back and do intensive research with megapodes. The Sera station was already generating return visitors who could look out for the infrastructure and sustain obligations with the Pawai'ia while I was in Miami finishing my dissertation.

As Deb and I finished our time in Miami, and Ross was heading back to New Zealand, we were actively looking for someone to take our place at Sera and start some new research there. We convinced David Bickford, a fellow graduate student at the University of Miami planning to study frogs in Costa Rica, that PNG was really where he wanted to be. Dozens of herpetologists had studied in Costa Rica, while Sera had much to offer that was new. One of our assistants from the US, Wayne Crill, had surveyed frogs in the study area, easily finding more than thirty species. Most were microhylids that lived on land. They laid their eggs in damp places: some stuck to leaves, others buried underground. The tadpoles developed and metamorphosed inside the eggs and emerged as tiny froglets. The males exhibited advanced forms of parental care, keeping eggs moist, protecting them from predatory ants, and even transporting the emergent froglets on their backs. David was sold, so all we had to do was sell him and frogs to someone who would pay for his research.

Our work had caught some attention at the Wildlife Conservation Society. Toward the end of our stay at Sera, the organization had provided us with supplemental funds to continue our research after other grant money ran out. We'd built the station despite the early disinterest of WCS, using mostly funds from the Fulbright fellowship, the NSF, and Deb's Maytag grant. With the station up and running, WCS saw the idea was worthwhile. Spin-off projects began to emerge around the Sera nucleus.

A young PNG organization, the Research and Conservation Foundation (RCF), was taking form with support from WCS. In 1987 I'd shared my camp for a while with Bill Peckover, one of the founders of RCF. We reviewed his draft plan for the organization together, talking at great length. Back then, RCF's founders had modest goals, along the lines of producing posters and stamps (Bill had helped set up the PNG Postal System) to promote conservation. I stressed the importance of conservation research to PNG and helped Bill revise a document setting RCF's direction. The organization's plans became more ambitious.

Another RCF founder, David Gillison, who'd built the house at Rutanabi, had worked with Mal in Goroka to develop the tourist lodge in Ubaigubi. David, being from New York, had brought the Wildlife Conservation Society into the picture, first as a partner with the lodge and then with the larger Crater endeavor. If you trace the whole Crater story backwards, David is the initial impetus and father of it all. Mal would tell us that WCS had proved to be no real help and possibly a liability for the lodge. The organization never produced the promised tour groups, demanded a cut of the proceeds, and sent a litany of inexperienced project managers—the worst of whom stole a human skull from a sacred Gimi burial place and nearly caused the lodge to be burned to the ground when the pilfering had been discovered. Indeed, Don Bruning actually later smuggled the skull back to PNG and returned it to its none-too-happy descendants. You can imagine Mal's skepticism when I first showed up at the Aero Club saying I'd been sent by WCS. Here I was naively thinking sponsorship by WCS was a mark of distinction, while everyone in Goroka was thinking, "Oh no, not another WCS tosser." I did not realize that due to my predecessors, I had a couple of strikes against me on arrival. It took a while for me to prove I wasn't just more of the same. Only then did I begin to learn what people really thought of WCS.

A good idea on paper, the Lodge at Ubaigubi had the backing of the local Gimi, tremendous scenery, and bird of paradise display courts viewed from special hides. In the animal world, these birds are the acclaimed masters of plumage and dance: they combine elegance, extravagance, and the utterly bizarre in a way few species anywhere can rival. A lodge where one might witness such unique spectacles up close should draw visitors. But its location led to high costs. Travel there required an expensive flight to Goroka followed by a helicopter drop. Everyone involved wanted a cut, from WCS to travel agents who booked groups to Mal to the Gimi. The project couldn't succeed with everyone expecting a hefty profit. The Gimi in Ubaigubi saw their expectations rise and then crash. They dedicated land, built a magnificent lodge, and designated special bird-of-paradise conservation areas. They fulfilled their part of the deal. It might work in South Africa. But in PNG there is little wildlife to see compared to Africa. Big Conservation has a rich tradition of transplanting models that work in one place to places where they cannot work.

The Gimi, like many other tribes around PNG, had their expectations raised by the conservationists, worked hard, and ended up with nothing to show for it. The people back in New York and in the travel agencies lost little. They simply moved on to the next project. But we saw the consequences: disenchanted Gimi who to this day put up their guard the moment you mention conservation. Well-intended conservation projects have left a trail of disillusionment across PNG and the world. Ecotourism is just one example. A string of similar projects—ecoforestry, bioprospecting, butterfly farming, and most recently various "carbon-credit-for-your-forests" schemes —have widely failed and soured landowners on "conservation." A different model was needed, one that could generate income over the long term without having to depend on a string of for-profit middle men like travel agents, green timber merchants, and butterfly traders. We had an alternative that worked: research tourism.

WCS backed the formation of RCF and its growing involvement with Crater Mountain Gimi and Pawai'ia communities. After our return to Miami, WCS sent Chris Filardi, another of our former field assistants, and Jamie James, a WCS intern, to talk with the Crater landowners about forming committees to work toward creating a large, protected area for wildlife. The Crater Mountain Wildlife Management Area did not yet exist. It would take several more years of effort for the area to be formally gazetted by the PNG Parliament. But in the promotional materials and publicity the Wildlife Conservation Society produced, the Crater Wildlife Management Area was portrayed as a real entity long before its official recognition in PNG. Big Conservation sometimes plays a little loose with the facts; its funding depends on a constant stream of success stories.

The big break, and perhaps also the downfall, for the Research and Conservation Foundation, Wildlife Conservation Society, and Conservation International came in the form of the Biodiversity Conservation Network (BCN), a USAID-funded effort. It was the zenith of the Integrated Conservation and Development (ICAD) mentality—the notion that by "integrating" conservation and development, by building ecotourism lodges, for example, people would embrace conservation because it served their interests. The ICAD premise often was that the local people presented the threat to conservation and thus needed to be induced not to destroy protected areas. Dirt poor people like the Pawai'ia and Gimi would profit from this so-called "integrated" conservation.

The BCN set up a network of sites, from India to the Solomons, with each promoting some sort of development (usually some presumably marketable nontimber forest product or ecotourism). Of the twenty million dollars it pumped into the network, a large percentage went to support Big Conservation administrative salaries and overheads, with the rest going to young national organizations like the RCF and their staffs. Relatively little actually trickled down to the village level and sites where the integration was supposed to happen. Places like Herowana and Haia saw the creation of guesthouses that attracted few visitors. The BCN explicitly considered this a huge experiment, a test to see if the "integrated" model worked. But it did not play out this way in the villages. No one said, "We want to conduct an experiment to determine whether ecotourism in your community promotes conservation." Folks like Deb and I gnashed our teeth from the sidelines, knowing the plan would never work and watching as our friends in the villages invested their time and effort in someone else's grand experimental scheme. They were little more than guinea pigs.

When big bucks are available from a source like USAID, Big Conservation scrambles for a place at the trough. What no one seemed to consider were the ramifications of a failed experiment. If the test run did not prove fruitful, the well-paid staff in New York and Washington, DC, would still have their jobs and would simply look for the next big donor. But in the villages, hopes were dashed, leaving people just as poor as before and also demoralized. In the national organizations like RCF, staff who bought into the ICAD myth and toiled for little pay were left with no support when the BCN funding ended. RCF staff were left to deal with the disappointed landowners who knew nothing about the funding behind the scenes.

The BCN fiasco began while we were in Miami and continued while I was working for Conservation International. Deb got some money from WCS (a tiny slice off the BCN pie) for surveys and training at Crater Mountain. At the time, we were still new to Big Conservation and keen to be promoting conservation in PNG. The BCN funding helped support David Bickford, as a scientist to help the Research and Conservation Foundation integrate conservation and development in the broader Crater Mountain Wildlife Management Area, at the center of which was Wara Sera. A stream of researchers moved in and out of Wara Sera. We were keeping it alive, but as happened with us, Bickford had to leave Sera in order to write his dissertation in Miami. He found over forty species of frogs within a couple kilometers of the station (that's over a third as many species as found in the entire USA) and wrote his dissertation on how males of different species care for and protect the eggs. He's gone on to become a well-established conservation biologist based in Singapore. Another important career helped by "The Sera Experience."

While working for CI my attention was mostly elsewhere. I alternated between time in the USA with Deb, at the CI offices in Washington, and in several places in PNG like Lakekamu, or on the Indonesian side of New Guinea, then called Irian Jaya. But I made it back to the station once for a poignant visit. I hiked out for a couple of days to check up on things. Ross was there with his girlfriend, Jackie, and another field assistant (Ross and Jackie warned me she was crazy). She stomped around the station a few times muttering and swearing incoherently, which Ross and Jackie calmly ignored. All was fine.

It was great to reunite with Mayabe and the other Pawai'ia. But when I sat on the verandah, looking across the Sera gorge to the ridge the B-Trail ascended, the memories came rushing back, filling me with a tremendous sense of loss. At this place, I had let the days flow by, carried along by the pace of the rainforest. Now I had an "official" job and had actually snuck out to Sera without telling my bosses back in DC. Things like this apparently led some of CI's more devoted pencil pushers to call me a "rogue biologist" when I was out of earshot. A bit of friction was caused just by dropping off their radar now and then, or by changing my scheduled returns and staying longer in PNG than initially planned. One of the Washington office bigwigs once pulled me aside and upbraided me for not being a team player. CI had a large PNG program with a large staff in DC. Only two of us, though, actually had the in-country experience needed to assess what was feasible in PNG and what was not. I found myself straddling the gap between the decisions made in DC and the reality in the field. Leaning too heavily on the foot in PNG with just a proverbial toe touching the US headquarters seemed to brand me, to a few key administrators, as a troublesome employee. Sitting on the verandah at the research station, listening to the familiar butcherbird song, the quiet roar of the Sera below, and the gentle patter of rain on steel roofing above, I pondered the contrasts in my life over the last few years. I was on a timetable, people were expecting me elsewhere, and I had debts to pay back in the US along with a dozen other obligations. In other words, I was developing a more typically complicated American lifestyle. I felt lucky to have experienced the freedom I'd had at Sera, and I savored the opportunity to get just a little taste of it again as the bosses in DC wondered where the heck I was. I knew I would have to find a way to get back to Sera.

Chapter Twenty-One

Epiphany: transformation from research to conservation

Nupela tinktink na turnim kain wok long risis i kamap mo long lukautim bus

Like many researchers, before I made the transformation from scientist to conservationist, I saw training as someone else's job. With so much to be done, I felt, individuals could legitimately assume specific roles and let someone else tie them all together to effect conservation outcomes. I would do research on rainforest ecology, someone else would do social work, someone else would train and build national capacity, and yet someone else would tie all those aspects and more together. These fields were too demanding for any one person to handle all of them. Science, I thought, is a special calling that requires a hundred percent of the scientist's effort. Someone else should convert the science to actual conservation.

Because I once believed this, I hope I can call this presumption a bit selfish, arrogant, and a tad lazy without seeming sanctimonious and pointing at others. My own selfish desires subconsciously drove this view. I liked doing research; I did not want to get caught up in the required social sciences and politics or spend my precious time teaching. At the beginning of my transformation to a "truer" conservationist around '97 to '99, I saw capacity building more as a distraction from the research path I'd set for myself. It was a means to maintaining the good will of my host country and a means to developing collaborations that would benefit my research. I'm somewhat embarrassed to be making this confession, as it implies I began training national students out of selfish motives tied more to my research than to conservation. I want to put this selfishness out in the open and admit to it, because far too many of my present colleagues claiming to be conservationists and conservation biologists have not made this transformation. The more time I spent in PNG, the more I came to truly appreciate two fundamental revelations: 1) that rainforest conservation in places like PNG would never happen unless it is driven by nationals, and 2) that nationals were fully capable of doing both conservation and top-quality research without Western supervision. My research, along with that of every foreign researcher in PNG, was totally superfluous on its own in terms of conservation. Without a strong national community of conservationists to drive actions, the scientific findings of foreign scientists did little other than build those scientist's resumes. My work was academically interesting in the field of ecology. But without Papua New Guineans to participate in the scientific arena and utilize science for *their* nation, it was all just a hollow intellectual exercise. To this day much of the rainforest science filling journals is interesting stuff, valuable for better understanding these complex systems. But it isn't conservation.

As my convictions evolved, I observed and experienced subtle opposition to the execution of these concepts from many senior Big Conservation professionals back in the US. Although it was politically correct to say that we needed to build capacity in the biodiversity-rich nations, at some fundamental level the conviction was not truly heartfelt. The subtle and insidious notion of Western superiority and the need for Western guidance in conservation has led to repeated and egregious failures of international conservation. Only by building local capacity to the point that the West is no longer needed in places like PNG can these repeated conservation failures be transformed into successes. Every US-based conservation organization working overseas should have an explicitly stated objective that it is a top priority to be OUT of that country by a certain date, turning all operations over to national management.

I came to realize conservation has almost nothing to do with the research I so loved doing. In truth, conservation is all about people. Conservation does not derive from a scientific publication, a good data set, or a stunning discovery. Those things are important, but they are science, and standing alone they are utterly pointless in terms of conservation. All conservation derives from a group of people changing their behavior. Whether it's a corporate CEO mandating a change in how her company treats its toxic waste or the entire population of the United States learning to turn their lights off when not in use, conservation requires a change in human behavior. Sure, research can tell us what changes should be made, like fencing livestock to keep them out of streams to benefit downstream water quality. But that's not conservation. Conservation means persuading, incentivizing, or even compelling people to change their behavior. Coming up with an "answer," like fencing streams, is not conservation. Conservation happens when people actually change their behavior—when, to continue the example, farmers erect fences to keep livestock out of streams. The person who put the fence up did the conservation.

Papua New Guineans had to be the ones advocating for changes in behavior on the part of Papua New Guineans. I had no more right to tell people in PNG how to manage their resources than they had to come to the US and tell us what to do. Given that their country retains 75 percent of its original forest, that their air is pure, their water potable, and their consumption of petroleum and coal negligible, one could easily argue they have more right to tell Americans or Europeans what to do than vice versa.

As mentioned earlier, Deb obtained some funding for biodiversity surveys and training in the Crater Mountain area. The training included landowners, some national professionals, and University of PNG students. The professionals worked at the national museum and had some fieldwork experience, but needed supplemental training. We enjoyed working with these guys, but they were somewhat set in their ways. Most had jobs they wanted to keep, but did not have much opportunity to move up. They were curatorial assistants, but lacked the higher education required to ever become curators.

We took on a few university students as interns at each survey camp, with some participating in more than one survey. We found several who were exceptionally bright, hardworking, and keen to do research and conservation. We began to see such students as the best investment for building conservation in the nation. One good student could go on to run a department in the government or lead a conservation organization. Some had real drive and optimism and we felt they could use the skills we could teach them throughout their lifetime.

On the third survey in 1996 we taught our first real field course. We brought about twenty University of Papua New Guinea undergraduates to our low elevation camp called So'obo. The logistics of flying everyone in to the abandoned Wabo Airstrip, transporting them by dugout canoe to the camp, housing them in tents, feeding them, and teaching in the rainforest were daunting. We, the instructors, even had to clear the airstrip ourselves with bushknives and a lot of sweat. I have a profound appreciation for the hard work it takes to maintain a grass airstrip in the tropics without a mechanized mowing machine.

Students at the university had few other opportunities to experience fieldwork. Chartering planes, hiring canoes, and buying the supplies for such an endeavor far exceeded what the school could afford, but was a fairly insignificant addition to big-budget conservation programs. Not only were field courses out of the question at the university, there was also no budget for faculty research. So students were rarely exposed to research or saw research in progress at the university. There was almost no chance to do their own research leaving most with little concept of what research is. This fundamental hole in their education left them unprepared to provide answers to problems facing the nation. We set our sights on closing that gap and building a core of competent conservation scientists who could eventually make Western scientists, like me, essentially superfluous. We did not initially advertise this objective very loudly, as most Big Conservation groups want the exact opposite—to build programs with a secure future for Big Conservation in PNG.

Chapter Twenty-Two
Hardships and danger

Ol hatpela samting na samting nogut

I can barely stand to watch many nature shows. *National Geographic*, once a bastion of quality nature documentaries, became a for-profit organization and, in doing so, apparently felt it had to pander to sensationalism to make a buck. Modern documentaries and "reality" shows portray rainforests as dangerous and foreboding. I saw one television episode in which a popular nature show host grabbed a large snake and seemed to have it well under control. Then the camera moved elsewhere and, in the next scene, the host was on the ground with the snake wrapped around him while he struggled to free himself from its death grip. It was pretty obvious they'd stopped the camera and wrapped the poor snake around him to create the appearance of danger. Most of the dangers and dramas on such shows are contrived.

Poor Steve Irwin, the Aussie "crocodile hunter" made his name grabbing dangerous animals and set a new (low) standard for the genre. While filming a documentary called *Ocean's Deadliest*, he was slapped in the chest by a stingray and died: a terrible tragedy that was entirely avoidable. He had to pander to an audience that expected to see people in danger whenever they were out in nature. I was in Queensland, not far from his home and zoo, when he died; it was a profound loss for Australians. Steve Irwin was an icon and hero. But he pointlessly put himself in jeopardy for the sake of sensational footage. Some folks called it a freak accident. But there was nothing freakish about it. He came much too close to a dangerous animal in order to stage a dangerous scene, and he suffered the consequence. Through a career of such stunts he essentially played Russian roulette; sooner or later, the metaphorical gun was going to go off. An ardent conservationist, Steve played a big role in raising people's awareness of conservation issues and their appreciation for nature. I just wish he could have done so without also promulgating the myth of danger lurking left and right in the natural world.

There is absolutely nothing more dangerous out in nature than what you find in any city, so long as you're properly prepared. There are a few possible exceptions. Tigers, grizzlies, and polar bears present very serious hazards. But thousands of people hike and camp in grizzly country every year, and those who make their camps properly, keep their food away from their campsites in proper containers, and don't surprise the bears are generally as safe as someone who follows the rules of the road on the highway. Drive the wrong way down the highway and you are in much bigger trouble than you'll get from most stupid blunders you can make in a rainforest.

Still, rainforest biologists do occasionally find themselves in dangerous situations and it would be foolish to ignore them. A proper understanding of the risks is necessary to stay safe. To underplay the risks would be as misleading as sensationalizing them.

Many nights flying ants would hatch out and come by thousands to the lantern inside the station and drop to the table. Note the "ant exclusion device" on the mug to keep the tea relatively ant-free. The secret to staying comfortable in the rainforest is to accept and live with such minor nuisances.

A friend and fellow graduate student at the University of Miami, Joe Slowinski, was an accomplished snake handler, but a single mistake in Myanmar cost him his life when he was bitten by a krait. But I know Joe would certainly have agreed, because we used to talk about such things over beers, that handling snakes was safer than driving in Miami. In fact, in 2001, the year Joe died, over 3,000 people lost their lives in car crashes in Florida. In my first year at Miami, my housemate, a student from Malaysia, died in a horrible freak accident in Costa Rica after he was stung thousands of times by an angry swarm of killer bees. People on the scene think he fell while running from them and knocked himself out, leaving him vulnerable. Every rainforest biologist has such sad tales of colleagues. But then, almost everyone knows someone who has died in a car accident.

How people perceive danger and what actually is dangerous are two very different things. Dangers that are unfamiliar assume a greater fear value than those we know. Every year, the US sees around twenty-three million visits to the emergency room for accidents. More than forty thousand people die in automobile accidents, over twenty-three thousand die from accidental poisoning, over nineteen thousand in falls, eighteen thousand in homicides, and so on. But about one or two people die per year in wild bear attacks in North America. Yet many see stepping into the wilderness as a much more dangerous proposition than pulling onto the Interstate. But there's no TV series called *The Highway Guy*. ("This week the Highway Guy braves Interstate 95 in Broward County. Watch as he navigates Exit 12 and merges on to Highway 1.")

Modern medicine can cure many of the ailments we encounter in the rainforest. In the days before antibiotics, a cut could go septic and you'd die of blood poisoning. But now, the bacteria you meet in the rainforest can usually be successfully ousted with standard antibiotics. We always had a good supply at Sera and never developed any infections that were resistant. The risk of encountering a fatal drug-resistant bacterial infection is highest in a US hospital, where bacteria evolve resistance to antibiotics almost as fast as the drug companies can come up with new ones. In a remote rainforest like Sera, bacteria have not been exposed to these drugs, so even good old amoxicillin or doxycycline still works miracles.

At Sera, with no upstream habitations, the water was pure. But I had typhoid many times when we lived in Goroka, where the sewage system leaked into the municipal water system. Typhoid was common. In the old days we took chloramphenicol for it, but later learned that was pretty hard on the ol' liver. Cipro became the cure of choice. We kept it (and a variety of other drugs) on hand in the medicine cabinet the way people in the States keep aspirin. Once when I was out at Sera and came down with typhoid contracted at Goroka I did not have any Cipro or chloramphenicol. As the fever set in, I tried to hike out to Haia to catch a plane back to Goroka. I took a boy along to act as a guide and to be available to get help if something happened. It's never a good idea to make that long hike on your own. I began the trek feeling okay, but a couple of hours in, the fever climbed and I became weak and incoherent. I should have turned back to Sera and radioed for a chopper. But one does not think clearly with a 104-degree fever. I forged on. Slowly. By evening I had made it only to the bottom of the mountain, following a level stretch along the river that usually took only three hours.

I collapsed, in my sweaty clothes, in an unoccupied bush house. The boy went off in the night and came back with some cooked potatoes from a nearby occupied bush house. I nibbled a little. Everything in my gut had long since run out, literally. I tried to stay hydrated by drinking water. The boy, who didn't want a dead white guy on his hands, looked very worried. The next day I spent ten hours laboriously hiking the rest of the route—a trip that ordinarily took four hours. I did it by making myself count steps. Fifty steps, rest. Another fifty steps, another rest. I rested standing, propping my chin on my walking stick, because I knew that if I sat down, I might not be able to stand up again. By the last hour, totally exhausted, I took only ten steps between rest stops, counting while I rested so I knew when to start hiking again. We'd learned from Deb's first bout of malaria years earlier how dangerous it was to be caught far from help without the proper medications. But it's hard to always be prepared for every eventuality. Every year we threw out drugs that had passed their expiration dates or grown moldy. When someone came in sick, we gave them what help we had. It was hard to predict and plan when buying medical supplies. Things ran out.

I had malaria on and off for years because none of the many doctors I consulted prescribed the appropriate dosages of the drug primaquine. For years I carried quinine because I could come down with a fever at any time, usually when traveling. During a layover in Amsterdam I walked from my hostel to the Van Gogh Museum. Before I could begin to enjoy the first gallery, a malarial attack came on so quickly I had to sit on the steps inside the museum, sweating buckets and shivering, my teeth chattering. My quinine was back at the hostel. No one paid me any attention, and I'm sure I looked like an addict in withdrawal. I remember watching the legs of people passing in my vision. I don't remember how I got back to the hostel and the quinine that eventually alleviated the symptoms. When new anti-malarials made from artemether came on the market I was very happy. They take effect within a few hours, rather than the twenty-four or more it takes for quinine to begin to work. And artemether does not have quinine's unpleasant side effects—ringing ears and bad taste in the mouth. After years of on-and-off relapses, I finally learned from a malaria researcher that instead of taking ten primaquine in one day as prescribed to me many times, I should take one a day for two weeks. After I did that, the fevers ended and the parasites were eliminated from my liver.

Other exotic tropical diseases came and left unidentified; dengue left antibodies, but I can't pinpoint when I had it. Flu-like symptoms are common in the rainforest; unless they take you into a real red zone, you endure them without getting tested. While undergoing a physical in the US, I learned that I'd had tuberculosis for some time without knowing it; the doctors said I needed to keep an eye on the calcification in my lungs. Another doctor visit revealed scar tissue in my retina from a fungus I never knew I had. In the rainforest, you get sick, you get hurt, you experience odd symptoms. You can't run to the doctor every time, especially if that means traveling to another country where better physicians and better tests are available. Most of my colleagues who do this sort of fieldwork have hosted and endured any number of odd ailments and parasites without ever really knowing the cause. I know I've hosted parasites and diseases that have not yet been identified.

Other tropical maladies loudly proclaim their presence. In Bolivia, bites of sand flies blessed me with the leishmania protozoans. Courtesy of these skin-eating microbes, I developed three large lesions, the largest eighteen centimeters across, where the skin was completely gone, exposing the red flesh below. The vein above the lesion on my left arm was completely blocked and hardened with dead tissue. I visited two US hospitals for treatment. At both, I became a big hit with the residents. My infectious disease specialist brought classes of students to observe me and then challenged them to make a diagnosis. Usually they started with lovely guesses like advanced syphilis. But once one of them asked my travel history (PNG, Bolivia, Guyana, and Indonesia in the past year), they'd hone in on leishmaniasis. By the time I got treatment I was changing the dressings on the lesions several times a day, because so much fluid was oozing out of the exposed flesh. In Guyana, an ever-present cloud of flies swarmed around my pant legs, drawn by the smell of decomposition. Probably if I had stayed in that camp much longer vultures would have started to circle above me.

As painful as these lesions were, the cure was worse. The doctors inserted a catheter in my right arm, snaking it all the way to my heart; once a day they pumped antimony into me, the idea being to kill the protozoans without killing me. At times I thought they might do the latter: antimony treatment causes some patients' hearts to stop. Regular EKGs indicated that my heart was fine. But sometimes, the catheter—called a PICC line—lodged up against my aortic valve, producing the feeling of imminent heart failure. During the treatment I stayed in my house in rural Pennsylvania, more than an hour from the nearest hospital. Not a good place to be when you think you are having heart failure.

Undoubtedly the most pernicious illness I came down with was filariasis. In my first year at Sera I suffered from almost constant low-grade headaches and feelings of malaise. My energy levels frequently dropped. Some days I could not walk more than a kilometer. I lived like this for a couple of years before getting the right diagnosis and medicines. With symptoms like low-grade headache and feeling like crap, doctors don't have a lot to go on. Filariasis was hard to diagnose, but simple to cure. I clearly remember Caroline, the wonderful tropical disease specialist who had earlier saved me from malaria, filling me in on di-ethyl carbamazide (DEC), the drug she used to treat me—which is, incidentally, the pill used to treat heartworm in dogs. Left untreated it causes elephantiasis, which grossly disfigures the body. Caroline told me the drug kills the larvae but not the adult worms which can live twenty years.

Great, I thought. I'll be dealing with these symptoms for another two decades. I'll have to continue to take the medicine for years. And, as predicted, there were times I'd slowly and imperceptibly begin to tire easily, feel a little less energetic and a tad more lethargic. Eventually it would dawn on me that the filaria were multiplying inside my body. I'd take the DEC and—poof!—within a day I'd feel dramatically better, almost perky. Unfortunately, the drug is not sold in the US (it isn't DEA-approved because that requires expensive testing and filariasis is quite rare in the US—so there's no money to be made). I buy the treatment cheap in PNG and carry it back to the US.

But of all the possible hazards—the diseases, the venomous snakes, sharks, crocodiles, flash floods, armed raskols, falling trees, falling off of cliffs or out of trees—undoubtedly the most dangerous was flying in small bush planes. I've lost two biologist friends to crashes in South America; they were doing exactly the same kind of flying we did all the time in PNG. On my first trip to Goroka the two crash survivors I met at the Lutheran Guest House were still in shock when I met them. I saw a plane crash and burn on the Goroka airstrip; the pilot survived and I later flew with him several times in New Britain. But many were not so lucky. Les, a pilot we flew with more times than I could count, died in a crash in a valley we'd flown through often. Another two MAF pilots who'd flown us in and out of Miyanmin (a field site I occasionally visited) lost their lives in a crash there. And several helicopter pilots I knew died, too. One had a heart attack in the air, one died when he hit power lines while crop dusting in Australia, two died when their long hauling line swung up and hit the tail rotor. A bush pilot in Alaska died a few months after I flew with him there. People make mistakes, and in bush planes and helicopters those mistakes can be instantly fatal.

In all our time at Sera, with all the assistants and visitors, we never had a fatality. With one exception. It happened during the heyday of the BCN grant promoting ecotourism in the area. I was back in the US and David was studying frogs and acting as the resident scientist at Sera. A prominent PNG lawyer, once the country's ambassador to the US, wanted to hike from Herowana to Sera. With her was an Australian friend, a doctor who was diabetic. She'd been warned that such an arduous hike was not a good idea, but apparently insisted she could handle the rigors. She was an experienced hiker. But most "experienced hikers" are not prepared for this hike. The trails go straight up and straight down. You follow riverbeds on slippery rocks and tromp over muddy, slippery land. If you are not experienced with this kind of hiking, the extra demands of maintaining balance and the steep terrain can quickly drain you. Add inappropriate footwear (e.g., almost all hiking boots) and you are bound to be exhausted. Unable to balance her food intake to the exertion, and because she wasn't carrying fast-acting insulin, the poor woman slipped into a coma. A Gimi guide ran to Sera in a few hours with a note from the hikers that did not fully explain the seriousness of the situation, as she had not yet slipped into a coma when written. David immediately radioed for a chopper. The first helicopter pilot could not find them in the sea of closed forest canopy and had to turn back when his fuel ran low. Mal came next, picking up David and finding their makeshift camp. He lowered the chopper into a dangerously tight treefall gap and hovered as David jumped out.

David cleared away some limbs so Mal could maneuver a little lower and they could get the hikers into the chopper. But by then it was too late; the poor woman had died.

After that I made doubly sure to vet everyone who planned to hike in, right down to checking the kind of shoes they intended to wear. More than once I told people the hike might be too tough for them and they should either skip their visit to the research station or shell out for a helicopter. Despite my harsh admonitions, many would not listen. Even if you have hiked all over the US or Australia, you will not have experienced a trail like that one: slippery and steep everywhere, with logs across ravines you walk across if your shoes and balance are good or, to be safe, you sit on them and shuffle across on your ass. A log over a deep ravine five hours from an airstrip is no place for stupid pride. Many people who ignored my warnings managed the hike in, but then paid handsomely for a chopper ride out.

But most people made the hike in fine condition. The record went to Henry, who was in his seventies when he hiked in. He loved it. We went at a somewhat slower pace, sleeping in a bush house midway. Imagine my surprise after that journey when he pulled out a thermos of pre-mixed martinis, plastic martini glasses, and a little Tupperware container with olives already on the toothpick. After the long hike, we sat high in the bush house watching the sun go down and sipping martinis. That doesn't fit my definition of dangerous at all.

Chapter Twenty-Three

Back to PNG at last
and shedding baggage

Mi go bek long PNG na lusim kargo

Once a year my Big Conservation employer, Conservation International (CI), brought many of its staff from around the world to DC for an annual planning session. A hundred people would be flown in from all over the world, half a hotel rented, meeting spaces leased, and so forth. CI came up with a new master plan for the coming year's global programs. And every year the organization would execute very little of the new plan before the next grand meeting, when new priorities would be established.

I participated in 1998. We all gathered in a huge auditorium. A professional facilitator, who charged an exorbitant fee, took the stage; management was agog because he had run meetings for Fortune 500 corporations. He must be good. He lost me when he started doing magic tricks. I am not making this up. This was how someone's donation for preserving biodiversity was being spent: on a magician.

We broke into groups to determine priorities for each country where CI worked. The idea was to pull together people from different parts of the world, with each adding fresh perspectives—a good information-gathering tactic, but not such a good method for making final decisions on policy and priorities. Countries vary widely in how one can approach conservation and what the challenges are. Some countries have strong government parks programs, others none. In some countries the main conservation threats come from logging, while others have few trees and desertification is the threat. Because I was the expert on New Guinea, I landed with a group of people who for the most part had no experience with this unique region. I explained that over eight hundred languages are spoken in Papua New Guinea alone, and that every tribal group and clan retained tenure of its traditional lands in PNG. I described PNG as a young democracy, comparing it to the western half of the island, then called Irian Jaya, which was at the time essentially occupied by a foreign military dictatorship, Indonesia. I explained that on-the-ground conservation in New Guinea would require working individually with tribal groups that rarely cooperated with other tribal groups, and that the national government had no ability to create and sustain small national parks, much less large ones. PNG's largest national park, Varirata, located just a half hour outside Port Moresby, comprised less than 2,500 acres and was constantly plagued by landowner problems.

CI's vice-president for the Asia-Pacific Region, hyped up on adrenaline, joined our group. He came into the meeting with the mandate that he wanted us to think BIG, as the magician had urged us to do. Thinking BIG was fine, I responded, but shouldn't we also think about what was feasible? Dismissing me as not being a visionary like him, he took command. He'd seen the ambitious plans the other groups were developing for national parks and corridors connecting them. He, and other senior staff, really liked the word "corridor." We needed corridors. There was money out there for corridors. I tried to explain that PNG, an amalgamation of eight hundred independent tribal nations, could not be unified with conservation corridors. The same problem again. What works in South Africa's Kruger National Park, Kenya's Serengeti, or Yellowstone in the US simply will not work in PNG. Members of tribal societies place their loyalties to their group before the state. This is a fundamental difference many Americans fail to grasp, from conservationists up to presidents who think US-style democracy will work everywhere.

By the end of the session, the VP had actually drawn a big ring around the entire island on our map of New Guinea. We would make a park system that not only ran the full 1,200 miles of the island along the north coast, it would also follow back around south of the central divide in a huge circle. Not only that, but it would extend out into all the major reef systems, from the Raja Ampat Islands just west of the New Guinea mainland to the archipelagos of PNG's Milne Bay Province to the east, stretching the length of the protected area to nearly two thousand miles covering many terrestrial and marine ecosystems. In a few hours, CI's priorities for conservation in New Guinea had ballooned from a few specific sites where we could work with tribal landowners to a giant national park system spanning around 7 percent of the circumference of the earth, encompassing lands and reefs of hundreds of independent tribal groups.

Our leader felt that we would not be able to land big donor contributions or big USAID grants by thinking "small," that is, dealing individually with tribal groups. "To get the big bucks, you have to think and act big," he said, or words to that effect. This frustrating mentality drives Big Conservation. CI's strategic planning had leapt into the realm of pure fantasy on the belief that doing so would lead to money. Despite all the fancy priority-setting workshops and the hiring of token scientists like myself, strategy was based on some VP's notions about what would bring in the biggest grants. Decision makers, like our leader, had to fund their departments and justify their large salaries. You can't do that sitting down on the ground and talking with village elders. No, you have to draw big (BIG!) lines on a map and boldly boast of what you plan to accomplish (so the donors/grantmakers will chip in a few million dollars). This is what CI got for hiring a magician to lead planning and a regional vice-president—who'd never visited the Pacific region—to guide us. At that moment I gave in to that little voice in my head. The one that had been growing louder and louder. The one telling me I was wasting my time. I'd thought I could add some science and a touch of pragmatism to a big organization's conservation actions. But it was clear that getting the big money and taking care of "competitive" salaries in DC was the real priority, while science-based conservation might get some scraps. The PhD New Guinea ecologist was window dressing, there to legitimize and execute the VP's vision, not to provide experience and pragmatism. Getting big money is what actually drives Big Conservation. Some conservationists sneer at the scientists who work for mining or development corporations, calling them "biostitutes." But the reality dawned upon me: I was a biostitute for CI. These organizations are not led by science, they are led by fundraisers and legitimized by hired biologists like me trying to nudge some conservation outcome from the funds left over after all the Important People are paid.

Of the four Big Conservation organizations with large international programs (Conservation International, World Wildlife Fund, The Nature Conservancy, and the Wildlife Conservation Society), I considered WCS the most science-based. With a large staff of scientists I respected, WCS followed a model of giving leadership roles in their programs in a given country to scientists with a great deal of experience in that country. Their strategy, I was led to believe, was to find the most experienced conservation scientists and let them build and lead a program they thought would work best in a country they knew well. The organization seemed to recognize that every country was different in terms of politics, society, and its biology. Only programs custom tailored to each situation would work. Issuing dictates from the headquarters in the Bronx, made by administrators inexperienced in the program country, would lead to failure. Country programs were fairly autonomous in WCS; when you looked at each one individually, they often stood out in their region as highly effective compared to the other Big International Non-Governmental Organizations, known in the trade as BINGOs. Putting the program country first and the Bronx administrative machinery second was, in my mind, a real vision and commitment to conservation. I approached WCS, looking for an opportunity to put my experience to good use. Little did I know, the organization was already on the same slippery slope CI had slid down. My story with WCS would not be one of frustration, of looking up that slippery slope from the bottom of the ravine. It would be one of scrambling against the downward slide to secure the program and station in PNG with a national staff while top-down direction and priorities for funding overheads in the Bronx gained more importance.

While CI provided me good pay and benefits, Deb's biodiversity survey funding from WCS only covered field costs. The WCS modus operandi was to give a small grant to dedicated people like Deb so they would do the field conservation work without requiring pesky perks like salaries or benefits. But Deb was covered through my CI health plan. In 1999 she and I traveled up to the Bronx to discuss the possibilities of us establishing a formal WCS country program in PNG. Until that point, WCS had supported some PNG programs, but did not have a cohesive country program there. The organization had used Biodiversity Conservation Network grant funds to send Arlyne Johnson to advise the new national Research and Conservation Foundation in PNG, but that grant was coming to an end. If we did not get involved, we feared, WCS would drop Crater and PNG. Big Conservation goes wherever the easy money is, and its big development staff in the Bronx would not break into a sweat over Crater Mountain. Deb and I needed to work for WCS so that we could actually raise the money needed to keep things going.

Our vision: focus on capacity building. After five training surveys in Crater, three field courses, and CI's Rapid Assessment Program training course in the Lakekamu Basin, we had the initial nucleus for a fulltime capacity-building program. The CI administrators felt they had met their obligations because to them capacity building was an event, not a process. It was a "deliverable" to check off on quarterly reports to the donor. But a month of training here and there clearly did not accomplish enough. Such courses met the obligations to donors and sounded good in reports. We were "giving something back" to the national conservation constituents. But what we were giving was largely symbolic; scientists are not trained in a month. I wanted to really work with the keen and dedicated young conservationists and biologists from PNG we'd been meeting. Simply teaching a course now and then was not enough. The young scientists needed mentoring. They needed the kinds of experiences I'd benefited from through years at good universities and working at the Academy of Natural Sciences. I had matured as a scientist with the help of accomplished mentors. In PNG, few such mentors were available in biology. We were ready to move there full time and do just that. In 1999, I believed that in ten to fifteen years we could create a team of scientists from PNG who could turn conservation around in their country—and without direction from foreign "experts," particularly experts in DC and New York who were so unfamiliar with the nation they could seriously suggest projects like "ringing the entire island in a park." Trained national conservationists could talk with village elders and tribal leaders as peers, not as pale-skinned aliens.

Deb and I pitched our vision to Josh, then head of the Asian program at the Wildlife Conservation Society. WCS boasted of having been around for generations. Originally called the New York Zoological Society, it had saved the American Bison and been part of the conservation revolution led by Teddy Roosevelt. In the 1970s, hoping to emphasize a grow-ing role as an international conservation group in addition to its primary function of running a zoo in the Bronx, the organization changed its name to Wildlife Conservation International. Now it was Wildlife Conservation Society to distance itself from Conservation International.

I saw some inefficiencies when we negotiated with Josh to start a PNG program, but we were so eager to enact our vision in PNG, to support the field station, and to really make a difference, that we would have overlooked almost anything. Knowing that, Josh had a pretty good advantage in our "negotiations," which in effect amounted to him dictating all the terms of the agreement.

There was no money, apparently, for us to go on staff. We could start on a temporary, renewable "contract" (even though we never got more than a verbal agreement). The unspo-ken reality was that staff, like Josh in the Bronx, cost more money. Hiring fulltime people without benefits would be more difficult in New York, but they could get away with it when their employees were stationed overseas. Josh assured us that while the budget was tight, we would almost certainly be hired as full staffers the next year.

Even though Deb would be Co-Director of the program, she started at substantially lower pay than me. It would be several years before I would actually go on staff, and more before Deb would; and her salary was always lower than mine, even though we did the same work.

But in 1999 we ignored these details because we were committed and *knew* we could make a difference in PNG. We'd been working there for more than a decade and, in that time, made a lot of mistakes and learned from them, even as we watched conservation organizations making the same mistakes over and over. Working effectively in PNG required a great deal of in-country experience—the sort of experience we were accumulating and that any national Papua New Guinean would have. Our desire to bring real conservation about in PNG coupled with our desire to help mentor students who could one day make a real difference in the coun-try drove our decision to take what WCS offered. If they would just let us accomplish the goals we'd set, we'd overlook the other issues. That meant putting the program in our hands and not burdening us with some idiotic vision like a ring of parks connected by corridors.

Our program would concentrate most fully on training young Papua New Guinean conservation professionals. They had access to places and people we could never reach. They had legal rights that we, as foreigners, would never have. They spoke languages we could not. They owned land while we were only temporary tenants. And, most importantly, nationals of PNG, or any country, have a right to lobby and act within their own political system. Foreign "experts" don't have that standing. Imagine an organization from Morocco sending experts to your town who then rent the biggest houses, drive the best cars, exhibit wealth far above that of 99 percent of the town's people, and then sit down in your town hall meetings and tell you how to run your county parks. Imagine those foreigners going into your governor's office and indicating the parts of your state that should be in parkland. Imagine them acquiring positions in the EPA or Department of Interior to act as "advisors" and tell the staff how to do their jobs better. That's how Big Conservation operated in countries like PNG.

Our vision was to work in a completely different way. We would not operate as advisors within the park system or PNG's Department of Environment and Conservation. We would not strive to be puppet masters for weak national NGOs. We would train national citizens to undertake conservation themselves in their own country, to set and implement their own priorities, and we would then get the hell out. It was a conservation strategy unlike that of any of the programs in the dozens of countries where WCS worked. Our method was realistic, achievable, and would have more conservation impact than anything else we or anyone from the US could do. And it would eventually make Deb and I unpopular with senior administrative staff back at their desks in the Bronx.

In preparation for vamped up training, we had bought everything we needed to run field surveys and field training courses in the US. We had fifteen tents, a hundred sixty Elliot traps, forty Tomahawk traps, flashlights, flagging tape, and so forth—all the stuff we needed but could not purchase in PNG. As the gear amassed in Philadelphia, we packed it up in crates and duffel bags that would be useful in the field for storing the equipment. I researched shipping options and found, surprisingly, the cheapest option was to take it as checked baggage. Each bag had to be under sixty-five pounds; we kept them to sixty-three pounds to allow for a margin of error. In all, we had thirty-eight large bags to check—about a ton's worth, not counting our carry-ons!

I called the airlines several times to re-confirm the price on excess baggage, and had them fax me the terms. We did not want to arrive at the airport and hear a different story at check-in. We had far more luggage than a taxi would carry, so I booked an oversized van, explaining about all our gear to the agent, who assured me the largest stretch van with the back seat removed would hold it all—no problem—and still have room for Deb and me. I was skeptical but I took him at his word. This was pre-9/11, back when you could still get through check-in within an hour or two. We allowed four hours just to be safe. Our bags were stacked and ready outside my office a little before 4 a.m., when the van was due. But instead of a stretch van, a normal-sized van pulled up, with all its seats in place. The driver, and I mean this with no disrespect, was mentally handicapped.

But he was a big guy and could heft the bags. Deb and I packed the front of the van, squeezing pieces in like the finely fitted stones of the Incan city of Cuzco. The driver piled up bags in the back. I was not sure they would all fit, but with bags packed all the way to the ceiling from the front seat to the rear door, we managed to squeeze in with a bag each on our laps. Hurdle two: check.

We rolled through the dark, sleeping city toward the highway. As we accelerated down the ramp, I noticed the road noise seemed to be getting louder. I looked in the side view mirror and saw a couple of our bags on the road. The driver had left the back door open and as we drove, we'd been leaving a trail of 63-pound bags, like breadcrumbs, across Philadelphia. I hollered and made the driver stop and back up the ramp. I jumped out, picking up and reloading bags as he drove backwards. Then we retraced our steps through the city. To my amazement, we recovered every piece. I re-fitted the last one in. Perhaps they weren't as snug as Incan rock walls this time, but I personally made sure the back door was actually closed. Through it all, the driver lamented that it was not his fault. The poor guy probably thought he would lose one of the few jobs he could expect to get. We reassured him we would not tell his supervisor. He really was doing the best he could with limited resources.

We got to the airport without further incident, spending the entire drive trying to calm and placate the poor driver. I was relieved to see him leave after we made one last check under the seats. We piled the bags onto several skycaps' carts and wheeled in to the counter, still well ahead of check-in time. One agent stood on duty at the desk; on her crisp uniform was a nice big badge that said "trainee." I walked up, armed with our tickets and documentation. Her eyes went from eager to worried to desperate as we rolled up cart after cart heaped with 63-pound bags and bundles of traps. Honest to God, this was her first day on the job; we were her second booking. I explained the situation, she fumbled around a little with the computer, and I started to watch the clock much more nervously. Fortunately, the shift supervisor came to her rescue. We formed a production line with one person weighing, another on the computer, and another tagging bags. By the time we finished, the comfortable margin of error had dwindled. The other passengers checking in watched us curiously, got their boarding passes, and moved on. Our bags were checked to Port Moresby, thereby avoiding Customs hassles in Australia. By the time we got on the plane for the first leg just to LA (followed by Sydney, Brisbane, and Moresby), we collapsed, exhausted. It was going to be a long flight.

Miraculously, all our bags arrived in Port Moresby! The bad news was that having so many bags meant we were the last ones to go through PNG Customs, which meant the Customs officers could take as much time as they wanted. The number of bags was not too unusual. Many missionaries arrive with huge loads. The New Tribes Mission near Goroka often has short "retreats" for Christian teenagers from the US; they usually arrive with a bargeload of luggage for their two weeks. We, at least, were setting up the equivalent of a field school for the university. When the Customs agents learned we were not missionaries and our bags not full of whatever missionaries carry, the agents took a little more interest.

Anyone who has traveled through Customs, in any country, knows that the worst items to have in your baggage are things the agents are unfamiliar with. I know from experience in the US that it is much easier to pass through with guns and ammunition (even post 9/11) than with scientific equipment. And forget about getting museum specimens through with just a couple of hours to make a connection. Bird skins or pressed plants are just too out of the ordinary.

So there we were with thirty-eight bags containing traps, nets, and all sorts of odd equipment. Because we had so much, the Customs officers assumed the goods must be for sale and therefore subject to PNG's high import duties. This is not to protect any industry in PNG, since the country has virtually no industry; it's just a way to make money off foreign visitors. Seemingly at random—no, certainly at random—the Customs agents confiscated about twenty-five of the bags and let the other thirteen go through. They said we would have to pay duty on items in the twenty-five bags because they were commercial, whereas the thirteen they returned to us were not, even though they did not even open most of the bags. What could we do? One never wins an argument with a Customs agent.

We went to a friend's house in Port Moresby and slept through the rest of the day, jet-lagged and exhausted. Then we spent the next two weeks trying to get our bags out of Customs. We photocopied the tariff codes that stated that educational materials were duty free, and got a letter from the provost of the University of Papua New Guinea stating that our bags were for teaching field courses. We obtained a letter from the prime minister's office stating that our bags should be duty free. We met, we called, we pleaded, and cajoled. No luck. Someone smelled a little cash under the table. This kind of corruption, when widespread, leads to national paralysis. I never paid such bribes in all our years in PNG. But apparently people do pay, especially at higher levels of government where whole mining and logging operations advance or stall depending on who tastes a little of the action. When everyone sees the top bosses getting rich under the table, the egregiously underpaid hard worker at the bottom of the food chain can hardly be blamed for wanting a little extra.

After days and days of this, we lamented about our dilemma to a national friend, Karol, who worked for RCF. One of the first Papua New Guineans I met when I arrived in 1987, he was very supportive. Back then he'd worked for the Department of Environment and Conservation, and had been instrumental in helping me get started. Sadly, now there was no one in government who welcomed biological researchers the way Karol had welcomed me. Foreign researchers are often seen with distrust or distaste, there to exploit the nation or tell people how to live their lives.

"Why didn't you tell me this?" Karol said when he learned of our luggage dilemma. My first thought was, *You didn't ask*.

He said, "I have a cousin who works at the Customs warehouse."

Karol made a phone call, then turned to us and said, "You can go pick up your things now." We immediately went to the Customs loading dock in a borrowed pickup truck and quickly loaded everything on board. There was no paperwork to sign, no storage fee, no import duty. Just a quick shake of hands and a heartfelt thank you. Papua New Guineans call this the *wantok* system, *wantok* meaning "one talk" or the people of one's language. Often referring to families or clans, it is the underlying system that works in PNG. The Western-imposed systems of governance and regulation often just do not work. Two weeks of effort accomplished nothing, but one call from a wantok got immediate results. No paperwork, no money, no bribe, and nothing anyone would consider illegal. Someone might have missed having his palm greased, but often a favor for a wantok trumps a bribe.

The wantok system depends on the ties of language, clans, and family. Those ties are invisible to Westerners like me, but evident to those who grew up with them. It's another reason Western conservationists can do so little where nationals can do much more. We are alien to the transactional systems that function under the surface of a dysfunctional government designed and put in place by Western planners and consultants. Time and time again, as we built our program in PNG, we would rely on the wantok networks of our students and staff. The bank would not be able to correct an error in our balance, but Anna would go in and talk to someone and the next day it would be fixed. The garage continued to keep our vehicle waiting for a part until Jephat spoke to someone; the next day the repair was made. Where resources and services are limited in supply, you often save what you have for the people who are likely to one day reciprocate—your wantoks. Business with a white foreigner might get you cash today, but it does not buy you that IOU that is likely to be needed down the road.

In the years ahead we would develop some quasi-wantok ties—not the binding ties of family and clan, but rather the small favors we could offer that someone might someday be called upon to return. A "loan" for a child's school fees. The use of our truck to haul pigs to market or a corpse to its burial place. These things buy some good will, but nothing binding. Even people whose lives we had surely saved by giving them medicine would lose any sense of indebtedness if immediate issues took precedence. We would find that some of our closest friends among the Pawai'ia, people we had known for more than a decade, could turn hostile in a second based on the lies of another Papua New Guinean. No matter what we did, we were still foreigners, outside the wantok system, and never to be fully trusted.

After getting all the gear to Port Moresby, the next order of business was flying it to Goroka, then transporting it from the airport to our house or office. When time came for a field course or survey, everything was repacked into smaller loads that a person could carry and hauled to the MAF hangar, then weighed and packed in the Cessna, and finally flown to the village. There we unloaded and moved it to a storage depot. From there, we'd hire and organize carriers, usually dozens for a single survey or course, then set out with the carriers to the campsite. Once there, we'd pay the carriers and unpack the gear. A few weeks later, when the fieldwork was complete, we'd do it all in reverse, ultimately storing the equipment at our base in Goroka. I invested much more time on logistics and moving food and supplies than actually doing science on a typical survey. A month of fieldwork entailed more than a month of shopping, packing, preparation, and transportation. Add to that the time required to write the proposals to secure the funding in the first place and then the time reporting back to the donors, and field surveys become extremely time intensive. Why did we need the research station? To eliminate many of these time-sucking tasks. With an established research station, the site was in place and equipped, housing ready to go, permissions secured. When we formally began our country program we wanted to be based in Goroka, the stepping-off place for the research station and the Crater area. Goroka is one of the most pleasant places to live in PNG. Goroka was not plagued with a crime/raskol problem with the severity of that of Port Moresby or Lae. In those cities you could pretty much assume your office and home would be robbed, and the best you could do was take precautions to avoid physical harm to you or your staff. Goroka has a beautiful climate, one that's ideal not only for growing some of the world's best coffee, but also for comfort. Brisk mornings turn to warm afternoons, which cool in the evenings to the perfect temperature for sleeping. Rainfall keeps gardens verdant, but the sun shines almost every day.

Everything was shuttled the ten-hour hike to the station with carriers.
Here a crew of carriers waits outside the house after the hike as we ready the pay.

You can walk everywhere in the small town of Goroka, as we did in the first decade of work in PNG. But when we started the WCS country program we bought a ten-seater Toyota land cruiser. Just walking from one side of town to the other could waste an hour. Originally the airfield was just dirt, pounded flat by the bare feet of hundreds of highland warriors directed by the Australian *kiaps*—the colonial patrol officers. But now it was a paved three-quarter-mile strip fenced to keep pedestrians out.

We needed the truck not only for moving all the supplies and students, but also because many chores done by phone, mail, or Internet in the US are best done in person in PNG. To pay your bills, you wait in line and get a stamped receipt because, if you mail a check, there's no telling if it will be properly credited to your account. It was common to arrive for a meeting and be asked to return in an hour. With the truck, such Melanesian ways did not end up eating your whole day. Once I waited in a long line at the bank only to find it was out of cash. The guy with the keys to the safe and strong boxes had gone home for lunch a few hours earlier. He came back the next day. Phones were often down or shut off for nonpayment. You might have to drive to the doctor just to schedule an appointment for later the same day. The ten-seater was a key piece of equipment, even if we never left town.

Less than two months after we purchased the vehicle, though, while it was parked on a steep, private street right next to our house, an inebriated driver lost control of his car, which slid across the lawn, landing on top of the hood of our Toyota. This was hardly an unusual accident in PNG.

In Goroka, we rented a house in the Pacific Estates, the housing compound Mal owned. In fact, the spacious house we rented, with a big verandah looking out on the lovely forested gardens of the estate, sat right next to his. There we entertained many scientists passing through Goroka or coming to work at the research station. Having sponged off many residents and friends when we were students, we wanted to offer the same opportunity to those now coming to PNG. Hotels were very expensive and often unsafe, so our hospitality ended up helping dozens of students and scientists. We did not charge anyone for what we offered, but I did ask people to bring a bottle or two of refreshing beverage. Despite the steady input of free liquor, we still had to buy quite a bit from the local bottle shop. In a town where going out at night was not the safest, and the nightlife options were two restaurants and two bars, we ended up staying in a lot and making our own entertainment. Two Australians, Janine Watson and Silas Sutherland, worked with us setting up the program and keeping it running until funding ran out for them. They were the best neighbors ever. We fitted up a second house on the other side of the estate as an office and safe living quarters for students. Their workspace, library resources, computers, and more were right there in the office-house: they could immerse themselves in their studies unlike anywhere else in PNG. At the university, it was not safe to walk to the library or computer lab at night. The model worked well, as we lived nearby and worked with the students every day. We developed a sense of family and camaraderie that still endures.

The program would grow and attract more and more top students. At its peak we rented three houses for students, one for Deb and I, and one for an office, and also provided housing allowances to half a dozen married trainees and several more support staff. What started as a combined house and office, dubbed the "BioLodge" by Banak, would become a small campus with its own satellite dish for Internet access, a small herbarium, an aviary for experiments, an excellent library, and work stations for a dozen trainees at any one time.

Chapter Twenty-Four

Finally, real conservation— capacity building

Konservashun tru i kamap—skulim smartim

We came to Goroka in July '99 with the goal of building a team that could eventually function without Deb and me and, for that matter, without any significant supervision from New York. There is absolutely no reason to believe someone in the Bronx can direct a conservation program in Papua New Guinea better than a well-trained Papua New Guinean. In our entire time running the Wildlife Conservation Society program, not one of the supervisors in the Bronx ever came to PNG. Imagine someone who had never been to the US setting the conservation agenda for a US-based organization. The only person to visit from headquarters was a lawyer. We wanted to hire a local lawyer to help us register the program legally in PNG. The New York lawyer came all the way to PNG in order to "interview" two of the potential law firms in Port Moresby we had selected—a task that took a total of two hours and resulted in the lawyer selecting the PNG firm I would have chosen. The cost of his trip would have paid one of our staff for a year.

Before 1999, WCS efforts (other than what Deb and I did) at building national conservation were centered on the Research and Conservation Foundation through funding provided by the Biodiversity Conservation Network. That one large BCN grant meant the PNG-based RCF grew quickly, hiring as its director a former honors student Deb had supervised. She had cautioned that he might not be ready, but because there were so few options,

WCS installed him in a leadership position at RCF, with an American, Arlyne, to provide him with support. But as the agenda was already set by BCN, RCF was little more than a subject in BCN's grand experiment to see if conservation could be linked to development.

RCF tried to find ways to make conservation pay. Guest houses were built in Haia, Herowana, and Maimafu villages. Hopes were raised, but few tourists came. The majority of visitors were the scientists and students attracted to the research station at Sera, and these usually settled in for long periods whereas tourists rarely stayed more than a few days. Members of the surrounding communities took note. With RCF backing the notion that they should be making money off their forests, other clans decided they could get income by building research stations on their land. They did not understand that the pool of potential researchers was limited and would not increase with more research stations. Instead, they saw cause and effect, the classic New Guinea cargo cult mindset: build an airstrip, planes come. Build a church, missionaries come. Build a research station, researchers come. It makes perfect sense.

By the time we arrived, the BCN funding was gone, RCF and CI staff in PNG were reduced, and the communities of Crater were expecting cash from their forests. Our long-term goal was to change the command structure so that Papua New Guineans would steer the conservation ship themselves. If communities saw advantages to "conservation" other than the false promise of cash, "conservation" might happen. If you replace the word "conservation" with "sustainable self-management of traditional resources," you have a clearer picture of where we wanted to take conservation. Saving species from extinction carried no significance. Improving hunting, diet, and health through better resource management did carry significance.

The field courses provided a good pool of mentorship candidates. Among those on the first few field training courses, Miriam Supuma had stood out as an extremely bright and hard working student. Vidiro Gei had shown a real interest in botany and had taken a temporary job at the national herbarium after she'd graduated from UPNG. Banak Gamui was already working for CI and trying hard to make their Lakekamu project work. Just as I had been tied to a Conservation International desk in the US, he was tied to one in Port Moresby—and just as frustrated as I had been. He took a big gamble and a big cut in pay in order to apprentice in our new program. Muse Opiang had thrived in one of our courses. His exuberance and enthusiasm for field biology would impress everyone for years, and still does. A tough street kid, he'd been tied up with some dubious gangs in Moresby for a while, but turned his life around. His grades at the university had been tepid, but when he got out in the field he became a dynamo. Paul Igag had shined on Deb's Crater surveys—he loved the long hours and hard work of setting and tending mist nets to capture birds. Katayo Sagata, who had a passion for entomology, wanted to become the nation's leading expert on ants. The world has only a handful of real experts on tropical ants—what an ambition for a student in Papua New Guinea!

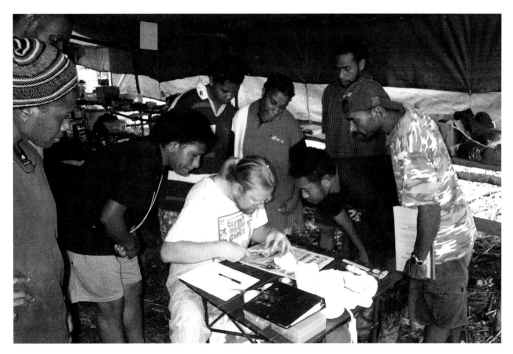

I am demonstrating specimen preparation on one of our annual field courses that began in 1996.
Eunice, looking over my right shoulder, went on to do a master's degree and now works for
the government on climate change policy.

You don't find students like these by looking only at their transcripts. Many of the students with high grades did not want to get their hands dirty. Many quite understandably said they went to the university to get away from the village and wanted a more comfortable Western lifestyle. Fair enough! We sought the few with a passion for fieldwork and the natural world. By getting students out in the rainforest for a month or more on our training courses, we could tell who had what it takes, and who did not. Those first six interns who helped form the program have all distinguished themselves admirably. As I write this, all have attained master's degrees, three are in PhD programs. Paul earned international recognition as PNG's first national ornithologist before dying tragically from a heart attack at home in Goroka. These exceptional individuals set the bar high for all future interns and took on more and more of the mentoring themselves—exactly, well almost exactly, as planned. And many interns followed. This superb team and the Sera research station created a magnet that attracted PNG's best and brightest young conservationists.

Arison Arihafa showed a real interest in forestry on one of our field courses. Quiet and shy, he didn't exactly stand out. But we were looking closely and could see he worked hard and performed well, even if he did not speak up in discussions. On this course we took the class to a huge cave that had a population of flying foxes. On the return hike, rain poured down and we had to cross a flooding stream. Partway across, Arison slipped underwater and lost his glasses. He never complained, but later we saw him straining to see the chalkboard during lectures. He did not have the money to buy new glasses. So when we got to town, Deb gave him some cash and sent him to the one little optometrist's shop in Goroka. Arison was ecstatic. Without that little bit of help he'd have been struggling for months until he could find the money to purchase new glasses, probably by borrowing from a relative (wantok). Debts like this are almost impossible to eliminate. The sponsoring relative might ask for ten kina here and there for the rest of Arison's life. Later, Arison would earn a scholarship to a master's program in New Zealand. When he wrote me after arriving, he said one of the best parts of being abroad was that he was no longer in fear of bumping into relatives who wanted money, as happened to him often the years he was in our program in Goroka.

Arison took on a three-year study of treefall dynamics at Sera. He regularly recorded the rate of trees falling across his transects and could quantify natural gap formation rates—a parameter very important for designing low-impact logging. (To mimic natural processes for lower impact, we first have to learn what those processes are). Arison plugged away at Sera for years, and between projects there participated in our classes and discussions at the Goroka training center. Through this period he slowly lost his shyness; the intellect and sharp sense of humor he had concealed came to the surface. He did so well in his master's program that the New Zealand faculty wanted him to continue on for a PhD; he would be one of the first modern PhD-level foresters in PNG. But the New Zealand government would not extend his visa to allow him to stay on. Rules! New Zealand and Australia give hundreds of millions of dollars in foreign aid to PNG, but relatively little of that aid money is spent to train PNG citizens and build national self-sufficiency. Scholarships are few and disproportionately go to build the business sector and, of course, lawyers.

Enock Kale first appeared on our 1998 course as a high school kid. His father had been a friend of David Gillison's in the long past of Crater. Normally we restrict our class to third- and fourth-year undergraduates. But we were teaching a field course at Herowana and Enock was from that village, so in deference to the village elders who asked us to enroll him, we allowed him to join us. We thought we could scale down some of the assignments for him, particularly the statistical training. But he surprised us by outshining most of the older university students and he proved himself a tireless worker both in the field and the classroom. Four years later, he graduated top in his class from the PNG University of Technology. He was not only the first in his family to go to high school, he was the first from his community to go to university. Most of his relatives were illiterate. He made it through by sheer doggedness. With little money for food or housing, he spent most of the four years sleeping on the floors of other students' places and literally studying by candlelight.

When we offered Enock a scholarship to join our mentorship program, he took the offer with alacrity, spurning numerous options for much more lucrative employment. Like all our trainees, Enock took our subsistence pittance because he was committed to learning and committed to conservation. We offered enough of a stipend to cover basic expenses and provided good housing on our little campus and twenty-four-hour access to the training center. You could go in to the office at any hour and find Enock or any of the others at work on a computer. The security in Mal's compound was great. (The guards carried bows and arrows and were very good shots. They lurked in the shadows and raskols in town knew they were taking a real chance if they climbed this particular fence at night.)

The real benefit we offered, one otherwise unavailable to PNG students, was that we supported our trainees in designing their own research and then we subsidized it—covering costs including travel, field equipment, food and wages for local assistants (extending the program benefits back to the Pawai'ia and other rural landowners). We supervised each project and worked with each student from his or her initial concept through design of the work to analysis and final writing of a thesis. After that we worked to get the research published. Especially important, we parlayed the students' extensive training experience into opportunities to apply for scholarships to top overseas universities. Competition for these scholarships was international, so our students had to stand out and prove excellence. At the time of this writing, around twenty students we mentored have received scholarships and obtained master's degrees in the US, New Zealand, Australia, and the UK. Muse, Samoa, Miriam, and Katayo are plugging away at PhDs.

Enock completed the first long-term population biology study of small mammals in New Guinea in a mark-and-recapture program at Sera. He established a large (15 acres) grid of traps at the top of the A-Trail, near the area I'd scoped out for the helipad in 1989. Under Deb's guidance, he set up a demanding schedule of nightly trap-setting. She and I talked it over; I feared his plan was too ambitious. Given the frequent heavy rains, the sheer volume of work, and the high likelihood of illness causing him to miss some fieldwork, I predicted it unlikely he could keep up with such a rigorous plan. We believed, however, that this was part of the learning process; that after a few weeks if he learned his timeframe was not tenable, he could redesign the experimental protocols. But to my surprise and delight, he carried it off perfectly. He did not miss a single scheduled trapping night, and tramped out at 5 every morning to check the traps. Not only did he execute the work flawlessly, he never once complained about the weeks of wet clothes, biting insects, and the steep climb up the A-Trail. I would challenge any top American student to execute such a project. Enock, like everyone on the team, had no sense of entitlement. He knew this opportunity was unique and he was not going to squander it. We trusted all our students with large cash advances and expensive equipment. We never once had a theft or even a slight misappropriation of funds. Part of their training experience was completing expense accounts for their field advances that could pass Deb's eagle eye. Enock, with his dedication, is the polar opposite to many students I see when I teach in the US who want to do the minimum required to pass and not an iota more.

Katayo Sagata had a huge smile that could light up a room. And he had a true passion for ants. Imagine that—the son of illiterate parents, first from his village to go to high school and on to college, is now close to being Dr. Sagata, the ant specialist. On one of our early training surveys, Katayo came along to sample ants. We were on the island of New Britain, undertaking one of CI's Rapid Assessment Program surveys to assist a group of local land-owners who wanted to start a conservation project. The surrounding lands had all been savagely logged by a Malaysian company. We built a camp in some magnificent remaining forest and were tasked with assessing its biodiversity in order to help strengthen the rationale for protecting the area.

On our first day, it poured heavily—nothing unusual for rainforest surveys! But it rained while we were building camp and everyone was quickly soaked to the bone. Even in the hot lowlands, heavy rains can be cold and raw, especially in the dark forest, well shaded from the warming sun. Katayo got chilled, which triggered a malarial outbreak. Most Papuans simply live with malaria. The risk of infection is near 100 percent in many areas, so even those people who do have access to medications that completely eliminate the parasites just contract the disease again. I quickly gave Katayo a dose of quinine, provided aspirins to reduce the fever, and made sure he got a dry bed. The next day he felt better, and I thought we'd dodged that bullet.

But later that night at dinner, Katayo vomited blood. Fortunately, a local colleague was in camp; he could escort Katayo to the Catholic Mission a few hours' walk from our camp. From there, he and Katayo could hop a boat to an airstrip and then fly to the capital of New Britain, Rabaul. Since I was not familiar with New Britain or the best way to get around there, Katayo was better off with our colleague. Later a messenger returned to tell us they had made the plane to Rabaul and that Katayo was recuperating. He'd recover and would later do a one-year field study at Sera, examining small ants that nest in small hollow twigs on the forest floor.

Not long after Katayo left, a representative of the landowners from surrounding lands, who wanted loggers to cut their forests down, came to our camp. The Malaysian loggers have this trick of paying cash to some people in a community and promising them more for the logging rights. They leave other people out of the deal. This creates rifts in the usual peace-ful village life. Jealousies and suspicions emerge and landowners begin to fight among them-selves. The loggers use the discord to secure a deal with the few landowners they've bought off. With a few signatures they can come in and log lands that were actually communally owned. They make only a few small payments and get out with valuable timber, breaking many promises in the process. What's left behind is a divided and shattered community with a degraded environment and less capacity to sustain themselves. We'd walked into the middle of this very scenario, and threats were now being made against our entire team. We had to abandon camp and pack out in a hurry. Our local friends were terribly upset, but agreed there was no other option. The threats and risks were real.

Miriam chose to do her research at Sera as well. On our training courses, we usually begin with the students standing up and saying something about themselves. Most told us what province they were from, and added something about their families. Miriam got up and said that in PNG, women are expected to marry young and start raising families right away. In many places, wives are bought and traded as commodities. Miriam said she would not follow that path, despite pressure from her parents. She intended to put off having children and concentrate on her career. She wanted to become a conservation professional because she felt the nation needed such professionals. Already in my mind I was saying "wow." She quickly proved my "wow" an understatement. One of the best students we ever had, she quickly overcame shyness and became comfortable conversing with me and the other instructors as an equal—a feat that typically takes our students, especially the women, a long time. Often back then teachers in PNG tended to exude an air of superiority and were unapproachable. Many students have told me they'd been strongly rebuked by teachers just for asking questions. Apparently, some teachers perceived questions as challenges to their authority and knowledge. So our style of direct exchange and eliciting queries from our students was often completely novel.

Miriam took our offer of a mentorship as soon as she graduated, designing a project to study growth and mortality of trees at Sera. Miriam came to the station and undertook the ambitious task of re-censusing the plots that Deb had established for her dissertation research. That meant first finding all forty plots, re-staking the corners and boundaries, then searching for all the tagged trees on each plot. She also tagged all the new recruitment—new trees since Deb's inventory—on the plots and obtained specimen vouchers to identify them. In the time it took to do the fieldwork and write her thesis, Miriam matured into a very competent scientist and advanced to a staff position in our program. We were thrilled when she landed a scholarship to James Cook University in Australia. When she returned with a completed master's degree, we hired her to help teach the younger students. With protégés like Miriam, we anticipated that by 2010 we would be able to turn over much of the teaching to former students as they returned with postgraduate degrees.

Miriam married while she was still in training. Deb and I were nervous because many traditional PNG men expect their wives to be subservient and produce children. Domestic abuse is a massive problem. Another of our students had a husband who beat her; we'd helped protect her several times. We feared Miriam's new husband might take her away. But Jephat proved to be as exceptional as his wife. An extremely bright, competent, and good-humored guy, he supported her career choices. We hired him to run the complicated logistics involved with simultaneously supervising a dozen honors students, each doing different projects and often in different places. Just manning the radio to communicate with students in the field occupied hours every week.

Some of the students used Sera as a stepping-off point for work in other areas of Crater Mountain. Leo Legra, for instance, wanted to study the New Guinea Harpy Eagle and become a world authority on these birds of prey. He also proved to be a top student after a month of grueling work on a field course, and when he graduated we offered him an internship. The New Guinea Harpy was one of the least known of the world's large birds of prey. To put its study in perspective, the US-based Peregrine Fund had sent a British ex-Special Forces hard-ass to gather information about the bird. He trekked all over the rugged Crater terrain and lived in tiny bivouacs trying to follow these secretive birds. But after more than a year of hard work, he had a total of about forty hours of observation. I told Leo he'd chosen a very difficult subject, but Leo was determined, and we were determined to let all our students pursue their visions. In order to ensure Leo would gather data, even if the eagles eluded him, we designed a project wherein he would study the sites and trees where eagles chose to nest. Local hunters could often take us to known nest sites, but the eagles were usually not actively using them. If nothing else, Leo could study the sort of habitat the eagles used for nesting.

Leo spent most of three years working the rough terrain of Crater. He worked primarily with two very shrewd guides, Smith and Amos, from Herowana village. Leo learned to climb trees using a single line and ascenders, initially from Paul Igag, my first student who had learned climbing techniques in his study of Palm Cockatoos. Leo's project was a tough one that sometimes required complicated logistics, which Jephat oversaw. Leo would be out in the forest, completely out of touch for weeks, then emerge in Herowana and radio us that he needed more food. Jephat would purchase the food and send it out to Leo on the MAF Cessna. The Peregrine Fund co-sponsored Leo's research and subsidized an internship for him in Panama working with large eagles there. Later, Leo took the initiative and landed an internship at Hawk Mountain in Pennsylvania. When he came back from this trip, it was apparent he was well on his way to being an authority on New Guinea's birds of prey. By virtue of his hard work, we were able to help him land a scholarship to the University of Kansas, where he earned a master's degree.

Another of the team who didn't base at Sera, Muse Opiang, wanted to study the long-beaked echidna—something we encouraged because the species is both biologically fascinating and a real conservation issue. It's being hunted to extinction, and no one is paying any attention. I'd bet most Westerners have never heard of this beast, which is perhaps the most primitive mammal in terms of evolutionary lineage. It still lays an egg, making it a monotreme like the more famous platypus of Australia. It has a long bony snout that it uses to probe deep in the ground for worms, which it can detect with electro-receptors. Covered in spines like a hedgehog, the long-beaked echidna is a tremendous digger, literally sinking into the earth as it spreads the soil directly beneath it with its powerful claws. It has the lowest body temperature of any mammal. Its milk does not come from teats, but exudes like sweat from the skin in its pouch. Only one lives in captivity and only a handful of specimens exist in all the museums of the world combined. It had never been studied in the field until Muse came along.

But the long-beaked echidna is incredibly difficult to study. This is one animal that makes cassowary research seem easy. Cassowaries, at least, move around by day and their scats are easy to find. Muse and his local assistants had to spend, literally, thousands of person-nights out in the rainforest searching for echidnas. He went through more flashlights and batteries than anyone can imagine. He and his merry team of Pawai'ia assistants would search and search every night. When they found one, it was just a matter of picking it up; echidnas don't run away or try to hide. I don't think they really can run. This docile and slow behavior makes the echidna very vulnerable to hunters and their dogs. There are no native cats, foxes, civets, et cetera. Echidnas survived quite well for millions of years, despite their slow habits, until humans and dogs arrived forty thousand years ago. Now they are in real trouble.

When Muse found an echidna, he then had the challenge of attaching a radio transmitter to it. We had the telemetry gear, but could not figure out an easy way to affix the transmitters to the animals. Echidnas don't really have necks, so a collar does not work. Scientists study their short-beaked relative in Australia by gluing transmitters to their spines. But long beaks have many fewer spines per square inch that they shed more easily. A harness will not work due to their bizarre anatomy: they are like an animal inside a bag, the skin is that loose. They can slip out of any harness. We finally came up with a viable design of attaching a small transmitter to a cloth bracelet around the rear ankle.

Muse was able to find and radio-track echidnas. He discovered their behavior could be even more unusual than expected. Muse's work grew in recognition and he showed so much personality that he eventually was interviewed on television and radio in Australia. Muse landed a prestigious East-West scholarship from the US State Department and went to school at the University of Missouri, where he earned a master's degree.

We developed a special relationship with the University of Missouri at St. Louis, which has an excellent tropical biology program then headed by Patrick Osborne—whom I'd met in 1987 in Port Moresby when he was on the faculty of UPNG! Here was a scientist who shared our passion for Papua New Guinea heading one of the best programs in tropical biology in the US. The first student of our program to go there was Banak Gamui.

Banak did a study at Mt. Stolle, where he put out seed and litter traps, dozens of them, and recorded what dropped into them for a full year. This, along with the growth rate of hundreds of trees he monitored, gave him a crude initial measure of the productivity of the forest. He separated all his samples into leaves, twigs, seeds, and so forth, then dried and weighed them. It was a big study, and one with interesting results particularly relevant to studying carbon sequestration by montane forests in New Guinea. Such information is growing in importance as the world tries to grapple with carbon in the atmosphere. Banak parlayed his honors research into a scholarship to the University of Missouri at St. Louis. He established a good reputation for our students there, and has since been followed by Muse, Enock, Kenneth, and Samoa, all of whom obtained master's degrees with top grades. Samoa has returned to UMSL for PhD studies.

The students' scholarships to study abroad usually covered their barest minimum expenses. We supported several who were married with families—Muse, Enock, Vidiro, and Katayo all had small children. It would have been a real hardship for them to go overseas for two years and be away from their families. So Deb and I often wangled bits of support for them from the grants we raised or from our nearly empty pockets so they could take their families along. Even my long-retired parents chipped in a small monthly check to support the students in St. Louis. The experience has been good for their spouses and children, making their families stronger. If they had been alone those years, I think they would have been extremely lonely and unhappy, diminishing the value of the experience.

Overall, the team has produced a huge amount of science in the process of doing training. Had Deb and I continued as pure researchers, as we had been when doing our dissertations, we would have accomplished far less on our own than we did through facilitating the students we mentored. Training students from PNG has been extremely gratifying and is the most important consequence coming from our research on cassowaries, even though on the surface it has nothing to do with that research. By virtue of having built the station so we could study cassowaries, we opened the possibility for the training program. It was a long process—first proving ourselves as scientists, then proving that a research station model can work in PNG, and then showing that PNG students can do as well as imported students (as we had been). The proof is there, but funding it is another matter.

We worked with other wonderful students in addition to those I've already mentioned. Kore proved herself an able-bodied fieldworker, studying cave-roosting bats in the back country of Crater. Kenneth, Junior, Samoa, and Aileen all studied the hunting habits of the Sokamin people, who lived around Mt. Stolle. Kenneth earned a scholarship to the University of Missouri program, overlapping there with Enock, then followed by Samoa. Junior went to Lancaster University in the UK and came back to expand his research on hunting. Eunice studied mangrove ecology near Port Moresby—she went to James Cook University because it has a good marine program. Paul Igag got a second degree in New Zealand after earning his master's in Australia. Mellie studied megapodes and secured a scholarship to pursue a master's in the UK. Michael Kigl came to us after having completed an honors degree in anthropology. Chris Dahl worked hard to become an expert on PNG frogs and parlayed that into a research position. Vidiro created a digital key to the trees at Sera, then went on to get a master's at James Cook University. She now is a lecturer at the University of PNG. All these successes and more are the result of bright and dedicated Papua New Guineans willing to work hard if given the opportunity to take their education to the next level.

Chapter Twenty-Five

InterOil arrives

InterOil kampani i kam daun long ples

Every year we hosted a big, American-style Christmas dinner. We would clear the large living room of our house in Goroka and set up a massive line of tables in an X-formation corner to corner in the big room. The students, staff, and their families were invited. We provided all the food and Christmas cheer people could consume. We put every oven on the campus to work, we cooked two large turkeys—for some this was their first taste of turkey —plus beef, pork, and a dazzling array of vegetables fresh from the Goroka market. We used home-baked bread to make the stuffing. All the plugs were pulled for this event. Father Christmas even showed up every year to hand out presents to the kids. We felt like one huge happy family. Christmas was the only time we could get the entire team together because it was hard to get everyone to return from the field at any one time. Students would be back from Sera, Supa (Muse's site for studying echidnas), Herowana, and other field sites. Often colleagues from overseas, like Jack Dumbacher from the California Academy of Sciences, took a break from their PNG fieldwork to join in the festivities. Mal, now governor of the province, and a handful of other expat friends in Goroka usually showed up too.

Since I could no longer be full time in the field at Sera, I often had research assistants from overseas helping out there. Many people inquired about volunteering at the research station. Over Christmas 2003, a very capable assistant, Steffen Oppel, staffed the station on his own. A hard worker and a self-starter, he was not interested in coming out for the festivities. We kept in contact via the two-way radio in the office, sending in food when his supplies ran low.

On Friday, the day before the big party, with cooking and preparation already in full swing, Steffen called in from the Sera station. Jephat in the office called me at home where I was busy in the kitchen and said I'd better come up to talk with Steffen. "Was it a medical emergency?" I asked. The reply was "No," but it was apparent that I'd better come up anyway. It was an emergency.

Our people were isolated at Sera; the radio was their only link to help. We tried to avoid having anyone out there alone. But when being there alone was unavoidable, we asked that they check in every day by radio. People had to be medevac'd out of the field with bad malaria, concussions, and, once, appendicitis. No one on the staff used the word "emergency" lightly. I ran to the office to radio Steffen. He was super tough and totally no-nonsense. If he called in with an emergency, there was a real emergency.

And there was. A helicopter had just landed at our helipad, Steffen said, carrying men from a company called InterOil. They flew in to let us know that on the following Monday they planned to begin drilling for oil nearby, at the top of our F-Trail. Helicopters would be coming and going regularly to and from a helipad they would cut in our study area, and that by the end of the next week, two hundred people and all their supplies would be shuttled in. They intended to clear about ten acres for the drill site. Steffen made them tell him their names, which they did not even offer. InterOil, they said, owned the prospecting rights for a huge area within the Crater Mountain Wildlife Management Area, including our Sera study area.

Hearing all this, I nearly dropped the microphone as a wave of nausea swept over me. I've never been more blind-sided.

As we would discover, this was a typical InterOil tactic. Deliver bad news on Friday afternoon and then close for the weekend. As soon as I got off the radio with Steffen I called the InterOil office in Port Moresby. No answer. Again, we would learn this was typical—they only grudgingly gave their contact details, rarely answered phones, and often changed their phone numbers.

A huge clearing and an oil well in our study area would spell disaster. Despite having established the station in as remote a place as possible, with the nearest road a three-day hike away and the nearest airstrip a grueling one-day hike away, we could still not escape the global demand for oil and oilmen looking to cash in anywhere and any way possible. InterOil was a US-based company headquartered in Houston but listed on the Canadian stock exchange because that country requires less stringent reporting for mining companies. The proverbial Texas oil company that did not give a damn, InterOil was well known in PNG. It had bought an entire oil refinery, one that was outmoded and considered an environmental hazard, then dismantled it and brought it to Papua New Guinea, where environmental regulation is only a vague concept. The refinery just happened to be sited in the district of the Minister of

Energy and Petroleum. In exchange for the promise of jobs, the PNG government not only gave InterOil a huge tax break, but also signed a deal under which InterOil would be the sole provider and distributor of gasoline, diesel, kerosene, and Jet A-1 for the entire nation. So much for free enterprise.

There was no source of crude in PNG for InterOil's refinery, so light crude was brought in by tanker from Singapore, refined, then shipped out to InterOil's exclusive distribution network in PNG (the former systems of Mobil, BP, etc., which InterOil now controlled). The deal was sweet for everyone but the consumer. With no competition, InterOil set its own prices. The one petroleum product InterOil did not produce was Avgas, the fuel used by many of the small planes, like those of Mission Aviation Fellowship, serving rural PNG. Since companies like Mobil could not distribute anything other than Avgas in PNG, their shipping and distribution costs went way up. Who paid this price? The rural and poorest people in PNG, rural coffee growers, rural schools, and rural medical clinics. Oil companies scream and holler about the evils of government regulation when it comes to matters like pollution or safety, but they sing a different tune when, as often happens, government regulations favor them.

InterOil, which calls itself a "vertically integrated business," believed that its profits could go even higher if it did not have to buy crude to refine. It began an aggressive program of prospecting. Under the terms with the national government, InterOil had promised a minimum number of exploratory drills. One of these promised well sites, they decided, should be Wara Sera. By keeping up the appearance of active exploration, InterOil could secure its leases almost indefinitely. At the time of this writing, nine years have passed since the oilmen moved into our study site and cleared a drill area, but they still haven't even flown in the drill and pipe needed for the well. They trashed our study area only for the sake of appearing to be exploring.

All those years of work establishing the research station were about to disappear. In such a vast forest, ten acres might not sound like much. Some natural landslips are larger than that. It was not the actual clearing *per se* that was so troublesome, but the inevitable consequences of a drill site and massive foreign intrusion on the social fabric of the Pawai'ia and Gimi. New strife in the community was now inevitable unless InterOil made an extraordinary effort to promote harmony. Some landowners would want exploration "development;" others would not. Some would make money; others would not. The ones not getting rich could turn jealous and bitter. Clans and tribes that once were enemies would rekindle old disputes. When you are as poor as the Pawai'ia, the arrival of an oil company seems like winning the lottery; or rather, more like being given a lottery ticket and told it is a likely winner. Everyone's expectations would skyrocket. We had seen it many times in PNG. I knew a total meltdown was almost inevitable. But I did not envision how quickly things could go sour.

This is what a drill site looks like. InterOil cleared the site in our study area, but then just sat there for years and never brought in the drill rig.

Deb and I conferred, and then we conferred with the rest of the team. Jack Dumbacher, our friend and colleague, was on hand and helped with advice, too. InterOil ignored our calls. This was the first we'd heard of InterOil's exploration concession in the region, and it was also news to the Pawai'ia—the actual landowners. Without advance briefing and community outreach, there would be pandemonium in the community. People get upset when helicopters land on their ground without prior negotiations. Picture a helicopter landing in a rural backyard in the US and discharging a stranger who announces he's setting up camp there— and, by the way, he'll be chopping down a bunch of your trees. American companies working abroad can behave in ways that would be seen as unconscionable in the States. It is no wonder so many people around the world dislike Americans.

Because it was Christmas, most of the Pawai'ia who worked at the station with Steffen had gone home. But the two present, he told us, were quite agitated. I hoped I could at least put off InterOil's onslaught, even though I knew the company's managers would not delay work simply to talk with us; it appeared they had no intention of talking with us at all. So I followed a roundabout route. Steffen reported the oilmen had arrived in a chopper chartered from Hevilift, the competitor to Mal's Pacific Helicopters. Hevilift had grown quickly under the ownership of one of the nation's former prime ministers, a man who, while in office, had acquired such wealth that he was now one of the richest men in the Pacific, including Australia. Not bad for a guy with a tenth-grade education in one of the poorest nations on earth. Politics can pay well in PNG.

We knew Hevilift would have the safety of its staff and equipment as first priority even if InterOil did not. I called the company's dispatcher in Mt. Hagen and explained that the work at Sera could potentially be disputed by the landowners, which could put Hevilift's pilots and helicopters at risk. Angry landowners might not welcome their arrival and could prevent their departure. The Pawai'ia were pretty agitated and angry, I told the dispatcher, adding that by Monday things could be really tense if InterOil did not first send in a crew to explain their plans, track down the papa grauns, and get some permissions. I think my long-term presence in PNG resonated with the dispatcher, another long-present expat. The dispatcher opted not to take chances based solely on assurances of Interoil's representatives. He agreed to delay Monday's flights until the situation on the ground was confirmed as stable. This bought us a little time and definitely got InterOil's attention! They were not accustomed to being outmaneuvered, even temporarily, by a "treehugger."

We carried on glumly with our Christmas party, putting a moratorium on discussing the InterOil invasion, and tried to make the best of things. But a sense of impending disaster underlay the festivities.

Our best hope for averting total calamity laid in working with InterOil and convincing its leaders to move their drill site farther from the Sera study area, and to drill as quickly as possible. If they did this, and found no oil, they might possibly pull out before the situation—not just the station and the ecology of the area, but the entire Pawai'ia way of life—was totally ruined. If the drillers found oil, likely dozens to hundreds of people would move in. With them would come HIV, guns, dogs, criminals, prostitutes, and all the detritus that collects around mine sites.

The story is familiar to every mining nation—witness the West Virginia coal boom, the California Gold Rush, the Klondike, and hundreds more in the US alone. Ghost towns from mining and logging booms still pepper my home state of Pennsylvania; Centralia gained worldwide infamy due to its miles of unmapped mine shafts burning underground and poisoning the town out of existence. PNG itself was still coping with a decades-long civil war on Bougainville Island over the policies and practices of what was once the world's largest copper mine. Over ten thousand people died in a conflict that became so intractable that the government once tried to employ foreign contract mercenaries for its dirty work. The Ok Tedi Mine to our west was turning one of the world's most pristine tropical rivers, the Fly, into one large meandering basin of tailing sludge. Wherever you go, boom and bust mining leaves devastated environments and people discarded like worthless tailings.

In PNG, people are inextricably bound to their land (and have been for millennia). When that land is depleted, they have nowhere to go and nothing to eat. The thought of this happening in my adopted Pawai'ia country—all my friends Joe, Ben, Phillip, Mayabe, Peter, and on, being displaced; all of the months of hard work Deb and I put into the station at Wara Sera being lost—was almost too much to bear. I easily could have just checked out and become the sort of catatonic drooling fool you prop up in a corner somewhere. ("Oh, him? That's Andy Mack. Something happened to him when they cut down paradise. Who's this Sarah he keeps going on about?") But I couldn't give up that easily. The team members looked to me in a way they never had before. Real leadership was needed. So I stepped up and made sure we emptied every bottle of wine and beer in the house. It was still Christmas.

Chapter Twenty-Six

Spivs and liars

Ol giamin man

The team met often to discuss the InterOil situation at Sera and map a strategy. I was quite demoralized at first, but Muse, Michael, Miriam, and the others all felt we could weather the invasion of the oilmen. Apart from the impending arrival of InterOil, the Crater Mountain Biological Research Station (the moniker we used in our scientific publications) was going strong. With a grant we'd secured a couple of years earlier from the National Science Foundation to upgrade infrastructure, we could build new station buildings, all with maintenance-free metal frames. A terrific team of Papua New Guinean biologists worked on site, joined regularly by international researchers. The vision we'd set in motion back in 1987 was in place. We'd already cleared the site for the new station upgrade when the first chopper from InterOil landed, and now were faced with a pressing decision: should we continue with plans to build the new station, or look for a new site?

Muse and Katayo scouted the Crater area looking for possible places to relocate the station—ones within a day of the airstrip, on reasonably level ground, with little human disturbance, etc. It was not easy to find a better site. The best candidate fell mid-way between Haia and Karimui, a large village on the flank of the next volcano along the ridge. Karimui had a reputation for having some bad characters. We felt putting the station within a day of that village would compromise our security and we would have ongoing security issues. One advantage of being remote, we believed, was the unlikelihood that raskols would hike for days through Pawai'ia or Gimi lands to reach us.

In the end we decided to build the new station at Sera. We considered the site ideal in many ways and had already done much baseline work there. The thought of starting over, even near Haia where the flora would be similar, was formidable. We determined we would slowly develop the new station and, at the same time, work hard to improve our relations with the Pawai'ia to ensure the station's secure future. Everyone knew InterOil would leave one day, but we would still be there. InterOil would be a flash in the pan, whereas we'd been there fifteen years and were committing to decades more. Four permanent steel buildings made a stronger statement of commitment than did our words alone.

In order to secure that future we spent a lot more time meeting and talking—what in the conservation business is called "outreach." Most of this outreach was done by the national staff, particularly Muse, Paul, Vidiro, Michael, and Miriam. These scientists had spent a lot of time at Sera as students before becoming staff, and they could communicate with the Pawai'ia and had their trust in ways Deb and I could not. The outreach worked well, and it looked as if the research station and the drilling could coexist. We were optimistic InterOil would not find marketable reserves and would then soon move on, if the company would just drill and get it over with. But InterOil had its own agenda, one that had nothing to do with actually drilling. By maintaining the drill site, it appeared to be adhering to the terms of its exploration license. Prompt drilling would mean the oilmen would have to move on to another site, at much additional cost. By keeping a skeleton crew at Sera, InterOil minimized its costs. We figured we could wait them out. We asked, and received, extensions on the NSF grant so we could put off building for a while. The last thing I wanted was to build the new station and then have InterOil actually strike oil, which would attract hundreds of camp followers to our peaceful study area.

But just the lure of oil was enough to draw some pretty undesirable spivs. "Spiv" is a British/Aussie term for what we in the US would call a scam artist. I like "spiv" better— what they do should not be called art. PNG is rich in natural resources that foreign companies extract—primarily timber, gold, copper, oil, natural gas, and nickel. Poor landowners are often eager to see these resources mined because it seems to be their only real chance at money. I certainly do not blame them, having lived with the Pawai'ia for so long. Even a few amenities, like a pillow and mattress, a pot to cook in, a lantern and fuel, would make their hard lives much more comfortable. Just getting a metal roof on a house can mean not sharing space with ten thousand cockroaches every night and not having to build a new house every few years. Money also buys medicine and pays for education.

But many rural landowners like the Pawai'ia are not versed in the ways of commerce and have no idea of the real value of the resources under their feet. Timber companies typically pay a few thousand dollars for hundreds of thousands worth of prime timber. Everyone in PNG has heard horror stories and wants to avoid being taken advantage of. In come the

spivs, fellow Papua New Guineans who convince landowners that they have experience dealing with mining companies and will make sure the landowners get a fair deal, for a small "fee"
of course. These smooth talkers know the vulnerabilities of illiterate and naïve forest people.
InterOil hung around long enough that the spivs started to move in.

Rex, the spiv ringleader in this case, was a bank teller in Goroka in real life. To the
Pawai'ia he held an exalted position in finance, and he was a national—they would trust him
over some guy working for the foreign mining company. Rex weaseled his way in via Herowana,
where he had some remote claim to kinship with some of the residents. Because wives are
traded and sold among different tribes, people like Rex can usually find some claim to a familial
link, making them even more trustworthy in the eyes of the locals. With lands bordering Sera,
some Gimi in Herowana were very interested in claiming part of the expected loot. Many of the
young men with nothing to do joined forces with Rex as their leader. They formed a landowner
association and began to stake their claims to the soon-to-arrive oil riches.

Rex and some of the Gimi drew up formal papers and took them to the Pawai'ia for
their signatures. They planned to rope the Pawai'ia into joining this landowner association
and giving it their potential royalties. In exchange, the association would represent them in
negotiations with InterOil. A few of the Pawai'ia were nervous about this and asked us to look
over the documents and discuss the deal in a meeting with Rex. Above all else, I wanted to
make sure the Pawai'ia got a fair deal. They should be properly compensated for the use of
their land and the mining of their resources. We arranged for a meeting in Goroka. Rex kicked
it off with a trick learned in Intimidation 101—make the adversary wait. Half an hour later he
waltzed in, followed by half a dozen of his tough boys. To me it was pathetic, but stunts like
this work well when displayed to naïve rural folk like the Pawai'ia.

The meeting included four Pawai'ia, me, Deb, Ross, Rex, and about a dozen of Rex's
boys and allies from Herowana. Rex claimed he had not yet filed association papers with the
government, so there was no cause for alarm. He boasted of all the work he had done and held
a sheaf of papers in his hands, but would not let me or anyone else look at them. The Pawai'ia
would just have to trust him and sign. Through a long and tedious discussion, Rex evaded
every question. Who were the officers of the association? What were they paid? Who were
the members? He ducked them all, and in the process became more and more irritable. He
had not expected us to be there and to be so demanding. He changed tactics and began intimidating the Pawai'ia at the meeting. Why were these foreigners interfering? The local people
had asked us to come, we told him. But under Rex's onslaught, three of the four Pawai'ia
started to wilt. His band of big, beef-fed town boys glared at the little Pawai'ia, who were in
town for one of the few times in the course of their entire lives. But when Rex glared at me, I
could not conceal my disdain. In the end, Rex and his boys walked off into the night in a bit
of a huff. He was obviously not happy—no one had signed his secret papers and it looked like
they would not unless the white guy looked them over first.

The upshot was that we showed Rex that we, at least, were not intimidated by him. His bluster worked with the Pawai'ia, but I knew who he was. In reality he was just a pissant scumbag trying to intimidate and rob our Pawai'ia friends of their deserved royalties.

For months after that I would now and then see Rex on the street in Goroka. He always had a couple of his tough boys with him. But I think he knew I had tougher boys behind me, even if they were not tagging along in a pathetic attempt to look important. He would not mess with me. I knew it, and he knew I knew it. So I met his evil stare with contempt or sometimes amusement. I refused to give him the benefit of thinking that I took him seriously. I knew when InterOil drilled and found no oil he would lose interest in the Pawai'ia in a blink. If the company did find oil, then so many spivs would arrive to cash in that Rex himself would be outgunned and marginalized. His only hope was to establish some credentials now and bank on future royalties. For me it was just a waiting game. If Crater Mountain held reserves of oil, there would be nothing I could do but retreat from Sera, keeping only my fond memories.

Chapter Twenty-Seven
Moving ahead despite InterOil

Wokim wok yet na lusim wori long InterOil

In the wake of the arrival of InterOil and the concomitant spivs, we did our best to move ahead. The real priority for our program was building skills in the team members so that one day Deb and I, or any other fulltime directors from overseas, were no longer needed. Perhaps facing this InterOil challenge now would help prepare them to handle other unexpected challenges in the future. In PNG you can pretty much count on things going horribly awry rather often. The focus on capacity building could continue, even if the main field site had a very uncertain future.

I've read that couples that lose a child often end up divorcing. Something similar happened with Deb and me. The strains of living in close quarters, our limited social lives as expats in Goroka, and the pressures of working together on a difficult program boiled over. We could not do it all and stay sane. The marriage gave out and we divorced, with little trauma, in 2004, continuing to work together as co-directors of the Wildlife Conservation Society's PNG country program. We tried not to let our personal lives interfere with our professional priorities, and to this day we continue to work together on some projects.

The team members carried on with their personal research. We continued holding field courses for UPNG students, we offered new internships, and our networks of colleagues in and out of PNG continued to grow. No one had as much personally invested in Sera as Deb and me, and everyone found ways to adapt to the uncertainty presented by the drill camp up on the F-Trail. We settled into our usual work patterns and tried to adapt and cope while waiting for news from InterOil that would be either very good or very bad. A bit like waiting for results on a biopsy. Was this thing in our midst going to spread or go away?

We couldn't wait forever for InterOil, and it seemed foolish to pull out on the assumption that things would go sour in the unlikely event the drillers found oil. Enock spent a year at Sera rigorously trapping, tagging, and releasing rats in order to measure their survival rates. Although studies like this have been done many times on virtually every small mammal in the US, this was the first time such baseline data had been collected for any of the 190-plus terrestrial mammal species in PNG. Arison kept up his study of natural treefall dynamics— data that could provide an interesting comparison to the huge disturbance made by InterOil. Vegetation in a small gap takes over and closes the gap in a few years, but the drill site would take many decades to recover.

Through all the years I endeavored to sustain my bird banding project, the only such long-term study ever conducted in New Guinea. Steffen and Doug Schaeffer provided months of highly competent volunteer effort to keep it rolling. I travelled into Sera regularly, helping on different projects, meeting with Pawai'ia landowners, doing maintenance on the building, and preparing the site for our new steel-framed buildings.

The epicenter of a burgeoning research program, Sera boasted a dynamic mix of PNG students, international volunteers, foreign graduate students, and experienced scientists. Silvia Lomascolo, an Argentinean from the University of Florida, came to study fruit-eating bats, figs, and seed dispersal. She worked at both Sera and Madang Province, making several trips to PNG and staying a long while. Silvia helped with our training courses and to mentor Kore Tau, a PNG student studying cave-dwelling bats at Crater. Ed Scholes, from the University of Kansas, continued his incredible research with birds of paradise around New Guinea. Starting at Sera and then moving around the country, he collected data on most of the bird of paradise species. He's still going strong. Brett Benz, also from Kansas, was doing a study of bowerbirds and spent time in several provinces. Libby Jones made several long trips to Sera from Yale to study seed predation by rats. Gretchen Druliner, a strong hardcore fieldworker, studied vulturine parrots. Ann Williams did some work at Sera then started a project in Manus Province studying endemic birds. Liz Pryde, an Australian student, studied *Elmerrillia* fruiting phenology at Sera and then went on to do a PhD on birds in New Britain. Paul Igag helped with the bird banding at Sera while studying cockatoos in Pawai'ia country and collaborating with parrot specialists in Australia. Nancy Irwin, from the UK, studied tube-nosed bats at Crater. Jack Dumbacher sponsored and mentored one of our interns, Susan Tomda, who was running experiments with captive birds in the campus aviary. If we build it, they will come. That had been our vision, and now it was coming true. Miriam and the entire team started a survey of feathers used for ornamentation by traditional dancers in the annual cultural show in Goroka. Our campus in Goroka was a constant beehive of activity, where international students and researchers mixed with national students. They all benefited from this kind of interaction.

The facilities of Sera and our campus in Goroka also attracted senior faculty researchers. Jack Dumbacher came every year; he and I were collaborating on a study of phylogeography, the genetic variation and speciation, of lowland birds across the island of New Guinea. He also resumed studies of pitohuis at Herowana, where with the help of the village elder, Avit, he discovered the source of the toxins found in this poisonous bird. Paige West, of Columbia University, and I collaborated on a study of hunting practices by the Pawai'ia and Gimi. Paige continues to be a fresh and underappreciated voice of reason in the conservation community of PNG. Dale Clayton came to study feather lice. Craig Symes from South Africa spent more than a year at sites between Sera and Haia studying birds in different habitats. Gary Dodson studied antlered flies. Steve Richards surveyed frogs at Crater and helped on several of our training courses. Michael Balke came from Germany to study aquatic beetles and also helped mentor and support Katayo. His collaboration led us to several very significant grants that supported the training program. Richard Cuthbert from the UK studied hunting practices among the Gimi in Herowana. A team from Brigham Young University came to collect fleas and other insects. Deb and I spent more and more of our time coordinating and facilitating research by a growing cohort of scientists, supplementing the very small existing pool of biologists with experience in the country, be they nationals or foreigners.

Through the construction of the Sera field station and development of the training program and campus in Goroka, we were in the process of transforming PNG's ecological and conservation research milieu. The training program and the Crater Mountain Biological Field Station served three important functions. First, we facilitated and encouraged overseas researchers who came with their own funding, which helped subsidize the research station. Our employers and donors in Big Conservation would not commit to its long-term support, so we needed to generate independent funds to help make it sustainable. Researchers from overseas paid a usage fee that helped pay for maintenance; they also hired local assistants and paid a fee that supported the Pawai'ia community. We were helping upgrade their airstrip and support the village school.

Second, by luring new scientists to the country, we helped build PNG's knowledge base, one of the most deficient of any nation in the world. Each new scientist visiting Sera added a new person to the pool of biologists who had direct experience with New Guinean ecosystems and biota. Each new project added information and knowledge to a very small and narrow database. Although still relatively modest, scientific output from Crater was building momentum and was unmatched anywhere in PNG for terrestrial research.

The third component of our strategy was the training of PNG students. The overseas scientists we drew, top experts in specialized fields, worked with our students, giving them experience and advanced training in diverse fields we alone could never provide. The country needed national conservationists with expertise and international-caliber training. When this corps of students matured and took on the conservation issues, we would finally see conservation progress in PNG. Deb and I were less interested in undertaking direct conservation; we focused primarily on training the outstanding students we met on our courses so they could handle PNG conservation themselves in ways that were more effective and culturally appropriate.

We realized early on that this strategy was working. But convincing donors to support our programs was a separate issue. Only The Christensen Fund provided consistent and lasting major support. Most other conservation donors and organizations look for parameters like "number of acres preserved as protected areas." They do not appreciate that the number and quality of trained national conservationists is the single most important parameter. I do not care if you commit one million acres to a "protected area;" if there are not adequate personnel to manage and sustain such an area, it means nothing. PNG and countries like it have huge catalogs of failed conservation efforts, many initiated and then dropped by Big Conservation and its foreign donors. If you look closely, you will usually find the ultimate cause of these failures was Big Conservation's over-reliance on ephemeral foreign expertise and failure to train and invest in national staff to sustain the projects. Success does not happen with just a nudge from overseas. Someone, a properly prepared someone, has to be on hand every day, year-round, to sustain success.

The dividends accumulated quickly. An uptick in scientific publications coming out of PNG included an increasing number authored by Papua New Guineans. Our students were capable of doing such high-quality scientific work and communicating the results so well that they could compete in the international scientific arena for precious space in peer-reviewed journals. We could also thank our many overseas collaborators and visitors for the increase in journal articles about work done in PNG. But most gratifying for Deb and me was the growing numbers of our students who competed successfully with applicants from around the world for scholarships to respected universities in the US, Australia, New Zealand, and the UK.

Because we made training our highest priority rather than some glamorous flagship species like tigers or jaguars, we often felt a bit of tension with our Wildlife Conservation Society bosses in the Bronx. A prestigious publication, a white paper, a government policy or law protecting a species, some lines on a map marking a protected area . . . these are the things Big Conservation headquarters and their big donors valued. But such outcomes are essentially meaningless. Conservation is not accomplished by a line on the map; it is accomplished by people. Laws do nothing in and of themselves; it takes people to put them into effect. Policy papers galore already sit in government files collecting dust. People enact policy. Without the right people, conservation will not happen.

As far as I am concerned, there is only one reason to justify the presence of a US-based conservation organization in a foreign country: that country does not yet have the human resources and technical capacity to manage conservation itself. Therefore, the top priority of any foreign conservation organization should be to train and develop national scientists so that foreigners are no longer essential. Any other vision is a subtle form of neocolonial exploitation.

The merits of our program and its output did not elude everyone. A representative of the MacArthur Foundation who visited called it the best capacity-building program he had ever seen. Reviewers of the proposal that earned us the infrastructure improvement grant from the National Science Foundation could see that the research station at Sera was helping to transform field biology for the entire nation, and awarded us the funds over competing proposals from prestigious universities and organizations with more substantial programs than ours.

Despite the risk posed by InterOil, we decided to move ahead with the construction of the new steel-framed buildings. Bundles of steel beams fabricated with pre-drilled holes were flown to Herowana in a twin otter—a workhorse plane that can carry about 1,300 pounds and land and take off from short grass airstrips. We also flew in pressure-treated timber for the floor joists, bolts, tools, a portable generator . . . everything we would need to put the frame up.

When we sent a charter to Herowana we paid the cost of returning the plane, thus we subsidized MAF's discounted rate for the villagers to send coffee to Goroka for sale to coffee buyers in town. Every time we did this, we saved coffee growers quite a bit of money. You would expect this would have bought us good will. But the plane could not hold all the coffee of every grower in the village, which produced 100,000 pounds per year. Our few charters carried only a small percentage of that. Consequently, under the logic of many Gimi, we seemed to be favoring those few who could send coffee out when we chartered a load in to Herowana. I fear we earned more ill will than good.

The village elder, Avit, tried to dole out the loads fairly, but there were always more disgruntled than pleased growers. I often had to meet with villagers to explain why not everyone got a break. Such things fester in PNG, usually out of sight to Westerners like me. All the good I did in Herowana—the work I provided to dozens of men and women, bringing in tens of thousands of kina to the community as well as subsidizing their discounted freight rate on coffee, were all easily forgotten; meanwhile, any petty grievance was retained, providing fodder for the conniving Rex to use against me. When a spiv insinuates himself into village politics, he can stir up long-buried clan rivalries and turn petty grievances into open, festering wounds.

The new, improved station was made with heavy steel beams that were brought in on a long line under a Bell 212 chopper (the Huey widely used in Vietnam).

Once the building supplies were gathered in Herowana, we waited for a clear day and called in a helicopter. Famous for their use in the Vietnam War, the Bell 212 choppers (that make the distinctive rotor *whap whap whap* you hear in every Vietnam movie) can lift a heavy load either externally in a sling or internally in their ample cargo space. In Herowana, we put loads in slings for our chartered Bell 212 to lift using a long line. The pilot shuttled each load to Sera, then set it down gently and hovered overhead while I disconnected the clevis and pin so he could return for the next load. In the meantime, we quickly unloaded the sling and had it ready to return to Herowana. Every fourth trip, the pilot would land so we could throw the three emptied slings in the cabin. In this way we shuttled in about a dozen loads—all the iron beams for one building, all the roofing iron for the three buildings, all the floor joists, and a massive pile of plywood, along with other miscellaneous bits. The steel for two buildings was left in Goroka in case we discovered a problem with the first one as we erected it.

When the last load was unslung and the slings packed in the chopper, the pilot flew off to Goroka, leaving me at the helipad with an intimidating mishmash of iron beams, wood beams, plywood, boxes of bolts, cables, tools, and all manner of building components of uncertain purpose. Rain began to fall, so we threw up a tarp to protect the plywood, generator, tools, and wood. The steel was left out to get wet. It was built to survive rain and would be seeing a lot more of it at Sera. I looked at all the pieces, feeling both daunted and extremely excited. I had been dreaming of building an expanded station since the day we set the first nail at Sera. To celebrate, I partook of my all-time favorite activity—sitting on the verandah watching the rain pour onto the forest canopy and listening to the light drum on the metal roof while sipping tea. There's nothing better in a rainforest that gets twenty feet of rain a year than sitting in nice dry clothes under a dry roof sipping a hot drink. Before long I'd be doing this from the new building and admiring an even grander view over the Wara Oo, looking up the F-Trail and ignoring the fact that InterOil lurked behind the ridge just a couple of miles away.

The next weeks presented an interesting challenge. How do you erect a steel beam structure without the benefit of crane or scaffolding? We had designed the structure in segments that were not too heavy for a team of strong Pawai'ia to move aided with tactical use of pulleys, winches, and levers. It was basically a mega version of the erector sets we played with as kids. Each footpad on the eight posts had to be exactly level, vertical, and the right distance apart; otherwise, when several vertical sections went up, the posts were either too far apart or too close at the top to align with the predrilled holes in the connecting floor beams. I had eight Pawai'ia to help me. None had so much as used a wrench before, so I gave a few lessons on basic tools and construction. I don't remember how many times we struggled to hold up two 150-pound beams, their drilled holes lined up, while my Pawai'ia assistant tried to bolt them together but persisted in turning the nut the wrong way. "Turn it the other way," I'd tell him, and he would pull the nut off, turn it around and then try threading that side the wrong way! There is no clockwise or counterclockwise for people who don't have clocks. Eventually they began to get the hang of it, some more than others.

We built scaffolding from trees lashed together with rope or vines so we could get up high enough to lift the heavy beams using a chain block. It looked awfully precarious at times—a steel beam swinging from a chain connected to a bunch of lashed-together trees. But piece-by-piece it came together. With creative use of levers and sledgehammer, we were able, bolt by bolt, to get the holes aligned and raise the structure. It took only a couple of weeks, and that was with a green crew and me figuring it out for the first time through a steep learning curve. There were no assembly instructions. By my estimate, the next buildings would go up in seven to ten days each.

Later, with the building near completion, I sat high on the metal ridgepole and remembered a similar experience in 1989, when I nailed the station's ridgepole in place and looked out from my tall perch across the canopy of the rainforest. This time I was building a research station that would last for fifty years. This time, I did not build it so "they would come." People were already waiting to move in to the new station. I imagined the classes and students we would teach there and how the place would become a center of research and learning. It was extremely gratifying to see my life goals so close at hand while in my forties. My friend Susan Klimas was there studying tree ferns and the future looked bright.

The steel structure for the new station, one of three planned identical buildings, is nearly complete.

But a few weeks later those dreams would shatter. The steel frame was still out there, but no more researchers or students came. No relaxed conversations on the new verandah with visiting scholars. No quiet stalking of cassowaries on the G-Trail and no more long-term monitoring of birds, mammals, and plants. Though the metal frame was strong and robust, the program would come crashing down.

Chapter Twenty-Eight

The Deal Breaker

Brukim wanbel

The InterOil people had been traveling around the broader Crater Mountain area conducting transect surveys (but still no rig or pipe for drilling up on the F-Trail). They cut many helipads, on both Pawai'ia land and Gimi land, hired local guides, and made extensive on-the-ground geological surveys. All this fueled the anticipation of great wealth among Pawai'ia and Gimi. But the Gimi feared they would not reap the same benefits as the Pawai'ia, since the drilling site was on Pawai'ia land.

When Rex came to Herowana to stir people up, he found a willing audience in early 2006. Many Gimi there had relatives who had married into Pawai'ia families. Even the most tenuous links through, say, a great aunt who was Pawai'ia on the mother's side, would seem to be enough reason for young men to now claim a right to Pawai'ia oil royalties as well as equal opportunity to work at the drill site.

Highland villages, like Herowana, had once been presided over by village elders who made decisions, settled disputes, and acted as leaders and even as police, judge, and jury. They gained authority through a series of rituals and rites, often affiliated with the "men's house," a special gathering place for adult men only. When missionaries arrived in PNG, most commanded that the men's houses be torn down, that rituals be abandoned and heathen art burned. They wanted no challenges to their Christian doctrine and power. But they could not serve all the functions the village leaders had performed. The churches collected money and worried about people's souls. Who was fighting with whom over a pig or cuckoldry were not matters for the missions. The result, in Herowana and in much of PNG, was the loss of relatively stable village social order.

Women work all day in the gardens. Many of the young men, with no elder authority guiding them, end up playing cards, bullshitting, and just hanging around. In that environment, it's easy for rumors and jealousies to blaze. A sense of unmet entitlement thrives, and a spiv knows just how to push the right buttons. Spurred on by Rex, young men began to feel robbed of their entitlement to oil revenues. What's more, it was personal. They felt I had deprived them of work opportunities by building the station on Pawai'ia rather than Gimi land, that I had cheated them of free coffee transport on our charters. In Goroka I counted one of the most powerful men in the country, Mal, as my friend and next-door neighbor. I had a campus of very dedicated staff. I presume Rex considered me a major obstacle to getting the Pawai'ia to sign him on as their leader, but getting rid of me was not an easy or risk-free undertaking.

So he cultivated lackeys among the disavowed Gimi, seeking a way to reach me and our program without risk to himself. Unfortunately, all of this became clear only in hindsight. While I was optimistically constructing a new building at Sera, Rex was just a day's hard hike away in Herowana, scheming to get me out of the way once and for all. While we were doing community outreach among the Pawai'ia, strengthening our foundations for a thirty-year formal agreement with the Pawai'ia landowners at Sera, Rex was in Herowana influencing the Gimi, weakening our base, and planning the demise of the project.

In an effort to be inclusive, we hired a work force of one Pawai'ia and three Gimi from Herowana to work with Enock, who himself was from Herowana. The Pawai'ia were not pleased to have Gimi living and working at the station, but understood the need to keep their volatile neighbors happy. We constantly balanced conflicting demands and objections by the Gimi and Pawai'ia in an effort to be fair and ensure no one was excluded from benefits.

In March 2006 everything changed. Rex sent a letter saying we had to come to a meeting to settle issues. I was in Fiji for a week lending a hand with a WCS project, and Deb was in Australia on business. One of our female students, Nina, was at the station with four local workers, but no other program staff or interns were there. We later learned Rex had been in Herowana stirring up indignation, then flew back to Goroka. The next morning, before dawn, five men with a shotgun and a pistol set out from Herowana for Sera, running fast.

They arrived in early afternoon in a light rain. The workers were tending the fire in the open-sided cookhouse beside the worker's house, and Nina sat in the station writing field notes. The men sauntered by the cookhouse and waved their shotgun at the workers. The three from Herowana knew them and were not about to raise any complaints. They would have to live with these men their entire lives, so they just let them pass. The Pawai'ia worker was so afraid of the guns he did and said nothing before running off into the forest. Not to get help, but to hide.

Nina went to answer the door, expecting it to be one of the workers. A stranger with his face painted black pointed a shotgun at her. The five men piled in, tied her up and put a bushknife to her throat. They demanded and took her money and anything else they wanted. But this was not a robbery. They then proceeded to brutally beat her. A small woman, she fought back as best she could until exhausted. Savagely beaten for an hour, expecting to be killed, she played dead, a tactic that probably saved her life. When they finally stopped they prepared to make their getaway, ripping out the satellite phone and cutting the wires on the VHF radio. Without these, getting help would require running to Haia and radioing for a helicopter, which would take at least a day.

The intended message was clear: *It is no longer safe here: Go away!*

Most importantly, Nina survived the brutal beating. But at that moment, the Crater Mountain Biological Research Station, and my dream for the previous twenty years, died. There was no future in a place that was not safe. We had built the station as far from the problems of the outside world as we could. Hundreds of times exhausted researchers pushed themselves over the mountains and through the river torrents just to get to an area removed from the corruption and environmental degradation of "development" in more accessible places. I knew keeping the world at bay was impossible, but thought if we went deep enough into the huge Pawai'ia forest, we would be safe. I could not have been more wrong.

No place is free of the petro monster. The demand for oil reaches everywhere and the problems arising from an oil-based global economy easily work their way into the most remote jungles of New Guinea. Behind the reaching tentacle of oil comes a monster with no compassion. Stand in the way and the consequences are severe. I tried to make sure the Pawai'ia got a fair deal and Nina paid the price. It had never occurred to me that Rex would spur this level of violence before there was even the smallest indication that Crater Mountain might produce oil. InterOil had not even begun to drill.

When the bastards left Nina for dead, they assumed the four workers who had seen them would say nothing. Guns are very intimidating. But Nina crawled to the radio and with her teeth and bruised hands managed to splice together some of the wires they had cut. Through a weak connection she could be heard in our office in Goroka. Paul took her call and, although it was largely inaudible and incoherent, he recognized the emergency and knew immediately what to do. Send in the cavalry. He called Mal, who had a protective, avuncular relationship with all our students. By the time Mal got to the hangar his engineers had a chopper fueled and running. He arrived at Sera in forty-five minutes—record time.

I would love to have seen those lowlifes when they heard Mal's chopper whipping in over the treetops. Despite an apparent promise from Rex to provide them with a lawyer if they ever needed one, seeing that helicopter zoom over their heads would certainly have scared them—and had they known Mal was flying it, they would have also known they were, as the Aussies say, stuffed. They ran through the night and arrived back in Herowana just before dawn. In the village there are eyes everywhere and no one leaves and returns unnoticed. The station had experienced a disastrous event, one that could easily have turned fatal—and neither Deb nor I were in Goroka. I'm very proud of the efficient way the team handled the situation. They immediately alerted the police in Goroka and made sure Nina had proper care, booking her on a plane to Australia, where quality medical services were available, once it was safe for her to travel. Deb made arrangements for her to stay near Brisbane and met her there. I booked the first flight out of Fiji. I was not even needed there in the first place—the project was in the process of being bungled by people in New York, but the Fijian staff could have handled things if allowed to do so. On my way back to PNG I stopped to see Deb and Nina in Queensland. Nina mostly slept. Deb stayed to help take care of her, and I went back to Goroka to face the repercussions.

Chapter Twenty-Nine

Things unravel quickly

Olgeta samting bagarap kwiktaim

When I arrived in Goroka I found the usually cheerful students and staff morose. We all knew that the attack on Nina and the station could spell the end. The heart of the program had been compromised; in a single act of brutality our shared vision for the program had been shattered.

The leaders in the Bronx immediately circled their wagons, leaving us outside the circle. They quickly told us not to discuss the incident with them via email; if we felt the need to do so, we should cc their lawyer so the communication could be considered privileged. I got the feeling that their main concern, once assured Nina had survived, was that the Wildlife Conservation Society might be sued. Senior staff suddenly became interested in PNG, and in particular whether the research station was administered by WCS or our PNG partner RCF. I was coached not to speculate out loud on ways the attack could have been avoided. Later, when we were called back to New York to discuss the catastrophe, our direct supervisor nearly had a fit when we told him we had given Nina money so she could get home with a financial cushion to support her while she got back on her feet.

"I didn't hear that, I didn't hear that!" he said almost childishly with his fingers in his ears. It might have been funny in other circumstances.

Apparently, providing money at such a time might be construed as an admission of responsibility if they were sued. Their priorities became ever more apparent, and they had little to do with the victim. The mothership always comes first.

In Goroka we met a number of times with the police. The senior investigator, Inspector Paul, was called in. Paul commanded respect along with a good deal of fear in the highlands. People sometimes disappeared in police custody, or died in transport from a crime scene to the jail. Villagers who hid criminals from the law sometimes came home to burned-down houses. In a tough and nearly lawless province with a handful of police for a quarter million residents, this is just the way things work. There are no special forensics teams, no crime scene investigators. The only real tool is talking with people. In most cases in PNG, someone saw what happened or heard what happened and knows where fugitives are hiding. Getting that person to spill his or her guts might be all it takes to solve a crime; and just the sight of Inspector Paul arriving in a village often elicited information.

The police had no money to pay for travel to Herowana, where the criminals were hiding out, so we agreed to cover helicopter bills. Mal put one of his choppers at the officers' disposal. On Inspector Paul's first trip to Herowana, the villagers promised to help find and turn in the fugitives. Many in the village were unhappy about the events at Sera, which spelled the end of a lucrative and beneficial relationship with our program. We had held many field courses and sponsored field research on their land. A rift formed in the village between those who wanted the bastards turned over to the law (or dealt with more harshly outside of the law) and those who were hiding and protecting them. Such disagreements split along clan and family lines and exacerbated existing tensions among families who felt other families had benefited disproportionately by our program. Someone always thinks someone else got more, and that alone is enough to make them sabotage or destroy anything that might be positive.

Avit, our friend in Herowana, reported by radio that some of the villagers were pulling their guns out of hiding. One day someone shot in the direction of Avit as he worked in his garden. Outsiders from a neighboring village were reportedly being called in with their weapons as allies in the coming dispute. The situation grew very tense.

Inspector Paul made a couple more trips to the village, finally convincing the culprits to turn themselves in—which they did, perhaps, because of Rex's promise to pay for a good lawyer. The five culprits showed up to discuss their surrender with Inspector Paul, who allowed them to go home to say goodbye to their families. Only four of the five came back. The ringleader fled to the forest, presumably taking his guns. The other four were transported to Goroka to be incarcerated until trial. But so long as the fifth was on the loose, there would be no trial. The inspector used this as a lever to get the families of the four in custody to pressure the family of the fugitive. For months he eluded capture, though we often had reports of his whereabouts. Certainly we could not go to Sera while this armed fugitive was on the lam.

Our friend Jack had just begun working with a grad student on a project at Herowana. They had to reel in their study and give up on fieldwork. The grad student returned to the US frustrated by how hard it was to get anything done in PNG. Already conditions for field research were returning to the state I had encountered when I first arrived there as a student myself. Without the Sera field station, cooperative communities, and a reasonable expectation of security, few biologists, national or foreign, would find field research in PNG an option worth pursuing. Several foreign researchers cancelled their plans for visits to Crater. Real opportunities for income among the Gimi and Pawai'ia were quickly drying up.

Four of the culprits waited in limbo in the Goroka jail, which was not a particularly pleasant place. I had no desire to see a speedy trial. Nina had left a statement with the police, but she was not eager to come back to Goroka to testify. The ringleader, we'd heard, had holed up with his wife in a very remote hamlet. But the community was not very supportive of him and he had to keep moving. No one wanted to harbor him for long, lest word of their complicity reach the inspector and draw his ire.

The Pawai'ia and Gimi share a strong belief in witchcraft, or *sanguma*, as it is called in PNG. Indeed, almost everyone in the country has a strong respect for *sanguma*. Well-educated people tell stories about things they have experienced and seen firsthand. After hearing these stories over the course of my many years in PNG, I am convinced of the power of *sanguma* as well. A practitioner can cause great harm to anyone who really believes in *sanguma*. People really do fall ill and die when they discover someone has placed a curse on them. As a scientist, I can envision mechanisms that could drive such a thing independent of any spirit world or supernatural powers. It does work, and I suspect there were people among both the Gimi and Pawai'ia who were using *sanguma* against the fifth man who continued to elude the inspector. Between being constantly on the move in harsh conditions and the strong dark medicine working against him, I knew he would not last forever. He would actually be better off in jail with his co-conspirators. It took more than a year, but he grew thin and sickly and eventually died out there. By late 2008 two of the four in prison had died. They had believed Rex would bring them wealth from InterOil, but had been nothing more than pawns in Rex's manipulations.

The team met several times after the attack to discuss what to do. At best, we could wait until things settled down and try to rebuild. If the communities banded together and turned in the criminals, then showed a true desire to have us resume work at the research station, perhaps Sera could be saved. But the Pawai'ia were still expecting wealth from InterOil. Men could get work at the drill site doing hard physical labor, and InterOil paid them more than we could. The research station and all our discussions were easily forgotten. We offered steady work for decades, income without destruction of the environment, work that was fun and easy (like looking for cassowary scats), and community involvement in the project. InterOil paid more, but promised little involvement, significant environmental impacts, and work that could end at any moment. But the lure of big money has driven people around the world and throughout time to take the big risks and ignore the sure bet, and the Pawai'ia were no different. Their apparent lack of enthusiasm for Sera did little to encourage us to return.

I agonized. I remember sitting on the verandah of our house in Goroka, as I had done so many times in the past with so many friends, sipping wine and talking with Doug Cartan, a

Canadian expat who had a long history of managing projects, consulting, and generally offering sage counsel. Because I was so close to the project and held it so dear, Doug told me, I was not seeing the obvious. From his perspective, the invasion at Sera was the "deal breaker." We could not resume working there after something so horrible had happened. Nothing would be out of bounds. When he said it out loud, I realized he was correct. The dream was over. Doug's advice provided the final nudge past the tipping point. No one would ever feel safe at Wara Sera again. I could never ensure anyone's safety there. I could never send a student there. Knowing that a survivor caused the criminals to be apprehended, any subsequent attackers would probably not leave survivors.

It was over.

We sent a helicopter out to the station with a team of men, Jephat, Muse, and Kamena, all of whom could be intimidating. Muse had run with some of the toughest raskol gangs in Moresby; he was no stranger to violence. Kamena was a Marawaka warrior, a member of the most feared tribe in PNG. No one would mess with them. We told no one they were going out there. It was a fast surgical strike to extract the transportable assets. They landed, packed up everything of value, and lifted it all and themselves out in the chopper. Years' accumulation of field equipment, a fully stocked kitchen, solar panels, backup generator, and the thousand-volume-strong library we had grown since 1989. The noted author David Quammen visited us for a week to learn about cassowaries and ended up writing about our eclectic library. It was all quickly bagged and heaved into the large belly of the Bell-212.

When they arrived it was apparent someone had already broken in and ransacked the place, even trying to burn it down. Our decision to pull out permanently was the right one. We had to leave the heavy construction materials for the new station. The men chained and padlocked what could not be lifted out; maybe we'd be able to remove it later.

Quickly the forest will close in around Sera. The houses will collapse without someone to replace beams as they rot. When they do, people will come to scavenge the roofing iron. Even the nails will rust away to nothing. The forest will grow up, leaving only an odd level spot where twenty years ago Deb and I and a small group of Pawai'ia dug into the wet clay. Someone looking very carefully might find the evenly spaced stones that had been the footings under the posts that held up the house. A few other incongruous river stones might be found high above the riverbed. The heavy cast iron stove will likely be the final remnant. Eight of us had carried it, laughing, from the helipad, slung beneath a long pole like some big game animal. Every Sunday we fired it up and Deb made bread and pizza while we sat beside it basking in the dry warmth. Now, it's a rusty iron box in the middle of a thicket of climbing second growth.

A little distance from this archaeological anomaly sits an odd steel frame rising up twenty-five feet. By now there are trees growing up through the frame and overtopping it. Just another monument to a lost dream. For a while, Pawai'ia who remember the story will tell it to their children. But life is short among the Pawai'ia. Moai and Pero passed long ago. Simeon, Cowboy, Luther—gone too. More than half of the men we hired to help us when we first arrived have already died. In a couple of short generations, the research station at Sera will be just another example of white people coming and leaving, just like the thousands of missionaries, the hordes of government consultants, the miners and loggers, and even the million soldiers and sailors who came suddenly during World War II and left just as abruptly. Like the rusting wrecks of planes and sunken ships from the war, the National Science Foundation–funded steel frame in the forest will stand for decades, a mute testimony to the struggle and unfinished dreams of two visitors from another world.

Chapter Thirty

Regrouping, yet again

Startim nupela, narapela taim yet

As saddened as we were by the loss of Sera, our work in Papua New Guinea was by no means over. The Goroka campus thrived and we had a full crew of excellent students, several of whom had already journeyed overseas and returned with master's degrees. Their level of sophistication and scientific capabilities exceeded that of almost every person I knew in the PNG conservation scene. And more were in the process of earning master's overseas. Collectively, our former students would be a force majeure for conservation. We also conducted short courses on campus, bringing in conservation professionals from across the country and working with them alongside our resident students. Financing the program was difficult, but we managed through near-constant proposal writing. We had strong support from the MacArthur Foundation and The Christensen Fund. Deb landed several major grants including ones from the European Union and the Darwin Initiative in the UK. Every new grant had us leaping for joy. When we earned three-year grants, we knew we had a bit of stability. Many donors give support for only one or two years, perpetuating the cycle of constant fundraising. Our program was developing an international reputation. In a nation with such a ridiculously inadequate educational infrastructure, we were building a community of conservation scientists on a par with one you'd find in much richer nations with top-notch universities.

By now the team took the lead in many of our projects. We shifted some of the student studies to other sites. We finally had our own satellite Internet access in Goroka—a chore that took years to accomplish because the government did not want to lose any income on its monopoly dial-up access. We provided broadband Internet and a fine library for our students. Every week the team sat down over pizza to discuss a current scientific paper. We'd been holding these discussions for years, but now they were led by senior team members like Miriam, Banak and Paul rather than by Deb and me. The caliber of the discussions had risen steadily to be comparable to that you would find in an American graduate school. When we began the practice, none of the students had any idea what they were supposed to do or say. None had even read a scientific paper. Now they were discussing published papers and even finding flaws in them, as if they had been reading scientific journals their entire careers. Although the geographic center of the program was lost, its heart remained, and it continued beating.

Conservation is about people, and it takes the right people to make things happen.

With the situation stable in PNG, the Wildlife Conservation Society management invited us to meet with them back in the Bronx to discuss the future of the program. Typically, when we made the trip to New York, we'd find our bosses, Colin, Peter, and Josh, were too busy to spend much time with us. Colin would boast that he had carved out a full hour for us and then take long phone calls in the middle of our conversations. "Sorry, I really have to take this; there's a crisis." Josh was notorious for taking calls and typing emails during meetings. I remember times when, after making the three-day trip from PNG for a meeting, we'd be subjected to "important" interruptions that turned out to be conversations with a spouse about what to have for dinner. But on this visit we managed to get a little more attention than usual from management. WCS was still worried about being sued.

We also got Josh's attention with our requests for pay equity. Since we'd started the program in 1999, Deb had been paid considerably less than I was, even though we were co-directors of the program. We did the same job for vastly unequal pay and I was vested in the pension plan while Deb was not. We explicitly told Josh that this situation could not continue. Josh danced around a lot and promised to see what he could do—the usual dismissal we got when we actually wanted something from the Bronx. We were told to submit applications for promotions at the end of the year. WCS could not simply correct her salary, but if we obtained promotions we would be eligible for boosts in pay. Given that I had just reached the salary CI had paid me six years ago, this was an attractive prospect.

Along with these discussions, Deb had one other big issue to bring up. During routine testing in Australia, doctors had discovered she had the most virulent strain of hepatitis C, probably contracted from the reusable steel syringe used by a local doctor in Goroka. She learned the hard way that hepatitis is prevalent in PNG. Deb had the choice of ignoring the disease and hoping it would not progress, or treating it before it caused serious damage. We wanted to talk with the WCS administrators explaining that she'd need a full year of aggressive chemo, with daily pills and weekly injections of interferon. This regimen would require constant monitoring by a specialist in Australia to ensure the damaging side effects did not become life-threatening. She also needed to avoid the chance of secondary infection in PNG. The "usual" bout of typhoid in Goroka could be fatal once the interferon compromised her immune system. But there was no shortage of work she could do from Australia. Deb handled all of the program's finances, wrote many of the proposals and donor reports, and edited student essays—and other tasks she could accomplish off-site with a good Internet connection. Now that the campus had its own satellite dish, it would be feasible for her to continue working full time while on the treatment. To their credit, the Bronx managers said she should undergo treatment and that she could work from Australia the full year.

We then met with four of the Big Leaders who supervised us, including the head of International Programs, and reviewed the total scenario of what happened at Sera, giving them our prognosis for the future of the program. They seemed satisfied that the situation had been handled well and were visibly relieved there did not appear to be looming liability issues.

Toward the conclusion of the meeting, they gave us an assignment. They wanted a vision statement of what we, personally, would like to accomplish in the coming years—a written account of our best hopes for the PNG program's future, without considering funding as a factor. Although we had not secured any real promises from WCS, we came out of the visit feeling that we had been heard. Our Bronx bosses had told us to apply for promotions, they expressed satisfaction with our handling of the invasion at Sera, and they asked us for a vision of the future in terms of our overall program of our personal careers.

We flew to Australia and set about the business of finding a place for Deb to live while undergoing the chemotherapy. The ordeal would be a long one. I traveled back and forth between PNG and Australia. I would stock up Deb's pantry, take care of any errands, go to Goroka for a few weeks, then return and repeat the process. An Australian friend of Deb's helped with many of these tasks also. Deb had a monthly appointment with a specialist. If her friend or I were in town we'd drive her; if not, she'd hire a taxi.

We scanned receipts and financial documents in Goroka and emailed them to Deb. She kept the books balanced and handled many complex financial obligations. I yo-yoed back and forth. The program ran smoothly, with no interruption in the training, classes, or research.

We held our annual month-long field course in Goroka, putting more emphasis on computer skills and data analysis than we had in previous courses. This adaptation was in response to requests and perceived needs of the students and faculty at the university. We did the course fieldwork at nearby Gahavasuka Park, a forty-five minute drive from town. The availability of electricity and a proper classroom gave us the option of providing many more lectures and nighttime seminars. Although not in the field full time, the students were totally immersed in training and getting more practice with data analysis.

During my brief stays in Australia, Deb and I worked on the vision statement and our applications for promotions. I felt optimistic: we had been raising about a half million dollars a year to run the program and pay our salaries—we were essentially financially autonomous, giving WCS a great program at minimal cost to them. The training continued to go well and to receive recognition. While most Big Conservation groups undertook "capacity-building" through short workshops that involved someone flying in for a week and then flying out, we built capacity through mentorships. We did not just deliver a message and leave. We lived the message, and we lived it with our students. People who visited the program praised it; we had many boosters. But convincing the Bronx managers of its quality and worth was not so easy. They had never come to PNG to see the campus or the research sites, or to meet the students and staff. They often told us that because our program worked so well, they did not have to come to PNG; they were busy traveling to the programs that, unlike ours, were in a state of crisis. We sent in our applications with a sense of pride over what we had managed to accomplish.

In the vision statement, we outlined an expanded training program. Our goal had always been to train nationals so that our presence would become unnecessary. Everyone entering the program was prepared to qualify for scholarships and admission to an overseas graduate school. Most chose this route, and those that did not still profited by the preparations. We did not set a time limit for this; some were ready in two years, others in four; some took their new skills straight into conservation-related jobs in PNG. But the idea was that everyone would sooner or later have the ability to earn a scholarship if they wished. We felt that we could add the most value by one day developing a leg of the program in the US that was affiliated with a good university where the students could come to work with us and other mentors. The PNG arm of the program would be run fully by nationals—the senior staff in Goroka. We would develop sources of scholarship funding and a graduate program dedicated to PNG students that would offer much that was not available in PNG, like a decent library, proper internet access, laboratories, a diverse faculty, international networking, and more. We envisioned such a program eventually taking on students from other developing nations. The idea was to build local capacity in the countries that needed it most. The developing countries have the most biodiversity and at the same time are home to conservation professionals that are arguably the most overloaded, under-supported, and most eager to build needed skills. We knew conservation in those countries would be handicapped if it perpetually relied on expertise from organizations in the US and Europe.

Our statement was not about stopping the proximate causes of biodiversity loss and ecosystem failure. We were not going to fight logging, fight the wild game trade, or combat invasive species. We were not going to work to save an endangered species or establish a park. We were going straight to the root of why there was so little progress on such issues. Ultimately, success on any of these fronts would rely on people in those countries who were native to those countries and who lived there full time. Organizations in New York and Washington, DC, can do no more for conservation in Papua New Guinea than a Papua New Guinean organization can act to create a park in the Adirondacks or save the California Condor. Conservation success in the US is not because Americans do it; it is because citizens do it. Many

American conservationists forget this when they move to international conservation.

Our vision was somewhat bold and unorthodox, but we saw it as a way to have the most positive impact on conservation in countries like PNG. With our demonstrated success in PNG and the clear need for more and better conservationists in other countries, we figured we'd be able to find major donors to support an expanded training program. But we'd misread the New York leaders. They clearly lacked any enthusiasm for developing a new generation of national professionals. Such people might eventually come into competition with them for the same donors.

In March 2007, while I was in Australia with Deb, the folks in the Bronx scheduled a conference call with us. They'd been sitting on our promotion applications and vision statement for months. We allowed ourselves to be optimistic. We might get promotions and raises and we might, at the least, get some feedback on our vision statement. If they did not share our ideas, we could always revise. It was, after all, just a draft where we were told to assume no financial limitations. The attack at Sera had been almost a year, to the date, earlier. Deb was halfway through her chemo. We had recovered well and were moving forward.

The call from WCS came in, with John Robinson and Colin Poole on the other end. They absolutely stunned us by announcing they were closing down the PNG program altogether and that Deb and I had one month left as employees to close the program. We had never had any indication from the Bronx of dissatisfaction with our work. Indeed, they had recently suggested we apply for promotions. We'd raised the funds for the program ourselves, and had enough grant money in the bank to keep it going another twelve months.

"What will happen to our staff and students? Can we at least use remaining funds to support our current students until they complete their degrees?" we asked.
After some discussion they agreed that "The current national staff could stay on to close things up and spend out the existing grant money." WCS would "honor its commitments to the donors" (even though that would be hard without Deb and me). Once the money was spent, there would be no program left. They said at best, perhaps a "skeleton staff" might remain as a placeholder in case WCS wanted to do something in PNG in the future. John and Colin told us the legal department would be in touch to tell us about our severance package, and with that they hung up. Two dozen students and interns, half a dozen staff, and hundreds of partners and collaborators in PNG were hung out to dry. Villagers from Crater to Manus to Mekil were suddenly out of work. The betrayal went far beyond Deb and me. In one phone call, WCS had broken the trust of our students and staff, our scientific colleagues around the world, and the local residents where we had projects—the people we'd been working with and living among for years. I suspect their Human Relations Department gave no thought to all these people while they crafted the terms of my dismissal.

Chapter Thirty-One

Closing shop

Pasim dua, pinism bisnis

On the day of our dismissal in early 2007, Ross, our Kiwi assistant, flew in to Australia to discuss the direction of the program. Although he presumably had no knowledge of what was about to happen, it is not unlikely that Poole and crew scheduled their call around Ross's arrival. We later learned that they had been in consultation with him prior to our dismissal. In a few short months he'd be in negotiation with the WCS Big Leaders about redesigning the PNG program and taking on directorship. A little over a year after they told us they were shutting us down completely, Ross would be back in Goroka, installed as the new-improved PNG country program director.

Colin made good use of his multitasking skills. While he told us the program was over, he sent an e-mail to a brand-new expat member of our staff, someone we had just hired to work as a trainer. His credentials looked good on paper, but he proved unstable in person. Shortly after he was hired and new in PNG, he screamed at my colleague and good friend Paige, who at the moment, like him, was a guest in my house. Apparently in my temporary absence, while helping Deb with her chemotherapy in Australia, he felt the house Deb and I had lived in for eight years became "his" and Paige should move out. A few weeks after arriving, he insisted on being given a role equal to or above that of Miriam, our most senior staffer—a demand he expressed by shouting at Deb and me. What really put the warning lights on for me was the way he talked with Ross about the women students on our training course, ranking which ones he would like to bed. I found it offensive and inappropriate, though they told me "all guys talk like that" and to get off my high horse. I was not about to leave him in charge. Yet Colin, who had never even met the guy, and knowing he had only been in PNG one month, emailed him to ask him to oversee the transition the same day he sacked us. The only apparent qualification he had was that he cost less than we did.

I flew back to Goroka right away and called an all-staff meeting. The usual jovial atmosphere ended immediately when I broke the news that the plug had been pulled on the program. Many cried, myself included. I said Deb and I would do our best to ensure that all the current students received enough funding to complete their honors degrees. There was just nothing more to say. I went home to my own misery. The house in Goroka was home by then; I had lived there longer than any place since I left my parents' home at seventeen. Soon, I would have to pack all my belongings and find a way to get them to the US. But not yet. First, I had to go back to Australia and gather a bit of composure and strength.

In our last official month with WCS, Deb and I appointed Miriam to take our places as director, joined by Banak as co-director when he returned from the University of Missouri in a couple months. She cut the new guy loose. He'd been rude and abusive to several of the students, and the team was already leery of him. He simply was too arrogant and condescending to them.

When I returned to Goroka to pack up, I found one of our students, Leo, there with a collaborator from South Africa. They had organized an expedition together to study a species of hawk of which very little was known, and had found success. I was encouraged. Leo had set up the hawk study entirely on his own. This was the sort of initiative and collaboration we were aiming for—students working independently, not acting as subordinates to and taking direction from a big organization in the US.

Still, packing was slow and painful. There were handmade *bilums* and crafts different villagers had given us as presents. Paintings and books that had been gifts. Photographs of the many friends with whom we'd shared so many good times. So many bits and things had accumulated that had rich memories associated with them. There were goodbyes to be said, to a handful of friends in Goroka, to our team, and of course to Mal, who had been like a fun-loving older brother to me for nearly twenty years. I'd heard some of his jokes so many times—heard him laugh each time he told one as if it were the first. The language he used to describe our former bosses in New York would have made a sailor blush. He'd lived in PNG almost his entire adult life and was governor of the province. He'd seen so many whites come and go, so many experts giving their opinions and then leaving. He had little respect for them.

I packed everything I wanted into cartons for Jephat and the team to ship to the US. The rest—the clothing, kitchenware, and so on—I gave away. I carefully doled out the electrical appliances so everyone on staff got at least one expensive piece. I threw one last barbecue on the verandah, building a fire in the yard to cook the traditional way, stuffing tubes of bamboo with meat and vegetables then shoving them into hot coals to roast.

A small part of the team we built in Goroka when WCS shut the entire program down.
We are having a barbeque and joking about being PNG "stakeholders."
Standing L. to R.—Miriam, Junior, Kenneth, Leo, Kore, Jephat; seated—Susan and Mellie.
Five of these obtained master's degrees partially thanks to the capacity-building program.

The next morning, all the students and staff came with me to the airport. We took many pictures and sniffled. I felt like I had when we left Haia after living at Sera as grad students, not knowing if or when I'd be back. Although it had been our plan all along to turn the program over to senior staff, this was a few years premature. If we'd been granted, as we requested, time to wrap things up properly and provide key training, the team would have been able to carry on without much help from us. Certainly there would be little assistance from the Bronx, as we were still operating under their word that they wanted to close the program down completely.

We'd come so close. First, we'd been on the verge of realizing our dream of building a permanent field station at Sera when it was snatched away, just as the plans came together. Now we had to close the program a very short time before it was ready to stand alone. There are few success stories in conservation, because true success usually requires decades of uninterrupted effort. There are no easy fixes. But the existing conservation infrastructure expects quick fixes. Donors fund one-, two-, or occasionally three-year grants. Big Conservation must continually come up with new ideas and new programs to sell to their donors. It's not easy to talk benefactors into funding an ongoing, ten-year process to train conservationists in a developing nation. Big Conservation fundraisers want a metric they can use to sell their organizations—numbers of acres preserved is one everyone wants to trot out. But such numbers are meaningless without people in place to manage protected areas. In order to keep the funds rolling, Big Conservation must constantly pitch new projects and proposals. This means large staffs in the US. Their role is to support the organization. The accountants, managers, supervisors, lawyers, development staff and more do not actually practice conservation. They make up a huge inverted pyramid that rests on the backs of people like Miriam, Banak, Muse, Enock, and Katayo in PNG. Yet that big burdensome money-making machine does not care to invest even modestly in the training to make those backs strong. This big machine feeds itself first before it feeds the workers in the field.

I don't attribute our closure to InterOil. We were working around the company's intrusion. I do not attribute it to Rex and the criminals who attacked Nina. We were moving on from their invasion. It is a testimony to the competence of the national staff that they were able to overcome such obstacles, and do so without any assistance from anyone in New York. But I do attribute the final closure to the resistance of Big Conservation to invest in the people at the forefront of conservation—the nationals in countries where conservation organizations work. A true conservation success story is one in which a national organization or agency forms and matures and stands completely on its own without input from the US or UK. Organizations like WCS should *never* boast about being in a country for the long haul or promise to be on hand there in fifty years. Any time a US conservation organization operates in a country for more than fifteen to twenty years, its work there should be considered a failure. Until the funders and drivers of international conservation embrace this philosophy, Big Conservation will continue to fail.

The conservation literature is full of analyses about priority setting. Which species? Which country? Which threat? Professional conservationists have spent decades of aggravation and hundreds of millions of dollars trying to answer these questions because of the professional mantra: "Because conservation funding is limited, we need to determine where that funding can be most effectively invested." That sentence, or something like it, is in the introduction of hundreds of research and policy papers. Most of them presume that if, by some magic, the highest priority can be identified, then Big Conservation can take on the problem. This ignores the fact that no matter what priorities you discover, no matter how you rank countries or species or parks or threats, nothing can be accomplished unless someone in the country in question, working with the species or park in question, has the skills, training, capacity, and clout to actually do the work. This should be the number one priority—to build the human capacity in those countries to act for the benefit of their species and their parks for their future and that of their children.

We were very close to demonstrating that this scenario can work, that Big Conservation *can* go into a country, even a country like PNG with poorly trained conservationists, and build the capacity to obviate the need for direction from the US. It took me years to fully appreciate the importance of this message. When I started as a graduate student I held the US-centric "we-them" attitude, as in "we need to help them." Had I bounced back and forth on short trips the way most US-based conservation decision makers do, I might never have realized how misguided that tactic is; how, in a subtle way, it exploits the conservation issues of developing countries for our own livelihoods. But I stayed long enough to become intimately familiar with the problems and the people who faced them. From the illiterate Pawai'ia hunter to the top university graduates, the Papua New Guineans had the ability to take on the conservation and management of their own resources without interference or direction (depending on your perspective) from the US. I saw not only that they could do so, but that they must. This is a lesson the conservation arena, from the donors to the Big Conservation leaders, must embrace if we have hope for any real and lasting progress.

I am optimistic about conservation only because I have worked with people like Banak, Miriam, Muse, Katayo, Enock, Junior and twenty more students we mentored, who work for real solutions in their country on their land. Given the resources currently being sucked up by Big Conservation, there is no telling what they could do if those funds instead went to the places that need them. A real Big Conservation success story would boast of leaving a country program to national management who had better skills and abilities than the initial foreign management. Thinking this way will require a huge shift in the conservation paradigm. The standard US-based Big Conservation leaders do not really believe developing nations can handle their own conservation. Indeed, their livelihoods depend on such nations not becoming fully competent. We came really close to proving them wrong.

Epilogue

Birth of the PNG Institute of Biological Research

Nupela kampani i kamap, ol PNGIBR

After packing up our personal belongings, I returned to Australia, where Deb was still undergoing chemo. As we were now both unemployed, we had no choice but to return to the US. Back in the States, Deb settled in what had been our old house in Pennsylvania before we divorced. I moved to the Pittsburgh area for an endowed position as a conservation biologist with the Carnegie Museum of Natural History.

Shortly after our return, the bosses in the Bronx sent their first representatives to PNG. Apparently they were impressed by the program they had decided, sight unseen, to close. Or perhaps they had always known it was a good program and had meant to keep their presence in PNG all along. Whatever their thinking, within a few months they were openly planning to continue our program and hired Ross as the new country program director. Ross had started as our field assistant at Sera in 1992. I had helped him focus his research on megapodes, which he took up as a master's study at Sera while Deb and I were in the US wrapping up our dissertations. We helped him get funding for that research and to keep Sera running. We then hired him to help run the WCS country program after it started to take off, making sure the Bronx treated him better than they had treated Deb. And when he wanted to follow his girlfriend, who got a job in Germany, and pursue a PhD there, Deb and I helped him secure a leave of absence from WCS so he'd have a job when he finished the PhD. In the years we worked together in Goroka, Ross had become one of my closest friends. But when he signed on to replace Deb and me, we felt truly betrayed, as did the entire staff.

The official WCS announcement that the program would continue under Ross's guidance was a further blow to our vision of national leadership. If, perhaps, WCS administrators had considered Banak or Miriam or Katayo or any PNG national capable of taking the reins, perhaps they could have salvaged things a little better. If they had actually undertaken a hiring search and let nationals apply for the position, perhaps they could have built some good will. But with the implicit statement that only someone from outside PNG could run such a program, the Big Conservation leaders in the Bronx alienated not only staff who had been with us for years, but most of the conservation community in the country.

There was a real team spirit and a shared vision for a different kind of conservation organization in PNG, one where conservation science could come from within the country. WCS spent out the existing grants we had raised. The team wanted little more to do with WCS or the new vision Ross and the Bronx would bring to the program. WCS administrators saw a lucrative future and opportunities coming through various mechanisms of carbon credit trading. They were going to build a program wherein they could obtain money from polluters in developed countries to support non-polluting conservationists in developing countries—in essence, prostitute themselves for big money from interests in the coal and petroleum industries. Many Big Conservation organizations have jumped on the bandwagon for such exchanges. Whether they do anything to reduce pollution is doubtful, but the cash-strapped organizations do stand to benefit. Banak, Muse, and the team wanted nothing to do with it. They decided to form their own organization.

They created the PNG Institute of Biological Research (PNGIBR). As WCS spent out the remaining dollars in the grants, the team used the time to lay the foundations for PNGIBR. From the US, we helped in many ways. Deb, particularly, invested much time and her own money to help get PNGIBR started and established. Paige West, a solid supporter of national-led conservation, joined in the effort. Her scholarly book *Conservation is our Government* was based in large part on how Big Conservation operated in PNG and particularly around Crater Mountain. From the US, Paige, Deb, and I joined Miriam, Banak, and Muse as founding board members for PNGIBR. When the time came for WCS to restart under Ross and the Bronx, the entire staff opted to take large pay cuts and a much less certain future. They virtually all shifted to PNGIBR.

The vision we had begun came to be, although not quite as planned, and prematurely. The team did not have stable funding and support when PNGIBR opened shop. But it had the best group of conservation biologists in the country and the real commitment that comes only from people working in *their own* homeland to benefit *their own* futures. The behavior of Big Conservation in PNG had demonstrated to them that if they truly wanted a stable future, one that did not simply follow the ever-changing whims of donors and Big Conservation leaders in far-away countries, they would need to take control for themselves. The team knew they could do more for conservation and do it for less, and they were willing to gamble their careers on the PNG Institute of Biological Research.

I'd tried to build more than a research station in PNG. The loss of the Sera station left an emptiness in me that remains to this day. My disappointment with my former employers and Big Conservation has only grown as I've watched them continue to waste money and fail in PNG. The end of this story would be, for me, quite depressing and pessimistic were it not for the national team we helped along in PNG. They are an inspiration and a bright ray of optimism in an otherwise bleak conservation landscape. The odds are stacked against them and they get little support from Western donors who sometimes treat them as subsidiaries. Many donors supporting international conservation only support US organizations. But if they can hang in there long enough, and if attitudes begin to change where conservation funding originates, they will be able to make major accomplishments in PNG where so many others have failed.

About the Author

Andrew L. Mack is Executive Director of the Indo-Pacific Conservation Alliance and founding board member of Green Capacity, Inc., and the Papua New Guinea Institute of Biological Research. He has worked for two of the largest international conservation organizations and two large natural history museums in the United States, convincing him that small national organizations are more effective for conservation. He has spent many years in rainforest camps studying birds and tropical ecology, and he has published more than fifty scientific papers. He is most proud of the many Papua New Guinean students he has mentored. He now lives on a small tree farm in western Pennsylvania.

More about the author at: www.cassowaryconservation.com

How to Help
Two nonprofits supporting conservation in New Guinea

Green Capacity, Inc. (www.greencapacity.org) and the Indo-Pacific Conservation Alliance (www.indopacific.org). Donations can be made through the web sites and are tax deductible. Funds go directly to support conservation in New Guinea.